THREE TIMES A COUNTESS

Three Times
a Countess

The Extraordinary Life and Times of Raine Spencer

Tina Gaudoin

CONSTABLE

CONSTABLE

First published in Great Britain in 2022 by Constable

13 5 7 9 10 8 6 4 2

Copyright © Tina Gaudoin, 2022

A CIP catalogue record for this book
is available from the British Library.

ISBN: 978-0-34913-482-6 (hardback)
ISBN: 978-0-34913-481-9 (trade paperback)

Typeset in Adobe Garamond Pro by SX Composing DTP, Rayleigh, Essex
Printed and bound in Great Britain by Clays Ltd, Elcograf, S.p.A.

Papers used by Constable are from well-managed forests
and other responsible sources.

MIX
Paper from
responsible sources
FSC® C104740

Constable
An imprint of
Little, Brown Book Group
Carmelite House
50 Victoria Embankment
London EC4Y 0DZ

An Hachette UK Company
www.hachette.co.uk

www.littlebrown.co.uk

For Noreen, Patricia, Ria, Win and all of the other
strong women in my life

'Nobody is a countess three times by accident.'

Julian Fellowes

Contents

Prologue: No Agenda

Everything she'd experienced, lived through, achieved and married into had been leading up to this moment. On 12 December 2007, Raine Spencer, formerly Lady Lewisham, the Countess of Dartmouth, Countess Spencer and La Comtesse de Chambrun respectively, London councillor, board member of the British Tourist Authority, chairman of the Covent Garden Joint Development Committee, chairman of the GLC Historic Buildings Board, divider of loyalties, rehabilitator of royal relationships and most latterly Harrods board director and sometime shop assistant, swept into Room 73 at the Royal Courts of Justice, Strand, London and took the stand at the coroner's inquest into the death of Diana, Princess of Wales.

As the late Princess's ex-stepmother, once vilified by the Princess, but later one of her closest confidantes, Raine had plenty to spill. She'd cherished three men in common with Diana: her late husband and the Princess's father Lord Spencer; Prince Charles – a long-time friend and Diana's former husband; and Diana's lover, Dodi Fayed, a close office mate of Raine's, who had died on impact on that steamy August night in Paris in 1997, in the terrible, tragic crash that changed history. The world was transfixed. Here was the chance for a uniquely intimate glimpse into the fateful life of the most famous woman on earth – a woman her brother Charles had described as 'the most hunted person of the modern age'.

An excitable air of nervous expectation hung over the court. After weeks of testimony from what could best be described as 'bystanders', mostly French, expectations were high. Here was someone the public, the press and likely even the assistant deputy coroner for Inner West London appointed for the hearing, Lord Justice Scott Baker, might have assumed was uniquely qualified to shed light on the reality of the Princess's relationship with Dodi Fayed, her distressed state of mind after what she had effectively termed a 'betrayal' by the royal family and the events leading up to her death.

Conspiracy theories surrounding the Princess's death ten years earlier were still swirling, like so much Dickensian fog. Operation Paget, a 2004 Metropolitan police criminal investigation unit set up to look into the allegations (made principally by Mohamed Al Fayed) that the Duke of Edinburgh and MI6 had colluded to murder Diana, Princess of Wales and her lover Dodi (Al Fayed's eldest son), had cost the public somewhere north of £12.5m, produced an 832 page document, and concluded in its first report in 2006 that there had been: 'no conspiracy and no cover up'. The Princess and her companion, it stated baldly, had been killed by a drunk chauffeur who lost control of his speeding car in a Paris underpass. And still the world wondered. Could it have been that simple?

Dodi Fayed's father, Mohamed Al Fayed, had already dismissed the findings as 'garbage' and a 'cover up', insisting that his son and the Princess had been 'murdered'. The crash had been, he claimed, a thinly veiled 'intervention' by a royal family – specifically Prince Philip – and a government concerned both by the Princess's associations and possible pregnancy with the Muslim son of one of Britain's most notorious shop keepers and her increasingly vociferous public stance on landmines; a position which was threatening government ties and policy in the regions she highlighted.

There were also the loose ends, which in spite of the conclusion of the criminal investigation were deemed too many to gloss over. Firstly there was the mystery driver and the white Fiat Uno car, which appeared from witness statements to have been involved in the fatal collision – neither had been conclusively traced. And then there were the unfathomably high levels of carbon monoxide found in the blood of chauffeur Henri Paul. Most significantly the Princess, who it had been suggested was pregnant and imminently to be proposed to by Dodi, had been painted by the press, commentators and even politicians, as a desperate, confused neurotic, blighted by failed love and circumstantial loss of position, poised to make a decision that would irreparably damage the reputation of the House of Windsor.

It was, despite the findings of the criminal investigation, not too much of a stretch to conclude that suggestions might have been made, 'off the record', that the matter of the Princess and the playboy needed to be brought to a swift close. In this it was suggested that the shadowy cabal of British Secret Intelligence Service (aka MI6) had been assisted by the American Secret Service. And then there was the much talked about phone call to the Princess from the MP for Crawley and close friend since childhood of Prince Charles, the Honourable Nicholas Soames, who, it was alleged, had told the Princess in no uncertain terms to 'stop meddling in landmines', threatening her darkly that 'accidents do happen'. The then portly bon vivant Etonian, Soames, a grandson of Winston Churchill and nicknamed somewhat unkindly at the time by the tabloids, 'Fatty', was scheduled to give evidence after the Countess.

What was required then at this investigation was the insight of someone who knew the Princess's heart, who was close to all sides

– the Spencers, the Fayeds and the Windsors. Someone who might have the courage, the fortitude and the clout to speak truth to power.

Cue Raine, Countess Spencer, a title she had settled on after her divorce from her third and final husband, the French Count, Jean-François Pineton de Chambrun.

The Countess had cut an iconic, divisive figure ever since she had been 'introduced' into society and voted 'Debutante of the Year' in 1947. With her enormous sweep of bouffant hair, her cut glass vowels and her demure yet forceful manner, it would not be an understatement to describe her as formidable. Certainly, the British public and the national press thought so. Everything about Raine – from her mother, the prolific penner of romances Barbara Cartland, often nicknamed 'the pantomime dame' for her putrid pink outfits and lurid makeup, to her much publicised feud with the world's most photographed woman, her stepdaughter Diana, was 'good copy'.

It was no surprise then, that when Raine's expertly made-up face – the artfully mascara'd hazel eyes, the glossy red lips – along with the trademark sculpted hair, with pearl and jewel earrings the size of quality scallops clinging to her ears, first came into view on the bank of 50-inch plasma screens, specially installed in the press annexe for the inquest, a burst of riotous, appreciative applause ricocheted round the room. The seventy-eight-year-old Countess, who had arrived in her chauffeur-driven Rolls, was manifesting a chic if slightly dotty eccentricity, in her black immaculately fitted woollen suit, and her pillbox hat and veil (a nod perhaps to the grieving Jackie Kennedy or the widowed Duchess of Windsor?). Her famous wit was subtly on display – how else to explain her chequerboard scarf which cheekily mimicked the cap bands of the Metropolitan police force?

As Raine was sworn in, the silence in the court room was almost audible. In the press annex fingers hovered anxiously over keyboards whilst all eyes were trained on the screens. Mr Ian Burnett, counsel to the inquests, had risen and was preparing his first question: 'Are you Raine Countess Spencer?'[1] he asked. The Countess, who appeared entirely unphased at the prospect of giving evidence at one of the most historic inquests of all time, slowly raised her veil, fixed the QC with a dazzling smile, moistened her already glossy lips and, taking a deep breath, perhaps for dramatic effect, began . . .

1

Mummy Darling

— •◆• —

It would have been surprising to anyone who knew her, that Raine would have given anything but a masterful performance at the inquest. 'Behind the saccharine image there stands an extremely able politician, a feminine but tough bargainer, who is prepared to fight for the moon to get half', the *Guardian*[1] had said of her earlier political career. Here was a woman who had been rehearsing her lines and managing her image for her entire life. Her first role was as the daughter of the globe's biggest pedlar of romances, the redoubtable novelist Barbara Cartland, known to her millions of fans as BC, who had at the time of her death written 723 books and sold more than 750 million copies worldwide.

Barbara Cartland must have made for a strange and challenging mother figure. Publicly, the novelist fashioned herself as the fairy godmother of love. She dressed the part in negligee-like pink dresses, enormous hats and sported Geisha makeup, applying boot polish to her false eyelashes, rather than mascara, for greater effect. Privately, she was, by all accounts, a controlling, domineering figure in her children's lives, happily stating on many occasions that she'd rather Raine had been a boy (she later had two sons with her second husband – the cousin of her first). 'I was disappointed by having a daughter', she told the interviewer Dr Anthony Clare, for his Radio 4 series, *In the Psychiatrist's Chair*, 'I should like to have had a dozen boys'. When Clare asked why, she replied snappishly, 'I don't like women very much. I think men are marvellous, they are the heroes in my books'.

Throughout her life Cartland doted on her boys as she had on her own brothers and as her mother had on her father. They in turn worshipped her, always calling her 'Mummy', returning to the fold at very regular intervals (her sons, Ian and Glen, live at the time of writing at Camfield, Cartland's former estate). 'I despise men who don't run their own households', Barbara told Clare, seemingly without a shred of irony – Cartland's own mother Mary (known as Polly) had more than capably run her own household after the loss of her father, and Barbara, similarly, ran hers with a rod of iron, brooking no interference from either of her husbands, her sons, or Raine for that matter.

At least two of Cartland's three children were bullied at school in one way or another as an indirect result of her own dominant relationship with them. Ian's miserable prep school experience was thanks in part to the fact that Cartland made him wear his hair long down his neck: 'the boys used to call me a girl. I put up with the teasing and bullying and kept my hair long just to please her'.[2] Later, Raine was bullied when evacuated to a school in Canada. 'Perhaps they didn't like the way she talked', said Cartland at the time, dismissing the bullying, which was more likely due to Raine having been home-schooled and unaware of how to socialise with girls of her own age. Matters between mother and daughter were no better at home. 'The mother–daughter relationship was always what you might call scratchy', says a friend who knew both mother and daughter.

If 'Man as hero' was the prevailing trope in the Cartland household, then fantasy was the key to success. Barbara Cartland's emergence onto the social scene was a story worthy of its own leather-bound publication. Despite her lifelong insistence that she hailed from an aristocratic family, in reality, her parents, Polly and Bertie, were solidly middle class. Born at her paternal grandparents' house, a pseudo-Gothic villa in Edgbaston, Birmingham, on 9 July 1901, Barbara always said her parents would have preferred a boy. When, during the difficult birth, the doctor asked Bertie Cartland whether to save the mother or child, he reportedly expostulated: 'Damn the bloody child! Save my wife!'

'"That's dead – throw it on the bed", my father said', was how Barbara described her father's reaction to her entry into the world, 'but' she added, 'I was determined to live.'[3]

Born into a new century and a new Edwardian era (Victoria had died on 22 January of that year and Edward VII was now King), the world that Mary Barbara Hamilton Cartland emerged into was swiftly changing. A young MP called Winston Churchill gave his first speech in the commons (the Empire versus the Boers), oil was struck for the first time in Texas, the Commonwealth of Australia was formed, Chekhov's *Three Sisters* opened at Moscow Arts Theatre, US Steel became the world's first billion-dollar corporation, the first Nobel Prize in physics was awarded to Wilhelm Röntgen for his discovery of X-rays and a little known English engineer, called Hubert Cecil Booth, patented the powered vacuum cleaner.

Later that year, across the pond, Theodore Roosevelt would be inaugurated after President McKinley's assassination.

Whilst her family might not have been anywhere near as aristocratic as Barbara might have later made them out to be, they were certainly 'muck 'n' brass' wealthy. She liked to tell the story of how her industrialist grandfather, James Cartland, having lost a fortune speculating on the Fishguard railway, shot himself one Sunday morning (18 October 1903). James was the proprietor of a brass foundry, James Cartland & Son 'sole manufacturers of Andrews, Peacock's and Pugh's patent lock furniture and Thorpe's ventilating sash fasteners'. Probate states that he died leaving an estate of £92,614.11s 6d. (roughly £11 million today) so he and the family were certainly very far from impoverished.

'You are selling yourself on the altar for seven and six', Barbara's maternal grandfather, Sanford George Treweeke Scobell, had repeatedly told Barbara's mother Polly after her engagement to Bertie Cartland was announced (seven and six being the cost of a marriage license at the time). Barbara was always at pains to point out the superior side of her maternal family – her maternal grandfather, she said, had been educated at Winchester and Trinity College, Oxford, and according to her he had been amongst the first men to scale Mont Blanc. And she would add, the family was one of the oldest Saxon families in existence – distantly related to the Sheriff of Nottingham. Whether this is true or not, there is little dispute that the family backgrounds of the bride and groom were radically different.

Unfortunately, Bertie showed little aptitude for hard work and it's easy to see why Sanford was soon fed up with his feckless son-in-law. After their marriage the couple would be forced to live on the £50 yearly that Sanford settled on Polly 'We were very poor', Barbara later recalled. 'We only had two servants.'

Sanford's legacy to his granddaughter Barbara seems to have been his ability to subject others to his torrential rages. Describing her grandfather as 'handsome and blue blooded' – from pictures the former was also likely wishful thinking – she often told stories of how she had been brought up witnessing his terrible temper. A particular favourite was her recollection that Sanford had died of a heart attack, brought on by one of his tyrannical rages after the local fire brigade had proved tardy in their arrival to put out a fire at one of his pigsties. 'I'm very disagreeable at times and I don't feel the slightest bit guilty', she told Clare.

For a while after her grandfather's death, Bertie began to contribute to the family finances; but not without Polly's prompting. A dinner at which she sat next to a high-ranking official yielded results. The official offered Bertie a job and he worked his way up to the position of secretary of the Provincial Primrose League. The group, founded by Lord Randolph Churchill to spread Conservative principles of 'tory democracy' throughout the nation and named after Disraeli's favourite flower, afforded Bertie a decent salary and a position in society which Polly so craved.

From then on, the family continued to live the sort of life to which they had wanted to become accustomed, renting Amerie Court, a run-down farmhouse in Pershore, from the Earl of Coventry. Bertie's salary did not extend to them affording horses, so they rode to hounds and to tennis matches together on bicycles. Polly polished the family silver herself to save money and keep up appearances. Bertie was more a liability than an asset, drinking excessively and gambling recklessly. A legacy from his mother also kept them afloat. By then there were three children with the addition of two boys – John Ronald (known as Ronald, born in 1907) and James Anthony (known as Anthony, born in 1912), both adored by Barbara who by then was boarding at Malvern, where she was bullied. 'The girls thought her uppish', says her biographer Tim Heald, 'she thought them noisy and rather common.'[4]

When Bertie was called up in 1914, it seems to have been a relief for the family. Polly promptly moved back in with her mother and Barbara was sent to Netley Abbey, which she described as 'finishing school' but was in reality a school run by the Misses Downie, who discounted fees for the daughters of Naval and Military Officers (by then Bertie was a major). Sixteen-year-old Barbara did not weep for her father when she was told of his death in action in 1918 – she did however make practical arrangements for the funeral, writing to her mother, 'I have had my coat and skirt dyed black. Would you like me to have my frock coat done?'

With Bertie gone they would struggle to survive. To make money Polly moved to London and opened a dress shop. According to Barbara, her mother took a 'tall and dingy' rented house at 20 Neville Street, South Kensington, in order for the young Barbara to 'come out' into society. In fact, there is no indication that Barbara actually 'came out' in the traditional sense. The process of presenting debutantes at court had been suspended during the war and there would be no dinners or balls in her honour, no presentation at Buckingham Palace to the King and no traditional Queen Charlotte's Ball. In any case, the family's finances and their social position would not have afforded either the social leverage or the lavish spending required to launch a young aristocrat – had Barbara been one – into society. No matter because the London social scene, which had been dramatically, if temporarily, fragmented by the war, offered for one brief moment a different sort of opportunity for women like Barbara – young, and socially ambitious, with aristocratic pretensions, but no so-called 'breeding' – to launch themselves into society.

Instinctively comprehending the situation, Barbara seems to have set out to exploit it to its full advantage. Recognising that to 'succeed' in early 1920s society meant either being aristocratic or at least being as close to aristocracy, both literally and metaphorically, as possible, Barbara announced to her brother Ronald with all the enthusiasm of a modern-day Becky Sharp, that she planned to get to know 'everyone in London'. Everyone worth knowing that is. She made it her business to attend the 'right' parties and associated almost exclusively with the moneyed, the socially and politically notable and the aristocratic. 'I was grown up. I was expected to be amusing, gay and attractive to men. And incredible though it seemed,

I was!', says Barbara in one of her five rose-tinged autobiographies, *We Danced All Night.*[5]

Her happiness was momentarily blighted by the breaking off of an early engagement to an officer in the Life Guards. The break was precipitated by Polly, who had taken it upon herself to educate her daughter about 'the facts of life'. Barbara was so disgusted and shocked by the realities of the sexual act, that when her former fiancé threatened to shoot himself, she simply ignored him and whirled on in a champagne haze of admirers whom from then on, she would keep very strictly at arm's length.

She took more than one turn around the dance floor with a certain Ernest Simpson, though she was soon warned off by his sister Maud Kerr-Smiley, who let the young Barbara know in no uncertain terms that her brother needed to 'marry money'. Instead, he married notoriety, walking a certain Wallis Warfield up the aisle – the woman who would later be responsible for the greatest schism in the British Monarchy, when Edward VIII abdicated the British throne in favour of their marriage.

Could a young girl like Barbara, with ambitions that greatly outweighed either her bank balance or her middle-class background, have 'broken through' and succeeded so readily at any previous moment? It seems unlikely. 'Apart from my face and my youth I had little to offer', she concedes in *We Danced All Night.*

The 1920s unleashed a post-war explosion of manic energy. With hindsight it seems to have been composed of guilt and relief, which within the upper echelons drove a highly charged, somewhat debauched society, determined to party away the terrible memories of the death and destruction that the Great War had wrought and the impending threat of another to come. Boundaries were blurred and class barriers much more readily breached. London society was fuelled by a cocktail of champagne, cocaine, jazz, gossip and illicit affairs, which allowed someone like Barbara with a social hunger, a good mind and a mission to be successful, to slip through the cracks.

Pretty soon Barbara was pictured at all the right places with all the right people, notably with her best friend Mary Ashley, later the Honourable Mrs Cunningham-Reid, who married First World War flying ace, Captain Alec Cunningham-Reid (they were described by *Tatler* as England's wealthiest girl and handsomest man). Amongst other friends were Mary's sister, Edwina Mountbatten, the Countess of Dalkeith and the famous society beauty and Cecil Beaton muse, model Paula Gellibrand. Gellibrand, Barbara notes, somewhat waspishly perhaps, 'became a sensation overnight when she lunched at the Ritz in a hat trimmed with Wisteria'.[6]

Accounts of Barbara's early relationships with the opposite sex are varied, and contradictory. She was fond of recounting her first 'encounter' with just the sort of man who would later appear in her novels. The dashing and renowned archaeologist and Egyptologist Howard Carter first clapped eyes upon Barbara queuing for a drink at the infamous long bar in Shepheard's Hotel in Cairo. The bar, so called for its length and as a result its tortuous wait times, was the watering hole of military officers, explorers and global roués. The dates are blurry and it was certainly not the sort of place one might expect to encounter a young English lady on her own (there's a possibility that the whole thing was fiction) but then, Cartland was not just any young lady. Even then she seemed to possess the knack of positioning (or perhaps 'telling') herself into the vortex of the story. After having dinner together (with Polly chaperoning – the two were staying at Shepheard's whilst visiting Cairo for the first time), Carter issued an invitation for them to visit his newly discovered Tomb of the Pharaoh in Luxor. Naturally they (or was it Barbara?) accepted.

When the visit occurred a week later, it would be without Polly, who was 'unwell' on that day according to Barbara, who was left to visit Tutankhamen's tomb alone with Carter. One thing led to another, and Barbara would later tell of Carter's advances, made whilst the two were resting on the sarcophagus. She claimed that she rebuffed him and scrambled back out of the tomb, blinking into the sunlight, intacta. Whether things ended there or not with the adventurous Carter, Cartland never elaborated, but the visit was meaningful, and not just because of her privileged access to such a momentous historical find. From then on, until her death, Barbara would be endlessly fascinated by the colour pink, espousing its calming benefits and enveloping herself and her home in various shades of rose, which she claimed she first saw adorning the walls of King Tut's tomb.

On 2 November 1920, Barbara's engagement to Terence Hume Langrish, nicknamed Pingo, 'late Irish Guards and RAF', was announced in *The Times*. The betrothal was short-lived and the reasons for Pingo's rejection all too poignant. After joining the Special Police Force, having been unable to find work in England, Pingo and his great friend Peter Ames, the fiancé of socialite Millicent Orr Ewing, had headed to Ireland, where the war of independence was raging. Ames was tragically murdered in the terrible Bloody Sunday massacres on 21 November 1920, which left tens of British and Irish dead (including civilians, amongst them two children). After Pingo telegrammed Barbara with the news, it was left to her to break it to Millicent. Unable to cope with the tragedy, Barbara broke off the engagement shortly afterwards. 'I knew that I was running away, but I couldn't bear being involved in death and murder, tears and unhappiness. I just wanted to dance, to forget wars and anything to do with them.'

Barbara, now dressed mainly in pink, would quite literally foxtrot, tango and possibly even shimmy her way through the roaring drink- and music-fuelled twenties – she was an elegant, accomplished partner and her reputation preceded her. On her dance card were likely to have been Edward, then Prince of Wales, and his brother

George (later the Duke of Kent). From the mid-twenties the debonair brothers were in demand, living a bachelor life together in York House, a part of St James's Palace. Edward, it is said, was responsible for weaning his brother, younger by eight and a half years and a notorious bisexual, off morphine and cocaine after he became addicted during a friendship with Kiki Preston, the American socialite known as 'the girl with the silver syringe'.

By the age of twenty-three, Barbara had published her first book, a romantic novel called *Jig-Saw*, disingenuously telling the *New York Times* much later in an interview, 'I was a debutante then and it was a serious book and debutantes weren't supposed to soil their lily-white hands'.[7] The book was a bestseller almost in spite of its tepid reviews.

Her big break came the following year when she met Richard Viner, gossip editor of the *Daily Express*, who offered her five shillings a paragraph for any gossip she could put his way. Soon her florid prose caught the eye of Lord Beaverbrook, Napoleon-sized, snaggle-toothed media magnate and proprietor of the newspaper. As Barbara tells it, after summoning her to his office, the press baron, described by Lady Diana Cooper as 'the strange attractive gnome with the odour of genius about him', offered to make her 'the most successful female journalist in the world'.[8]

The inevitable catch was that she'd also have to be his mistress: an offer she says she swiftly declined, 'besides he was terribly old'[9] (Beaverbrook was forty-four). Undeterred, he decided to take the aspiring journalist under his wing – or that's the way Barbara told it. Soon she was hanging with the 'Beaverbrook crowd', partying at the press baron's invitation in Deauville with Noël Coward and the Marchioness of Queensberry, swiftly becoming a gossip columnist for the *Daily Express*. Beaverbrook impressed upon her two things: the need for short sentences and the heady elixir that a liberal sprinkling of aristocratic names could add. Barbara was introduced to the paper's readers as a young woman who 'exemplifies in London Society, the charming and intellectually exuberant type she describes'. In other words, young Cartland was a crashing snob and a namedropper, establishing herself in society by association, rather than, to use one of her favourite terms, 'rank'.

As the new 'favourite' Barbara also became a regular at Lord Beaverbrook's Hurlingham mansion, where lunch guests included Winston Churchill, Lord Birkenhead and Lord Castlerosse. Beaverbrook continued to make passes, but she was, she said, resolute and the two became close friends, with Max personally editing her snippets of gossip and later her columns, instructing her sternly to 'never be boring'. This made all the more sense when she comprehended that her readers were increasingly appreciative of the short dialogue they were hearing first on radio and later on television. 'I then reduced all the paragraphs in my novels to about three lines – if they were longer the reader skipped them.'[10] In other words, she was writing novels in the form of newspaper headlines.

Barbara didn't let historical matters like women's suffrage trouble her short-sentenced narratives either (though she was certainly the model of the modern self-supporting female herself). None of her heroines reflected the fact that whilst she was writing her early novels, women over the age of twenty-one would gain the right to vote in the Equal Franchise Act of 1928. The first tranche of over thirties females who met the property requirements had already to great uproar won the vote in 1918. If society was moving on, alas Barbara's fictional women were not. They never would.

Barbara was a studious ignorer of the zeitgeist – her heroines would, to a woman, fall in line in support of the ancient trope, that a woman's place was in the home. In reality, throughout Britain, the new-found freedom and liberation that women entering the workplace during the First World War had earned for themselves, could not now be contained by a post-war society desirous of a return to the 'old normal'. In direct contradiction to the burgeoning female empowerment movement and of critical importance in all of Barbara's 728 books, written over seventy-five years, was the notion that the heroines of her novels should define themselves by having lovers and husbands who were titled, rich, or best of all, both.

And, whilst the 'Bright Young Things' represented in literature by F. Scott Fitzgerald's Gatsby, P. G. Wodehouse's Bertie Wooster and Nancy Mitford's Radlett family, whirled each other around the dance floors of the jazz clubs and ballrooms of London, sipping cocktails and chomping on canapes, either trying to forget those that they had lost, or in giddy relief at having been a tad too young to fight themselves, the rest of Britain, particularly the lower classes, were struggling.

By 1925, when Churchill returned Britain to the gold standard, maintaining high interest rates, making exports expensive, and the cost of living almost prohibitive for the working classes, the collective relief and goodwill fostered by the end of the war had been exhausted. Unemployment had risen to over two million and in the North it stood at some 70 per cent of the population, thanks to the paucity of coal reserves (all of which had been used during the war) and the lack of investment in new mass production techniques in industry. By 1926, the workers had little option left to them but to strike. For Barbara, the event of the 1926 General Strike itself was the beginning of a growing insight that her own hard won, seemingly gilded life, could in the course of a few wrong turns (or possibly the wrong marriage), return her to the instability and genuine poverty from which her mother had sought so diligently to free them all. 'We were brought up by Edwardian women with narrow restrictive social customs, nurtured on snobbery and isolated from any contact with or knowledge of people outside our own accepted class', she later wrote in *We Danced All Night*, acknowledging a childhood free from the influence of men. At one point she even admits to her own financial challenges: 'We all wore large shawl-capes of fur which were really wide stoles. Mine was completely unidentifiable and although I longed for a muff I couldn't afford one.'

The poverty that she witnessed whilst running an errand to a vicarage on the Harrow Road during the General Strike (during which she wielded a truncheon to keep order) seems to have stunned her into a momentary realisation that all was not well outside her bubble. 'The dirty streets, the dilapidated, mean little houses badly in need of repair, the ragged children running about with insufficient clothes and bare feet.' At this parlous state of affairs she was forced to wonder, 'if the miners were not justified in refusing a cut in their wages?' She empties her purse of money to help a woman she meets in a hallway who cannot pay the rent. 'How long would it last to feed a family of five children?' She wonders in a rare moment of empathetic reflection. 'And how many families were there without help, without hope?'

Unfortunately, her compassionate insights endured no longer than the end of the General Strike and they were never to surface again in the same way, although charity would be one of her métiers. Perhaps the weighty expectations of her mother at that time were making themselves felt? Certainly, the young novelist must have realised that without a husband to provide financial security, her circumstances were parlous. She could not, unlike her titled friends, rely on trust funds, inheritances or 'daddy' for assistance. 'Marriage was the goal, the prize, the grand finale of our hopes and aspirations. There was no continuation of the story because there was no question of there being a divorce later', she told her biographer Tim Heald, admitting that she would not allow any suitor to kiss her unless he proposed beforehand.

Small wonder then that she had forty-eight proposals of marriage before accepting the forty-ninth. He was Alexander 'Sachie' McCorquodale, of Cound Hall, Shropshire, heir to a printing fortune.

'He was rich', she later said, 'his father's company printed all the Government's postal orders.' Whilst Sachie was not titled he was handsome, an excellent sportsman and he had 'prospects' (for which read he stood to inherit a fortune).

Surprisingly the only cloud on the horizon was Polly, 'Is he really worthy of you darling?'[11] she asked.

Barbara's powers of persuasion were already as impressive as her mother's. Having convinced Polly of Sachie's suitability she went on to persuade the young Norman Hartnell, then a fashion student, and later the exclusive designer to Queen Elizabeth II, to create a wedding dress to her own design (which she later described as a 'disaster'). The wedding, on 23 April 1927, was held at St Margaret's, the church next to Westminster Abbey, thus ensuring maximum exposure and an implication by location and guest list that this was a 'noble' media-worthy wedding. The desired press photographers were in attendance. As if to underscore her status, Barbara's twelve bridesmaids and three pages included the daughters of the Marquis of Queensbury, Viscount Scarsdale, Viscount Monsell and Lady Domville. The girls were outfitted in fairy-tale pink confections modelled on a dress worn by Mrs Dudley Ward, mistress to the Prince of Wales.

Barbara and Sachie set up house in Culross Street, where *Tatler* announced 'Mrs McCorquodale, an accomplished hostess, will be one of London's leading social figures this season'. She quickly became pregnant and, obsessed by having an attractive baby, placed a picture of her ideal baby next to her bed. 'I was determined she should be beautiful', she said later of her daughter, 'and I not only looked at Beauty but thought it.' On 9 September 1929, Cartland gave birth to Raine McCorquodale. The circumstances of the birth are not recorded, but her Gaelic name was chosen, said Cartland, because it was 'beautiful and original'. *Tatler*, 9 October 1929, ran a picture of a dutiful mother leaning over a cradle with the caption: 'Barbara Cartland (Mrs Alexander McCorquodale) and her daughter.

The famous young authoress of *Jigsaw*, *Blood Money*, *The Mayfair Review* etc, with her new daughter, who is to be given the uncommon name of Raine.' The pun was unintended. Eager to get back to her writing, Barbara swiftly hired a nanny who pushed Raine out in a custom enamelled black and white pram mirroring the colours of her own Rolls-Royce, given to her as a wedding gift by Sachie. 'What a lovely fat baby!', the young Princess Elizabeth is said to have exclaimed, coming across the infant and nanny at a birthday party, 'and what a funny name'.

Barbara was radiant. Her future was assured. She had a beautiful baby, a flourishing social life, a career as a novelist and titled friends. She cemented her reputation by organising a series of vast charity dinners, culminating with the infamous '*Britain and Her Industries*' dinner at the Royal Albert Hall, following the pageant of the same name. During the pageant itself the aristocracy vied for superiority by flaunting vast dresses illustrating British industry – each one more fabulous and indulgent than the last: Lady Ashley in black sequined tights as 'Coal', Lady Scarsdale in an outlandish woollen crinoline as 'Wool' and Barbara in the pièce de résistance – an enormous dress, sponsored by a cruise line and crafted to look like an ocean liner (with a train modelled on the ocean, so large it was positioned on a trolley, in turn rolled by three titled female attendants). The pageant and ball were a triumph for which Barbara was personally and very publicly congratulated by the Prince of Wales, who whirled her, sans train, post dinner, onto the dance floor. It was the apotheosis of her young career. She had success, she had social cachet, she was widely accepted, even without a title, as London's foremost hostess. And now the icing was on the cake: she was the woman who had danced with the Prince of Wales.

In stark contrast to the blissful marriages which she detailed in her novels, Barbara's own would not go the distance. Sachie, she had swiftly discovered after their marriage, was a lascivious drunk and serial philanderer who, she later claimed, was barely capable of performing the sexual act: 'I was never in the slightest danger of getting pregnant by him',[12] she told one interviewer, promulgating the premise (mostly her own) that Raine had been fathered either by the fifth Duke of Sutherland or by Prince George, the Duke of Kent.

By 1930, Barbara knew that the marriage was over. Her expectations of the physical side of marriage were, in fact, greater and more informed than might have been expected, given her initial proclaimed horror of the sexual act. 'Well I may write about innocent virgins', she told one journalist shrewdly, during her later years, 'but I wasn't one when I married.'[13] She lost her virginity, she later admitted, to Hugh Lygon, Viscount Elmley, the son of the seventh Earl Beauchamp, Lord Warden of the Cinque Ports, whose home, Madresfield Court, was the model for the house in Evelyn Waugh's *Brideshead Revisited*. (Elmley was broadly acknowledged as the study for Lord Marchmain, with his second son, the Honourable Hugh Patrick, as the model for Sebastian Flyte). Barbara claimed not to have found Elmley attractive enough to marry; this was fortunate because soon after, his father, Lord Beauchamp, was forced to resign all of his offices and leave England under a cloud, heading for the continent, after being outed as a homosexual and as Barbara so delicately put it, 'buggering the footmen'. (Homosexuality in Britain would remain a criminal offence until the 1967 Sexual Offences Act decriminalised homosexual acts between men aged over twenty-one.)

Barbara's own behaviour had not been perfect during her marriage. Later she admitted to the aforementioned dalliance with the Duke of Sutherland (his second wife confided to Barbara at a London lunch party in 1963, that she was sure the Duke was Raine's real father). She also had a relationship with a married Mayfair neighbour, Lieutenant-Commander Glen Kidston, one of the racing Bentley

Boys of the 1920s, who died tragically when his borrowed de Havilland Tiger Moth bi-plane broke up in a dust storm over the Drakensberg Mountains in South Africa. When locals found Kidston's broken body, they discovered lying nearby the six photographs of Cartland in Nile blue leather frames that he carried with him everywhere. They were later returned to her by Kidston's grieving sister. Not all of Barbara's dalliances ended in disaster. A fling with Lord Mountbatten (at least as described by BC) turned into a life-long friendship. They were at work on a book together when he died at the hands of the IRA in 1979.

Perhaps Barbara greatest claim was to have bedded Prince George, later the Duke of Kent: 'PG, as I called him was twenty-five at that time and absolutely adorable', she said, 'as well as being the most amazing lover. In my heart I have always believed he was Raine's father. I was shattered when he too died in a plane crash, whilst on active service during the war.'[14]

Against this tempestuous backdrop, with numerous allegations of out of wedlock fatherhood including a royal, Raine would hardly have been permitted to be a retiring wallflower, even had she so desired it. She did not. The media were as entranced by her as they were by her glamorous mother. When the *Daily Sketch* ran a light-hearted weighing-in of top society babies, Mrs McCorquodale's Raine was ranked at number two: 7lb 10¾oz, behind Lady Alington's Mary: 9lb 4oz and ahead of Lady Diana Cooper's Julius: 7lb 4oz. The *Glasgow Evening News* described Raine as 'one of the smartest babies in the park'. Her first party was of course her christening, reported thus in *The Lady*: 'The christening of Raine McCorquodale at St Margaret's by the Bishop of Chelmsford was followed by a very gay party indeed.'

But Raine was not an easy baby and in private Cartland was less than delighted with her. 'Not only was Raine a girl, she was also the child of that disastrous first marriage', notes her biographer

Tim Heald. She was also in poor health for much of her infancy. An enlarged thymus meant that she required delicate handling and in her early years she would sleep with a large radium pack strapped to her chest: 'expensive', noted Cartland tersely. She suffered from severe eczema too, a physical sign of weakness, something which Cartland, for whom keeping up appearances was all, would not have been happy about. Despite being warned that any sudden shock could potentially kill Raine, Barbara decided to raise her as a normal child, explaining that she wanted to inure her to the stresses and strains of everyday living, otherwise 'a rabbit pops out of a hedge and the child dies of shock'.

Raine claimed to remember little about the first major event in her life, the very public divorce proceedings of her parents. Whilst she was only four when the divorce was first petitioned, it seems unlikely that, even as a young child, she would not have sensed an underlying tension in the house, and her parents' mutual disquiet over the scandal which enveloped their lives. She did remember though 'being given lots of sweets as a distraction' but even those were soon 'snatched back' because they 'gave me spots'. No prizes for guessing who was doing the 'snatching'. Even in her darkest hour Barbara always held that it was a woman's responsibility, no matter her age, to look beautiful and to act as her husband's (and her mother's) best asset. 'It's your fault if he goes off the rails and to another woman', she later declared to Anthony Clare, conveniently skimming over her own fateful divorce and the circumstances leading up to it.

The events surrounding the Cartland/McCorquodale divorce were nothing short of scandalous and they were treated as such by the press. When Barbara discovered Sachie's latest affair with a major's wife and fellow alcoholic, Mrs Helene Curtis, via a batch of letters left in his unlocked desk drawer, she immediately offered him a divorce. Sachie forcefully resisted, worried about the amount of money and loss of reputation the whole affair would cost him.

He hired private detectives to spy on Barbara, reasoning that he would turn the tables and sue her for divorce instead.

It was Barbara's brother, Ronald, later to be misidentified as her lover in the divorce papers, who discovered Sachie's plot, when he engaged one of the private detectives lurking outside the house on Culross Street in conversation. The divorce came to court in November 1932, with allegations and counter allegations splashed across the press. Sachie overlooked his suspicions that Raine was not his biological child and counter-petitioned for custody of her.

The couple had guaranteed a very public divorce, by engaging the services of the two leading KCs of the day. Representing Barbara was former Attorney General, Sir Patrick Hastings, one of the best paid KCs in the land. Representing Sachie, the 1st Baron Birkett, later to become the alternate British judge at the Nuremberg trials. Hastings took the trial gratis having been incensed to learn from his daughter, who was dating Ronald at the time, that Sachie was hoping to crush Barbara by hiring Birkett. Fortunately for Barbara, Birkett was Sir Patrick's nemesis and he relished the opportunity to take him on in a high-profile case. The two prima-donna KCs used the McCorquodale trial to flaunt their legal skills and expertise. Sachie's legal bills – and presumably his blood pressure – rose ever upwards.

The papers trumpeted the story – a lurid exposé of upper-class life – for weeks: 'Divorce Suit by Novelist', 'Husband's Cruise in Liner' and 'Cousin cited in cross-petition'. The aforementioned cousin was Hugh McCorquodale. Barbara and he, it was reported, had become 'close' during Sachie's endless drunken indiscretions. In an admirable display of fictionalised truth, worthy of the best-selling novelist she had become, Barbara managed to persuade the court that Hugh's visits were harmless. He would, she said, simply admit himself to the house via a key she had provided, join her in her bedroom, kiss her on both cheeks and together they would drink cocktails. In retaliation, Sachie produced their ex-butler, 'Finney', who said that on taking tea up to Barbara, he had found 'Mr Hugh sitting beside Mrs McCorquodale in a very familiar manner'.

Barbara gamely dismissed the claims, telling the court that all of her friends 'behaved in this way, not just Hugh'.

'You have seen Mrs McCorquodale and you can judge for yourself whether she was the sort of woman who would throw herself into another man's arms in a profligate way', said the judge in the summing up, gesturing towards Barbara who sat, looking baleful, wearing (on her lawyer's instructions) little make-up and a restrained black dress. The jury took just fifteen minutes to deliver a victory for the lady novelist. She and Hugh would continue their relationship and marry discreetly in 1936.

Hugh McCorquodale, forever known to Raine as 'Uncle Hugh', had, like his cousin, been educated at Harrow and similarly went on to Sandhurst, joining the Cameron Highlanders. During the First World War he had been badly wounded in the Battle of Passchendaele and awarded the Military Cross. He had, he later proclaimed in a statement worthy of one of Barbara's fictional heroes, loved her since the moment he had set eyes upon her, at her wedding to his cousin, Sachie. After the divorce, Barbara, Raine and later their two boys – Ian born in 1937, and Glen in 1939 – would be Hugh's lifelong focus. He had the sort of character required for a life with Barbara: long-suffering, kind, loyal and devoted. He was either thick-skinned or forbearing enough to withstand Barbara's eccentricities, her demands and most importantly, her exceptionally close friendship with her brother Ronald, with whom she once famously and rather uncomfortably proclaimed that she 'shared everything but sex'.

Sachie had agreed in the divorce to fund a nanny for Raine, which freed Barbara up to continue her working life and her socialising. She needed the money. Despite having authored twenty-one novels over the preceding sixteen years, the couple were stretched financially. Sachie's family, both scandalised and incensed by the divorce and Barbara's subsequent re-marriage, had confiscated his fortune, which left Barbara with just the £500 a year she had secured in the divorce settlement. Approximately £25,000 in today's money was nowhere near enough to live in the manner to which she had, in her younger years, been determined to become accustomed. Hugh's income was not in the same league as Sachie's, so both the house and the Rolls-Royce were sold to pay the lawyers' bills.

In the autumn of 1936, after the couple married, they moved with Raine to a flat in Half Moon Street, W1. If the young Raine ever registered their change in circumstance, she never acknowledged it, although it may not have been coincidental that she would marry three men who would bring with them not only titles, but various large and impressive homes to boot. Much later, Barbara conceded the trial had been tough on both mother and daughter. 'In those days', she told the *New York Times* in a 1981 interview, 'people didn't have "divorces".'

Barbara was already beginning to position Raine for her entrée into society. She had plenty of contacts. Her social world was one in which Emerald Cunard, perhaps London's greatest hostess at the time, gave sensational parties, only to be 'out sensationed' by a fellow American hostess and Cunard's enemy Lady Colefax. 'The oldest joke at the time', says Barbara rather spitefully in *We Danced All Night*, 'was that the only sound in the King's Road was Lady Colefax climbing.'[15] In 1933, Raine had starred in a round-up of 'Society Children' published by *Vogue*, which reported that: 'the little daughter of Barbara Cartland is a perfect hostess for the after-tea visitor . . . she has achieved a pretty dignity of manners which should stand her in good stead later'. Raine's nursery, we were told, had a fine view of Curzon Street, with a mantlepiece covered with invitation cards: 'and her engagement diary must be almost as full as mother's'. This would have been a physical impossibility. Barbara spent most of the 1930s, when she wasn't giving birth, writing or partying at the fashionable KitKat and Embassy jazz and dining clubs (both of which she'd had a hand in revamping) with her precious brother Ronald, for whom she nurtured not only an undying love but also an ambition to see featured at the heart of political power.

Though she favoured Ronald, Barbara adored Anthony too. The brothers were both schooled at Charterhouse and the three had been close all of their lives. Anthony had accepted a commission into the army after leaving school, whilst Ronald seemed to be destined for the type of career in politics that Barbara almost certainly, at some level, wished for herself. If her brother was full of self-doubt, she was not. She spent a great deal of time and money campaigning successfully for him to become an MP. In 1935, at King's Norton, Birmingham, Ronald was nominated to stand for the Conservatives. In addition to funding him, Barbara had found him a sponsor and stumped for him exhaustively alongside their mother Polly, who even attended Ronald's selection committee with him.

When Ronald won a surprise victory over his Labour opponent, G. R. Michison, whose wife the infamous writer Naomi attended the result hatless in high Russian boots – confirming their reputation as an outré pairing (they had an open marriage) – Barbara felt vindicated. From then on, she and Ronald were an inseparable political duo. He discussed and rehearsed every political speech with her, and was swiftly identified as one of the most promising parliamentarians of his generation. 'The trouble with most women today is that they will not realise that women can only succeed when they are the inspiration of the shadow behind men: that men become great through them. That is the secret of women's power', she later said almost certainly referencing herself.

The sources for inspiration and motivation in Barbara's life were threefold: her brother Ronald, her writing career and her daughter Raine. The three would intermingle and fight for attention throughout her life, even when, in Ronald's case, they were deceased, or in Raine's, when relations were strained and difficult to the point of no communication.

Despite Ronald's misgivings that Barbara's marriage would change their relationship, it did not: 'You know what you have meant to me these last five years – much more than I can ever tell you . . . Now, after today it can't be quite the same – our relationship', wrote Ronald to Barbara on the morning of her wedding. He urged her in closing: 'Don't ever lose the memory of these last few years; the struggles as well as the victories and don't forget darling, all the happy hours we've spent together.' For his part, Hugh had no objections to his wife's close involvement with her brother. Whilst brother and sister holidayed on the Riviera for example, with Barbara pregnant with their first son, Ian, Raine was sent to her beloved grandmother Polly in Worcestershire, to whom she was devoted (she later credited Polly for her 'can do' indomitable attitude), in order that Hugh could pursue his twin loves of shooting and fishing in Scotland.

Ronald's star was on the rise. In his parliamentary maiden speech, he attacked Prime Minister Stanley Baldwin's apathetic attempts to bolster aid to distressed areas of the UK. He was vociferous too about Nazi persecution of the Jews, something he and Barbara had seen for themselves on a walking holiday in Austria. In 1939, he was amongst a group of Conservative MPs who publicly opposed the government's policy of appeasement. When he left the chamber in frustration over Baldwin's weak leadership he had bumped into Winston Churchill who urged him to return to the chamber, because 'we have everything to fight for'. As a result of that encounter, Ronald impassioned speech in favour of intervention – 'We are at

the point where we are going to fight and we may be going to die'
– caught the mood of the nation perfectly, speaking for an entire
generation of young men, whilst his fellow backbenchers barracked
him incessantly. His reputation as a potential leader was cemented
and Churchill later described him as 'a man of noble spirit who
spoke fearlessly for Britain'.

When war broke out in 1939, Ronald joined Anthony in military
service, becoming a lieutenant, then major in the 53rd Anti-Tank
Regiment of the Worcestershire and Oxfordshire Yeomanry.
Anthony, a captain in the 2nd Battalion, Lincolnshire Regiment,
was already in France. Very soon, without their knowing it, the two
brothers were fighting the same enemy, not twenty miles apart from
each other, in the retreat to Dunkirk.

Barbara was prepared for the worst, or so she thought. 'I'd seen
in a dream that he was missing', she later told Anthony Clare,
adding, 'I'd had premonitions throughout my life'. In her dream
she reported seeing Ronald lying dead with a hole in his forehead.

On 6 June 1940, Polly received two telegrams from the
Secretary of State for War, informing her separately, that her sons
Major J. R. H. Cartland MP, RA and Captain J. A. H. Cartland
were missing in action. The worry and the waiting was almost too
much to bear for mother and daughter. It would be a year before
they learned the truth.

At the end of June 1940, with the potential loss of both brothers
on her mind and with the threat of Nazi invasion all too real,
Barbara needed her wits about her again. The family was vulnerable
in London and after much debate, she decided to evacuate Raine,
now eleven, and her two half-brothers Ian and Glen, to Canada,
taking up the offer of a cabin from her friend, Lady Dunn. She was
not alone in making this decision – thousands of children from
well-bred families were sent overseas out of harm's way. Winston
Churchill publicly disapproved, 'I entirely deprecate any stampede

from this country at the present time', he told his then Home Secretary, Herbert Morrison. Barbara was conflicted between patriotism and her children's wellbeing. In the end, Hugh persuaded her to take the offer from Lady Dunn, whose husband Sir James, a member of the cabinet, was warning of an imminent German invasion – the likelihood of which Churchill, it was said, was now also convinced. The family sailed at the end of June from Tilbury on the overcrowded Canadian Pacific liner, the *Duchess of Atholl*.

Canada was a shock for Raine, not least because she had never seen the inside of a classroom. Whether she had wanted complete control over her young daughter, or felt that as a girl she was not worth the school fees, is unclear, but up until that point, Barbara had home-schooled Raine with the combination of a governess and a good deal of her own intervention. 'She was trying to make me the perfect person and didn't have very good material to work with', Raine later said with admirable self-awareness. 'Ponies, learning to swim, governesses. It was a lost cause. Mother was determined I should be a sporting girl and had me taught riding, but I was terrified. I'm an indoor girl. I was always last in the local gymkhana.' She remembered hating being 'squashed into a school uniform' for the first time at her school in the smart resort village of Metis Beach overlooking the St Lawrence River. She was badly bullied – a fact of which her mother was all too aware, although she did nothing to help. 'The other girls kicked her with their boots, I can't think why', said Barbara dismissively in a later interview. 'Maybe it was the way she talked?'

Little is recorded about the family's Canadian sojourn, princi-pally because it was so short-lived. Barbara felt lonely, cut off and desperate, despite completing two lecture tours and accepting a commission from a millionaire to ghost write his life story, for which she received the sum of £250. She cabled Hugh saying she felt that it was 'unpatriotic' to stay away, and that she was 'underemployed and cowardly'. In reality it was more likely that she felt lonely and missed the company of friends and family, not to mention the 'buzz' of her newspaper columns. The urge to return was such that she endangered the lives of herself and her children with an impetuous decision to take a boat home from Montreal. Despite restrictions, she managed to obtain a permit to return from the Canadian Government – travelling across the Atlantic against the advice of the War Office, which had forbidden commercial travel, because of the severe risk of German U-boats, ramping up Atlantic patrols after the Battle of Britain. On 17 September 1940, the SS *City of Benares* had been torpedoed on its way out of Liverpool to Canada, with the loss of eighty-seven children and 175 adults. The shocking incident brought the process of evacuation to Canada swiftly to a close. Returning from Canada was now judged to be simply too danger-ous for anything other than troop carriers. But Barbara, headstrong as ever, ignored the advice of everyone (including Hugh and James Dunn) and decided to take the risk anyway.

She would pass what some would charitably call her blind deter-mination and others downright selfish pigheadedness on to Raine. It would later prove to be one of the defining characteristics of her daughter's success.

Upon their miraculous safe arrival, Barbara, Hugh and the children made their way to the tiny country cottage in Great Barford, Bedfordshire that they had bought before the war. Here, the young precocious Raine set to work amusing herself by reading every volume on the vast bookcases lining the walls of the cottage, save those that were forbidden – *Candide* by Voltaire and *The Dark Island* by Vita Sackville-West. 'Well, *Dark Island* we can understand, which is about ladies liking each other', she later said. 'But *Candide* is a rather moral book. Anyway, never mind, by twelve I'd read everything else: Jung, Freud, Shakespeare and Dickens. Whether I understood it or not . . . I read Karl Marx, all 600 pages. It was incredibly boring.'[16]

The evacuation marked the end of Raine's home schooling. From now on she would attend the local Owlstone Croft School, housed in an old stately home. Serendipitously, it was also the evacuated outpost of one of the smartest schools in London. Raine was bright and focused, often coming top of the class. But Barbara had very little time for formal education where females were concerned. 'Do tidy your hair, darling. No man wants a clever woman', she would intone to a grumpy pre-pubescent Raine.

In 1941, the family received the news they were dreading, and Barbara suffered what she later described as 'the greatest setback of my life', when despite having hoped and prayed otherwise, they received confirmation that Ronald and Anthony had both been killed at Dunkirk within a day of each other. Ronald was found, as Barbara's dream had foretold, with a bullet hole piercing his forehead.

The loss of Ronald, whom Barbara had described as 'like her twin', left a lifelong unfillable void. Like so many others, the Cartland family had suffered the almost unthinkable fate of losing two generations of men to the two world wars – Barbara's father in the first and her beloved brothers in the second. 'War is horrible, cruel and devastates so many lives, particularly women's lives', she later said. In a moving testimonial to Ronald, Anthony Eden declared: 'he had the true qualities of leadership, vision, courage and faith. Of all the younger men I knew, his was the fairest future'.

Trying desperately to distract herself from a looming depression over her brothers' deaths, Barbara went back to work. This time it was not for herself, but on behalf of the war effort. She became Chief Lady Welfare Officer for Bedfordshire and created a charity for women serving in the forces, which enabled them to be married in a traditional long white wedding dress rather than uniform. At full swing, Barbara had collected a thousand wedding dresses for lending. Later in her life she was fond of relating just how many of

these wartime brides wrote to her on their golden wedding anniver-
saries to thank her for their white weddings. It was the perfect
metaphor: the penner of dreamy romances makes real women's
dreams come true.

In 1945, with the war over and nothing to distract her, a bereft
Barbara claimed her world was 'in ruins' – she had lost her beloved
brothers and had finished the war without even a 'measly MBE' for
her efforts. She turned down not one, but two Conservative
associations, who invited her to stand in the 1945 election, saying
that her children (Glen aged five, Ian now seven and Raine fifteen)
needed her at home. She never fully recovered from the shock of
Ronald's death, claiming that he appeared to her in visions or
dreams for the rest of her life. In reality, Barbara was likely saving
her energies for what she knew lay ahead. She would not allow
even her profound grief at the loss of the man closest to her, to
distract her from her greatest mission: launching young Raine into
society, with the intention of finding her exactly 'the right' husband.

2

The Deb's Progress

———— •◆• ————

Barbara had spent the years leading up to 1947 – the year of Raine's eighteenth birthday – moulding her in the image of one of her storybook heroines. Raine had been 'finished' (for which read polished) in the manner of all traditional upper class and aristocratic females, first at the Monkey Club on Pont Street, a kind of 'anti-university' billed by its founder Marian Ellison as a place to 'provide post-school education for girls, full or part-time in a wide variety of subjects'. Here Raine learned to type, cook, speak German and French in the 'British Way' – that is with perfect grammar but a permanent English accent – and, perhaps most importantly, how to run a large house. The motto was that of the three wise monkeys, explained in the prospectus as 'from the carving of three monkeys over the door of a temple in Japan suggesting that "humanity should not absorb evil through the senses"' – or, in the common vernacular: 'see no evil, hear no evil, speak no evil'. Once the languages were mastered, Raine was sent to Mürren in Switzerland to improve and to learn to ski. She hated her time there, which was marked out only by two things: the meeting of a young, tall, dashing man on the slopes with the surname of Legge and a visit by her mother who having heard a rumour that Raine had become enamoured of her (much older) art teacher, had motored frantically across Europe in one of her vast limousines to defend her daughter's virginity. Later Raine would confide to her great friend Michael Cole that she found her mother's hysterical arrival, clad as she was in British tweeds and a fur cape, hilarious. Naturally BC was unrepentant. She no doubt took the opportunity to continue her practice of pressing her daughter into giving spontaneous speeches at every available opportunity in order to prepare her for 'society'. On her return from Switzerland, Raine found the tension in the family home that spring almost untenable. Much was riding on the summer of 1947: Raine's coming- out ceremony and subsequent 'season' was to be the fruition of all of Barbara's hard work and she was not going to let Raine fall at the final hurdle. 'She had perfect features and a lovely figure, so I decided I was going to produce her as a beauty', she said, with the calm, deliberate, detached tones of a marketeer selling a new product. 'She was still going through a very scruffy period and at times I really used to bully her and become absolutely furious with her – as I suppose mothers often do with daughters . . . of course, the bullying worked and soon she was starting to make the most of herself, which was really all that mattered.'[1]

Barbara would need all of her wiles to mastermind Raine's presentation at court, in the notorious 'coming-out' ceremony of Britain's post-war debutantes. The field was crowded and competitive. A seven-year war break in presentations at court had led to what can best be described for the times, as a bottleneck of brood mares. Twenty thousand eager debutantes of marriageable age (many exceeding the traditional age of seventeen, because of the delay) would be lining up for the presentation ceremony, followed by a party, at which cake and champagne provided by Buckingham

Palace would be served.[2] The pressure was increased by the fact that many of these young women were being presented at court by their widowed mothers, all desperate to unload the expense of an extra daughter into the hands of someone who could afford her. Prohibitively high death duties, two world wars and no provision for death in combat had decimated some aristocratic families who had lost three or four males in the space of just over twenty years. As Raine's great friend Anne Glenconner, who would come out in 1950, wrote in her memoir, 'the problem with being "out" in society in the early 1950s was that there weren't any likely husbands around, as there weren't many men. My generation had either died in the war or were still away doing National Service'. Strict rules of 'entailed' primogeniture also meant that daughters could not inherit titles or estates and everything had to be passed down to and through the males of the family, no matter how distantly related they were.

An official at Buckingham Palace, foreseeing the potential disasters that thousands of frenzied debutantes and their equally keen 'presenters' could wreak, neatly circumnavigated the problem of overcrowding by arranging for debs to be presented 'en masse' on specified days and times within the Palace State Apartments and in the royal gardens, at what were effectively 'Garden Parties'.[3]

There were 19,999 other debs and then there was Raine McCorquodale, who, whilst not aristocratic from birth, was an odds-on favourite for the highest honour of the season: Deb of the Year. With her winning smile, her exquisite dresses, her excellent dancing skills and her 'pushy mother', Raine had all the right connections, almost in spite of her birth. She would be presented by her mother's great friend Mrs Michael Bowes-Lyon, sister-in-law to Queen Elizabeth (Bowes-Lyon), allowing Barbara to neatly circumvent her own spurious 'coming-out' claims. Mrs Michael Bowes-Lyon was something of a rock star of the age – she'd had a dazzling wedding, as Miss Betty Cator, at St George's, Hanover Square, where the surging crowds captured on black and white celluloid, thronging to catch a glimpse of 'the royals' attending the wedding, had all but flattened the police cordon.

As early as the 1900s, there had been a rumbling of snobby dissent over the opening up of 'the deb system' to include those non aristocrats, like Barbara, whose families had made fortunes in industry and commerce. In other words, high society was in danger of becoming more of a meritocracy: 'As entry into politics and the diplomatic service became elective and civil service appointments subject to competitive examination, both originally preserves of the upper classes, the fundamental power base on which Society rested was weakened', writes Lucinda Gosling in her book *Debutantes and the London Season*. Amongst those with starry reputations but not necessarily 'presentation worthy' backgrounds were sisters Rosemary and Kathleen (or 'Kick') Kennedy, daughters of the American Ambassador Joe Kennedy, and sisters of John F. Kennedy, presented at court in 1938. Kick became the pin-up girl for generations of 'new debs' when she married William Cavendish, heir to the Duke of Devonshire, proving that if you were pretty, connected, wealthy or better still all three, you too could snag a duke.

Capitalising on the new monied debs was practically a blood sport, not just for penurious sons of the aristocracy, but also for a number of elderly aristocratic ladies who were down on their luck. Many made a tidy profit by accepting money for introducing the daughters of the wealthy (but untitled) to court. Here was an early indication of the way the wind was blowing. 'Industry and commerce' were marrying into and shoring up the aristocracy and aristocracy was making way. 'Society', once referred to as 'the ton', no longer constituted just the top hundred ducal families in the country. As industry and wealth increased, 'society' expanded – it couldn't afford not to.

In 1955, just eight years after Raine's debutante season, the aristocratic Nancy Mitford (herself a former deb and daughter of a baron) would spark social uproar and characterise the uneasiness within both the upper and the new middle classes about the blurring of the class divide, with her magazine article, published in *Encounter*, 'The English Aristocracy'. Amongst other things, Mitford included a perceptive commentary on the identification of the aristocracy via their use of 'U' terminology (false teeth instead of dentures for example) and of the middle and lower classes by their 'non-U' terminology (home instead of house and so on). The article was so successful it was swiftly incorporated into a book, *Noblesse Oblige* (1956), which included articles by Mitford, a letter from Evelyn Waugh and a poem by John Betjeman.

Fascinating and humorous though it might have been, the book also revealed a deep-rooted snobbery and an underlying panic within an upper class which effectively knew its tenure was limited. *Noblesse Oblige* underlined the fact that the tiny sector of society which once had dominated Britain (and the world) could now hope to differentiate itself with little more than the ability to speak differently and its ownership of property, a concept to which it clung with the maniacal belief of a tribe convinced that enough fields, grand homes and grazing cattle would protect them from the onset of social progress. And then there was the title of course. In the words of Professor Alan Ross of Birmingham University, upon whose thesis Mitford based her article, 'It is solely by their language that the upper classes nowadays are distinguished since they are neither cleaner, richer, nor better-educated than anybody else'. This was not quite true. But, if anything, the introduction of families like the McCorquodales, with their ready money and eagerness to spend it in the right way, was what was keeping the British social circle afloat, and aristocrats in their crumbling stately homes, long after the American socialites of Edith Wharton's *The Buccaneers* had been consumed by the very society the book satirised.

Many members of the aristocracy had, in any case, irrevocably damaged their reputations in the lead up to the Second World War with their love affair with Hitler. Until the end of the 1930s, upper class British girls were still doing 'the season' in Germany, as a means of either finding a wealthy German husband or as a dry run for the British version. Many were 'finished' in Germany, lodging with impoverished German aristocrats who needed the money, learning the language and taking in the culture. Intermarriage was even suggested as a means of maintaining the peace.

The 'German' label had been problematic for the monarchy too. The royal family had, after all, changed their name from Saxe-Coburg-Gotha to Windsor in 1917, when British feeling was strongly anti-German. George V was distinctly un-British in terms of his background, though he had been born and raised in the country. His parents, Queen Victoria, daughter of the Duke of Saxe-Coburg-Saalfeld, and Albert (her cousin and husband), had communicated in a mix of German and English. George, for all of his faults – he was known as a grumpy, shy, irritable ruler – understood that the requirements for a successful monarch were a dull, steadfast reign and, post-1914, the ability to empathise with 'the British people', or at least appear to. Hence he and his wife Queen Mary (formerly Princess Mary of Teck) embraced the Windsor title and the implicit 'Britishness' that came with it. The move proved sagacious. Over the next twenty years the royal families of Russia, Spain and Greece would be overthrown by a populous aggrieved at their elitism, wealth and a lack of connection with their subjects.

What then would the old king have made of the idea of the new one? Witness George VI – applauding Chamberlain's return from Munich heralding 'peace for our time'. From the meeting of the Duke and Duchess of Windsor with Hitler in 1937, to Nancy Mitford's sister Unity's appearance at the Führer's side when he announced the Anschluss in 1938, and the black and white video footage of a young

Princess Elizabeth apparently giving the Nazi salute alongside her mother, (which on July 18, 2015 made the front page of the *Sun* newspaper), the aristocracy's renewed fondness for Germany and the Führer was well-documented. Later, many aristocrats would claim that they simply hadn't noticed the strengthening of Nazi forces during time spent in Germany. This was implausible, to say the least. The attitude of Lady Elizabeth Montagu Douglas Scott, daughter of the Duke of Buccleuch, who later married the Duke of Northumberland, typified that of many young aristocrats. She had spent two months in Munich before the Second World War, preparing for the Scottish season. 'I'm afraid I didn't give a thought to what was going on outside. I was sleeping, eating, chatting, dining, dancing. That was all', she later confessed with startling stupidity.

Despite (or perhaps because of) the weakening of the aristocracy's grasp on social change, the rules surrounding Raine's presentation, at the Queen Charlotte's Ball, would prove as pernickety as ever. Barbara not only approved, she revelled in the antiquated systems and procedures. The first Queen Charlotte's Ball was held in 1780 by George III in honour of his wife Charlotte of Mecklenburg-Strelitz, and it funded the Queen Charlotte's and Chelsea Hospital (formerly known as The General Lying In Hospital). From then on, the ball went from strength to strength, with numbers growing in response to a changing society, in which the mothers of young women would take it upon themselves to seek a suitable match for their daughters.

During the Second World War, the ball had actually taken over from the traditional court presentation, which had been cancelled. At this point debutantes were forced to substitute bobbing a curtsey to the crown for curtseying to 'the cake' (which for reasons of rationing had been created using dried eggs). Once the traditional location of the Great Ballroom at Grosvenor House Hotel had been requisitioned by the American army as their headquarters, the ball had shifted to a smaller location and was thrown twice to accommodate numbers. In 1944, rationing was so severe that the caterers had simply given up and debutante families brought their own food, with the whole thing descending into a giant aristocratic indoor picnic. And still the band played on. The bandleader, Bill Savill (RAF), who began conducting his orchestra at a debutante ball during the Second World War, was still providing the dance music for the last Debs' Ball in 1958.

The application process for a debutante's presentation followed a strict procedure. An approach would first be made in writing directly to the Lord Chamberlain by a relative or friend who had themselves been presented. The Lord Chamberlain (or rather his office) would in turn approve the application and reply with the most important invitation (or stiffie as they were nicknamed) of the season: a stiff buff card with raised gold insignia stating 'The Lord Chamberlain is commanded by His Majesty to summon Raine McCorquodale to a presentation party at Buckingham Palace'. This was the starting gun for Barbara and thousands of other mothers across the country. The next few months could and probably would, decide their daughter's future and, by dint of association, their own.

'Coming-out' was a marathon and not a sprint. The season ran from May to July and a girl needed stamina, style and social connections to be truly successful. Once the summer season had concluded there were Highland balls and shooting parties north of the border to attend. Only when she had been presented to the monarch was a girl truly 'out' – on the marriage market and able to enjoy the parties, balls and rituals of the season: Ascot, Eton's 4th of June, Henley and Goodwood.

Once upon a time the ritual that Nancy Mitford's sister, Jessica, had described as 'the specific, upper-class version of the puberty rite', had been linked to menstruation's onset at the acceptable age of sixteen. All that had changed, but the reasons were still valid:

these were young fertile virgins of marriageable age, urgently seeking the right match. There was a whiff of communion about the whole thing too, and whilst the traditional white gowns with long trains and white feather headdresses were no longer required at court, long white gloves and fancy long ballgowns remained the order of the day.

'Presentation was the key event in a formalised connection of the monarch and the court with the Season and society. To put it at its crudest, the curtseyers were in, the non-curtseyers were excluded from the myriad royal enclosures, members tents and other well defended spaces, in which the well-bred were separated from the riff-raff', writes Fiona MacCarthy in *Last Curtsey: The End of the English Debutante*.[4]

The curtsey itself was not easy. Raine attended Madame Vacani's School of Dance, where all good prospective debs went to learn the 'lock and drop' process that was the key to a good curtsey. Betty Vacani (born Elizabeth Joan Church in Bombay, 1908) had taken over from her aunt Marguerite in teaching Princesses Elizabeth and Margaret, and later Prince Charles, to dance. This was royal warrant enough for every debutante in town. 'One locks one's right knee behind one's left and bends deeply with the front knee, with the object of the exercise being not to wobble', instructs a former deb. The procedure was not without its challenges. The willowy Lady Clodagh Anson, at court in 1898, found being presented to Queen Victoria something of a problem. As a peer's daughter she was due a kiss on the cheek rather than a simple hand grasp (peer's daughters were at the head of the queue). 'You had to make a deep curtsey to get down low enough', she said diplomatically, referring to the need to bend almost double to draw level with the diminutive monarch. Curtseys were due to any member of the royal family who might be present. Later, in the reign of Queen Elizabeth II, that would mean bobbing also to the Duke of Edinburgh – a famous dissenter who described the process as 'daft' from the get go. Stories abounded of debs in competition to catch the eye and garner a wink from the debonair, bored, raffish duke.

There were three things Barbara would urgently need to organise once Raine was in possession of her invite from the Lord Chamberlain: a dance of her own, outfits for the entire season and an official photograph for distribution to society magazines and newspapers. Society photographers such as Madame Yevonde, A. V. Swaebe, Bassano and Lenare specialised in porcelain complexioned girls looking wistfully divine in sparkling jewels, with ball gowns allowing just enough décolletage to suggest a burgeoning sexuality.

Never mind that parts of post-war London were still flattened, that displacement and homelessness was rife, rationing was still very much in effect and Britain was in the grip of persistent, unrelenting grey fog and drizzle, after the coldest winter on record. Raine was to have not one, but three dances thrown in her honour. 'The aristocracy', says one Londoner of the time, 'could always find a way through – even in the darkest of hours. If you knew where to look and you had the money there was always luxury to be found.'

A deb's 'coming-out' dance, thrown by her parents or a close relative, depending upon whose house was grander, was a giveaway in terms of a girl's real wealth and standing. Those without the means would often share dances or cocktails, those whose parents had significant funds, heritage or both, would have dances thrown at both of their homes – in London and at their country estate. If a girl was aristocratic enough, she could count on an appearance from royalty: Anne Glenconner's coming-out dance, given at her parents' stately home – Holkham Hall in Norfolk – with the King, Queen and Princess Margaret in attendance, held one disappointment. Princess Elizabeth (the future queen) did not attend because it was her birthday, 'something my father had overlooked when making the arrangements'.[5]

The Cartlands didn't have a stately home, but they did have money. The first of Raine's three dances was to be given by Barbara and Hugh; the second by old friend and MP for South Bedfordshire, Alan Lennox-Boyd; and the third by one of Barbara's oldest friends and Raine's godfather, the Duke of Sutherland, at Sutton Place, his Elizabethan house near Guildford (later famous as the English home of Paul Getty) where *Tatler* waxed lyrical about Raine, who looked 'enchanting', but also about the Bill Savill band, 'which played superbly', and 'the beautiful gardens where the herbaceous borders were a blaze of colour'. Her dances had the virtue of ensuring that Raine would literally be everywhere that season – not only did she steal three of the key evenings for herself, everyone invited to her dances was required by unspoken rule to invite her to theirs, whether it be a cocktail party, a shared ball or the whole overblown thing. The measure of a girl's success (and thus her mother's) was the weight of the 'stiffies' under which her drawing room mantle groaned.

The real point about the number of stiffies was that it spoke volumes not just about a girl's popularity, but also about the chances of her making a suitable match. Those chances increased exponentially with the arrival of every invitation proffered by the butler on a silver platter, before breakfast. Why? Because at the myriad dances, drinks parties and social events of the season, would be gathered Britain's most eligible, marriageable bachelors, all looking for the same thing: a wife.

Naturally, Barbara oversaw the making of many of Raine's gowns. For her debut at the Queen Charlotte's Ball, Barbara commissioned the House of Worth to copy a dress originally worn by the Empress Eugenie. She had them make it in yards of white tulle she had perspicaciously brought back from her 'mercy dash' to Raine in Switzerland. Rationing was still in place and it was impossible to buy such materials in England. Lucky Raine. Anne Glenconner came out in a dress made of dyed pleated parachute material bought by her mother from a local aerodrome. One of Barbara's friends possessed a crinoline and she decided to capitalise on the anachronism, making it part of Raine's signature look – one that Raine would perpetuate into her seventies.

'We had to think up all sorts of ways of making Raine look striking', Barbara told her biographer, Henry Cloud.[6] 'Artificial flowers were free of coupons; we bought a big wreath of daisies, poppies and cornflowers and sewed it round the neck of a dress of blue taffeta which she had bought at school from a friend for £3, adding a wide velvet hem. Over the crinoline it looked lovely and the American ambassador said it was one of the prettiest dresses he had seen in London.' The most photographed of Raine's dresses designed by Barbara herself – a green tulle with pink roses at each shoulder – was befitting of any fictional romantic heroine, not least Scarlett O'Hara, from whom Barbara seemed to have taken direct inspiration.

The dances themselves were fraught with the potential for monumental social faux pas and moments of excruciating embarrassment. Amongst the worst was being 'a wallflower' – in other words, not being asked to dance. Hundreds of debs each season would end up whiling away endless hours in the cloakrooms of the fancy ballrooms, where they would cluster for fear of being seen without a dance partner. On arrival at the dance, small notebooks were handed out with pencils attached – these were effectively dance cards which urgently needed filling. Some rituals made it easier than others: if a man was invited to the pre-dance dinner, etiquette dictated that he would then dance with every woman who had also been at the dinner table. On the other hand, if the girls on offer weren't deemed exciting enough, then all bets were off. It behoved every mother worth her salt to invite not only a hoard of 'eligibles', but also every male family member she could think of, to act as back up dance partners. There were undesirables too, but the mothers had found a way to weed them out by holding meetings in advance to swap names in order that the 'right sort' of man would attend.

If there was a cynicism on the part of the debs' mothers, it was matched only by that of the young eligible men who turned up. Many saw the dances as literally a meal ticket, donning their white tie in return for the dinner beforehand and a quick whip around the dance floor with the deb whose dance it was, before repairing to bed (alone) or going on somewhere much more fun, like a jazz club where they would mix with women who had done something more exciting with their lives than riding ponies and learning to curtsey.

Mothers were quick to share the names of those whose acronyms were inappropriate: NSIT (not safe in taxis) or MTF (must touch flesh). They or another family member would chaperone their daughter to every ball, the theory being that before a young girl was 'out' she could not go anywhere unaccompanied. This rule lasted for a year, after which the outed deb would be allowed to go out alone, provided that the 'suitable' man who accompanied her home in a taxi, stayed in the car whilst she made her way to her parent's front door.

For 'suitable man' read eligible and as Anne de Courcy notes 'there were never enough of these to go around'.[7] Inevitably it would be Barbara who would find a way to neatly circumvent the shortage by holding an all-male dinner before one of Raine's debutante dances, much to the fury of the other mothers: 'I heard about it yes', confirms family friend and art and antiques dealer, Frank Partridge. 'The story went that Barbara Cartland invited Britain's twenty most eligible bachelors to dinner. She sat at one end of the table and Raine at the other – no other women were present.'[8] Amongst those gathered were the three Johnnies – Johnnie Marlborough (11th Duke of Marlborough), Johnnie Spencer (Viscount Althorp), Johnnie Buccleuch (Earl of Dalkeith, direct descendant of Walter

Scott and heir to the largest private landed estate in the UK at 280,000 acres) – and Gerald Legge, upon whom Raine had already confided to her mother, she was keen. Pulling off the dinner had been a remarkable feat of social engineering for BC. Etiquette required that during 'the season' equal numbers of males and females should always be present at social dinners. Barbara had characteristically disregarded social norms and cleared the field for her daughter, ensuring she was the sole focus of attention. 'It was jolly well done', laughs Partridge, who marvels at Cartland's chutzpa, 'and of course, Raine would end up marrying two of the men at that very table!'

Raine was everywhere during the 1947 season, dancing her way into the social history books, she was presented to George VI wearing a 1934 vintage Molyneux blue lace which Barbara later admitted had come from a second-hand designer clothes shop in South Molton Street. In this at least Raine was ahead of her time, although her 'overblown appearance and her bloody pushy mother', as one acquaintance puts it, did not make her a favourite amongst the other debs. But neither mother nor daughter were ever out to win any popularity contests and both were thrilled when Raine was named Deb of the Year. Society magazines could not get enough of her – all of them carried her official picture, which captured her in her radiant glory. Hair primped, lipstick applied and mascaraed eyes upturned rapturously towards a distant star, or perhaps simply the gaze of an admiring onlooker? 'Eighteen years old with a face the shape of a heart, Miss Raine McCorquodale turns dancing eyes upon the world. Eternally smiling – at Ascot in Bond Street, at dances and at parties, she reminds us of another age when there were courts in Europe when a girl came out in a recognised manner and one of them was hailed as the Toast of the Town' raved *Leader* magazine. A full page of picture of Raine in *Tatler* was headlined 'Youth and gaiety at the Queen Charlotte's Ball'.

Barbara was in her element, her daughter was officially the most popular girl in England, beautiful, stylish and socially prominent. She could have wanted nothing more – Raine had gained what she had not, social acceptability and the potential to make a great marriage. But Barbara's good fortune did not end there. When a women's magazine read of Raine's prominence, it contacted Barbara and asked her to write a historical romance. Such was its success that *The Hazard of Hearts* – with its rags to riches story, dashing hero and unscrupulous villain – became the template for the millions of Barbara Cartland romances which have sold across the world since.

And what of the future of the debutantes? It wasn't obvious at the time, but Raine's season would be only a decade away from the entire proceedings drawing to a close. (A revived one would appear a few decades later and still exists today, but its anachronistic presence in a post-modern society has been the focus of well-deserved derision). By 1958, the Duke of Edinburgh, an infamous moderniser, and entirely sick of the procedure which he found tedious and trite, got his way and the palace announced it was to end the practice of presentations at court. In truth, it was more likely a polite way of saying what Princess Margaret famously told a friend: 'We had to put a stop to it. Every tart in London was getting in.'

3

The Eminently Newsworthy
Mrs Gerald Legge

———— •◆•———

The Honourable Gerald Humphry Legge, heir to the Earl of Dartmouth, was just the sort of man that Barbara Cartland's romantic heroines ended up marrying, after first having been ill-used by a dashing blackguard. The tall, straight-backed, dark-haired, Old Etonian Legge, was descended of outrageously good stock. William Legge, the 1st Earl of Dartmouth, had been the Lord Privy Seal (1713–14) and the 2nd Earl, William, was best remembered both for his role as Secretary of State for the Colonies (1772–75) and as namesake of Dartmouth College, the American Ivy League university. The 6th Earl had a more mainstream appeal: William Heneage, Gerald's grandfather, was purported to be the model for Lord Emsworth, P. G. Wodehouse's infamously eccentric peer in the *Blandings* novels. Just like Lord Emsworth, the 6th Earl had kept and revered a prize boar during the 1920s. Gerald's own father, Humphry, later the 8th Earl, was no slouch either, a former Naval officer who had received the DSO during the First World War, he was Chief Constable of the Berkshire Constabulary until 1953. Gerald's mother was Roma Ernestine Horlick, daughter of Sir Ernest Burford Horlick, 2nd Baronet.

Gerald's choice of post-war career was the unadventurous field of accountancy, but he had distinguished himself during the Second World War as a captain in the oldest continuous serving regiment in the UK, the Coldstream Guards (known both for its ceremonial duties and its weighty ranks of landed gentry) and had been 'mentioned in dispatches'. Admittedly, the earldom that Gerald would finally inherit seemed a long way off: his uncle William, then the Earl, was still alive but he was without a son, and the title would pass first to Gerald's father Humphry, before being passed down to Gerald.

There are two equally entertaining versions of Raine's engagement announcement, each as unlikely as the other. The truth is likely to be found somewhere in between. But first there was divine intervention, as Angela Levin records in her book *Raine and Johnnie,* Raine later said on Radio 4's *Thought for the Day* that it was God who told her to marry Gerald: 'We were standing on the ski slopes. I said to myself "God has chosen this man for you". It was love at first sight.' For God read BC. Raine was under no illusions as far as her mother was concerned. She knew very well that her mother's mission had been to 'bring her out' and 'marry her off'; to suggest otherwise was disingenuous. Was Gerald the perfect man? No. Friends thought him too weak for the bombastic, effervescent ball of energy that was Raine, but he was upright, patient, loyal and kind with good prospects. And kindness and patience had thus far been in short supply in the young Raine McCorquodale's world. And then there was the rather more uncomfortable but salient fact that he was offering. Unlike Barbara, Raine was not showered with a rush of proposals and she seems to have taken a pragmatic approach. It was a sentiment and to some extent a practice that would characterise her entire life, with a few notable exceptions.

One version of the Raine–Gerald engagement is that it was announced during one of Raine's coming-out balls, at which point Barbara ordered the waiters to stop serving champagne, called a halt to the band and effectively told everybody to go home. Anne Glenconner remembers the details, having heard them from her husband Colin Tennant. 'Colin was rather late getting to the party, which he was looking forward to because he liked Raine immensely. Rushing up the stairs to the ballroom he saw Barbara Cartland standing at the top "You are too late" she bellowed, "Raine is engaged and the party is over". Colin was rather disappointed.' In another version, Raine accepted Gerald in January 1948 whilst her mother was in New York with Hugh on a publishing trip and sent her mother a telegram with the happy news. Given Raine's deference to BC, this story seems rather unlikely. If it is true, one can only imagine the uncomfortable transatlantic conversation between mother and daughter, which must have taken place after the telegram was opened. Either way, Barbara must have been delighted although she gave a rather 'huffy' quote to the press, saying that she thought Raine was 'too young'.

There was no hiding her delight though at the smart society wedding of her daughter, held at the twelfth-century St Margaret's Church, Westminster, on 21 July 1948, just seven months after the young Princess Elizabeth had glided down the aisle at the next door Abbey with the newly dubbed Duke of Edinburgh, formerly Prince Philip of Greece and Denmark.

'The bride who was given away by her father wore a crinoline gown of white tulle, trimmed with bunches of orange-blossom and white satin ribbon and a Brussels lace veil held in place with a diamond tiara and she carried a bouquet of stephanotis', reported *The Times* of the Legge-McCorquodale nuptials, the next day.

'I suppose I was pretty', remarked Raine, years later, reflecting on this period of her life. The bridal gown had reflected the practicality and romantic inclinations of BC – it was actually Raine's 'coming-out' frock, with the blue ribbons replaced with white and bell like frills added to the sleeves. The bride, who didn't seem to mind the lack of a new frock, had the sort of tiny nipped-in waist and faultless décolletage that was much admired. 'I looked like something out of Winterhalter', she later observed. The string of sixteen bridesmaids (two more than Princess Elizabeth) read like a society 'Who's Who', with three Ladies (Caroline Thynne, Pamela Mountbatten – also one of the Princess Elizabeth's bridesmaids – and Evelyn Leslie), two Hons (Joan Spring Rice and Grania O'Brien) and the rest from notable families such as the de Traffords and the Bevans. They were outfitted, according to *The Times*, in 'white tulle crinoline frocks, trimmed with silver sequins and headdresses to match and they carried bouquets of flame-coloured sweet peas'. BC had overseen the organisation surrounding the wedding with meticulous detail, including the curiously designed bridesmaids' dresses, with their back ruching resembling breasts, which as *Life* magazine tactfully pointed out 'made it difficult to know if the bridesmaids were coming or going'.

The two pages were Raine's half-brothers: Ian and Glen resplend-ent in the McCorquodale family tartan with Ian recovering from a bout of mumps: 'I was ten at the time that Raine married Gerald and eighteen-year-olds don't have much time for their brothers who are after all so much younger', recalls Ian, 'but I do remember that Raine looked wonderful – so glamorous and she had so very many bridesmaids. I also seem to remember that we looked pretty good in our kilts!'[1] A black and white picture of Ian, standing distracted but resplendent in tartan and lace amongst a bevy of twittering tulle-attired bridesmaids in a cavernous ballroom offers a striking record of the scale of this society wedding. Another snap shows he and his mother laughing joyously: she very much the mother of the bride in deep blue cashmere, fur and jewels. 'Mummy was very happy when Raine married Gerald', Ian recalls, 'we all were.'

Gerald's best man was the dashing Rognvald Richard Farrer Herschell, 3rd Baron Herschell, a train bearer at the coronation of King George VI and Queen Elizabeth in 1937 and a Page of Honour to the king from 1935 to 1940. Old Etonian Herschell, who fought alongside Gerald in the Second World War, was another of society's most eligible bachelors. He would later marry Gerald's sister, Lady Heather Legge, who gave birth to one daughter, the Honourable Arabella Jane, in 1955. The Baronetcy became extinct on Herschell's death in 2008.

The reception, for nine hundred or so guests, was held at the palatial Londonderry House – the Park Lane home of the Marquesses of Londonderry, designed in the 1760s by Scottish architect Athenian Stuart for Robert Darcy, 4th Earl of Holderness, and inspired by Robert Wood's *Ruins of Palmyra*. Once called Holderness House, the home, with its vast central staircase, palatial ballroom, opulent chandeliers, statues by Antonio Canova and its tripartite yellow drawing room with an elaborate bird painted ceiling, was just the place for a fairy tale wedding. Guests could peruse the carefully notated array of wedding gifts – a break from tradition, but a rather ingenious method of illustrating one's connections – including Raine's gift to her husband (a gold cigarette case) and BC's gift to her (an aquamarine diamond hair clip and matching bracelet). Thereafter the trend for displaying wedding gifts at the reception would take off. It wouldn't be the last time Raine would set a trend. Later, when *Tatler* described the wedding in their 4 August 'Bystander Column' as 'one of the most brilliant of the season', and Raine was duly proclaimed by the magazine as 'Bride of the Year', both mother and daughter must have breathed a long, low sigh of relief.

Outside the tiny bubble of the aristocracy, with its champagne-soaked balls and weddings, Britain was gradually emerging from its post-war fugue. It seems hardly possible that with rationing still in place and 30 per cent of its buildings bombed out and craters pockmarking the brutalised city, just eight days after Raine was married, London would host the games of the XIV Olympiad – the first summer Olympics since Berlin in 1936. Known as the austerity games (Wembley greyhound stadium was converted into a running track with the use of 800 tons of cinders; athletes were housed in former RAF billets and London colleges; and Canada donated two pine diving boards for the swimming pool), the Olympics were a triumph of determination over the national debt, which already stood at 250 per cent of GDP. The television rights for the games were sold to the BBC for £1,000, which seems like a bargain until you consider that only 100,000[2] people in the UK had TVs at that time.

The games were a success, national mood was rising, and fundamental post-war social change was beginning. In 1951, the Festival of Britain, with its vertical Skylon, celebrated 'New Britain' long before Tony Blair tried and failed with the Millennium Dome.

Britain had arguably begun the long slow road to recovery in 1945, when Clement Atlee's Labour Party won a landslide victory, succeeding a war-worn Churchill. The ambitious launch of the National Health Service, a global first, offering free health care to all, by Health Minister, Aneurin Bevan, in the same month as the Games, illustrated the ambitions of the first ever Labour majority government, with a self-professed mandate to govern 'inclusively' – offering help to everyone in Britain, based on the level of their needs, rather than on an individual's wealth or class. A New Towns Act in 1946 had led to the expansion of modern new conurbations to house an expanding population and provide owner occupied homes. Britain was the most urbanised and industrialised country in the world, accounting for one quarter of the world trade in manufacturing. The country and the working classes paid the price. Working conditions and squalid housing, particularly in the north, spawned illness and dissatisfaction. In London the 'Great Smog' caused by the city's reliance on coal for production and heating, lasted for five days and killed more than four thousand people with pre-existing lung and heart diseases.

Seemingly a world away, a stucco, white-fronted, George Basevi designed Georgian house at 12 Chester Street, off leafy Belgrave Square and a decent stone's throw from Buckingham Palace, was to be the Legge family home. It was hard to imagine a more socially acceptable address for a young aristocratic couple. A couple of years later, the *Manchester Evening News* would tell us who else lived on Chester Street, 'At Number 8 Rt Hon Nancy, Lady Vivien, At No 15, Princess Stanislav Radziwill, At No 18, Pamela Countess of Lytton and at No 27, Surgeon Squadron Leader, Samuel Segal'. But, hyperbolised the report, 'at No 12 they have in their midst "a national figure" – the eminently newsworthy Mrs Gerald Legge'.[3]

The first few years of marriage were typical of upper-class newlyweds. Raine dutifully presided over a household of five staff and oversaw the decoration of the house by a young up and coming interior designer named David Hicks. 'She is the sort of person you either like or dislike. I admire her for her intelligence and style', he later told Angela Levin. He admired her bravery too where interiors were concerned: no colour was off limits at Chester Street. 'Her homes were always like her clothes – bright shades such as pink, orange and apricot, she hated gloom in any way', says Nicolas Norton, a long-time friend and director of S. J. Phillips, one of the oldest family-owned businesses in the world (also known to some as the billionaires' jeweller).

Raine dutifully gave birth to two children in swift succession: William in 1949, and Rupert in 1951, closely mirroring the birth pattern of the children of the monarch to be. The *Tatler* faithfully recorded both christenings, but it was the first, for the heir apparent which drew attention: 'I have never seen more friends and relations attend any christening than filled the pews of Grosvenor Chapel when the infant son of Mr and Mrs Gerald Legge was baptised', their social diarist reported breathlessly.

The Legges were remorselessly social – more it would seem thanks to Raine than to Gerald, who a friend suggests 'rather preferred the quiet life'. He was rarely mentioned or seen in the social pages of the day. On 26 April 1950, *Tatler* reported on a rare Gerald sighting. He was at Viscount Furness's birthday party, thrown for him by Mrs Reginald Vanderbilt, with a birthday cake decorated with the Furness coat of arms. Otherwise, he kept a low profile, so much so that he garnered a nickname: 'Left Legge' which referred to his 'at home' status whilst his wife energetically worked the social circuit.

Beyond the upper class bubble, things were far from effervescent: the 1951 general election had returned Winston Churchill to Number 10 by a tiny margin, reflecting the views of an increasingly vocal society resentful of continued rationing, oppressive state regulation and stratospherically high income tax. Though they lost, the Labour Party garnered a higher proportion of the vote than ever before, and from now on the Conservatives would need to be on their mettle in a chilly Cold War environment, with an increasingly vocal and demanding populace, who had become, since the war, more and more aware of the inequities within society. It was said that as the victory bells rang out for the end of the war in 1945, the Earl of Radnor commented to his Countess wife that whilst this moment signalled an upturn in the fortunes of the lower classes, 'now our personal problems begin'.

If societal changes were required (and the need for them would become increasingly pressing) no one, it seemed, had informed those who revolved in London's glittering aristocratic circles. Raine's own image and reputation were developing at pace. On 8 October 1952, *The Sketch* featured a full-page picture of 'Mrs Legge and her two sons, Rupert and William', in front of her china collection. 'Mrs Gerald Legge has the almost archaic reputation as being the best dressed woman in England. Her beauty and chic would more than stand comparison with places further off and inevitably smarter than our island fortress' opined the journal.[4]

But Raine had already made the decision that she did not want to be known as just a fashion plate (though later in the year she made headlines wearing a 'grass muff' at Ascot). Mirroring her mother, she set about becoming a society hostess, throwing her first charity ball at the Dorchester in aid of the Girls Clubs and Mixed Clubs, with the sort of precision and exhaustive endeavour that only the upbringing at the hands of Barbara could have produced. Her work yielded the predictable plaudits in a social world still hungry for post-war escapism. The Golden Cage Ball, held on 11 February 1953, was 'the best run and gayest charity ball for years' according to *Tatler*, due to the hard work and original ideas of its chairman, 'one of the most popular "young marrieds"', who greeted her seven hundred guests wearing a scarlet lace crinoline with a 2ft-high silver bird cage containing a red bird (to match her dress) perched on her head. Guests included Lord Leveson, the Duke of Rutland, the Marchioness of Dufferin and Ava, Lord and Lady George Scott and Douglas Fairbanks.

Just as in her mother's day, guests had gone to enormous lengths to dress the part: the Marchioness of Douro had tiny white doves in her hair while Lady Bridget Clark wore a headdress of organza and white ostrich feathers. Miss Fiona Campbell-Walter, in white tulle and elbow length gloves, won first prize for the cleverest headdress – a feathered confection with a tiny crown all attached to a sequined cat eye mask. The prize included a gold and silver cigarette case given by Boucheron. The chairman had left nothing to chance reported *Tatler*. True to form, Raine had chosen the dinner menu herself and interviewed the chef beforehand. Lord Porchester sang a love song, the Crazy Gang, Chesney Allen and Bud Flanagan entertained. It was roundly hailed as the event of the season.

As commoners (Gerald did not succeed to the title of Viscount Lewisham until 1958) the Legges were not on the guest list for the biggest social event of the decade – the Coronation of Queen Elizabeth II on 2 June 1953. Raine scored somewhat of a coup though when 'Mrs Gerald Legge' made the cover of *Tatler* a month before on 6 May, attired in what would have been regarded at the time as a rather outré crimson red chiffon gown adorned with white pompoms. In the build up to the coronation the *Tatler* featured the Queen and the Queen Mother arriving at what its indomitable Social Editor, Jennifer, billed as 'undoubtedly the biggest and the most resplendent private dance that will be held in London in coronation year', the coming-out ball thrown for debutante Elizabeth Ward, at Hutchison House. Also spotted at the party was Mrs Gerald Legge, 'looking pretty in midnight blue'. With Raine, reported Jennifer, 'were her dinner party guests including the Earl and Countess of Dalkeith, Lord and Lady Ogilvy, Mr Gavin and Lady Irene Astor, Lady Pamela Mountbatten and Mr Billy Wallace'.[5] Of Gerald there was no mention.

That Raine would be ardently royalist was never in doubt. Despite the abdication crisis in 1936, the monarchy's influence in Britain was still strong and pervaded all classes. The coronation of the young Elizabeth II marked a psychological turning point in Britain, although its imperialistic tone, with representatives from the colonies in jarring traditional headdresses and costumes, belied a nation in the process of busily divesting itself of many of those former colonies. (Burma, India, Pakistan and Ceylon had recently been granted independence for example.)

The coronation was a global turning point for communication. At Prince Philip's insistence, the whole event was televised for the first time. More than twenty million people across the globe watched the service (surpassing the numbers listening via radio) and marked the moment that television became mainstream. Watching the broadcast herself, Mrs Gerald Legge cannot have been insensible to the power of this new medium. Indeed, she would go on to use it to maximum effect herself over the course of the next two decades.

Whilst she might have fought against the aphorism (and by now their relationship was becoming increasingly tetchy) Raine was her mother's daughter. Witnessing her mother working hard to make ends meet had sharpened her awareness of at least two of BC's deadly sins: sloth and idleness. 'Raine was definitely different and whilst there had been absolutely no doubt that she would make a good marriage, we should not forget that she had been brought up with a mother who had provided for them all. Raine had seen this with her own eyes and she was not insensible to the idea of hard work', says author and social historian Anne de Courcy.[6]

In reality, Raine was never going to be happy with a traditional upper-class life spent overseeing the servants, attending her dressmaker for fittings, her hairdresser for a 'set' and taking tea at the Ritz with friends, passing the time waiting for the inevitable evening dinner parties, cocktails or balls to commence. This was still a society in which women did not meet for dinner and certainly not for drinks in bars or cafés. When night fell, they were supposed either to be at home or attending functions on the arm of a husband. For as much as she didn't want to be idle, Raine also didn't care to possess every other upper middle class girl's dream: a town house in London and an estate in the country. For one thing she detested mess: 'I'm a city girl', she would say, once pronouncing to friend, Michael Cole, on the environs of her later perch: Althrop House.

'All that mud. Ghastly. I much prefer the pavements of Mayfair beneath my feet.' [7] For another she liked to be active.

'I felt very much that she needed to do something to help people. She felt it too', said BC. As a result, Raine signed up as a Council Voluntary Care Committee worker for Wandsworth and Vauxhall and also as a member of the Citizens Advice Bureau for Central London. What she saw shocked her: She later described the children she had witnessed coming home from school to unparented homes: 'Their mothers were at work, there was mass deprivation and those haunted-looking children had to rely on strangers to unlock their front doors, because they were too small to reach the keyholes. I was turned into an angry young woman by all that I saw. Yet I felt so impotent.' In response she launched her fledgling political career by joining the London Conservative Union, nervously giving her first speech to twelve Tory ladies at St Saviour's Church Hall, Herne Hill, in November 1953.

'Raine was very intelligent. She didn't want to sit by the fire, she had nannies and cooks for the house and she was like my mother a crusader – she wanted to help people and she decided she was going to do this through politics', says her half-brother Ian McCorquodale.

'You go into politics for two reasons: one is to do something and the other is to be "someone", that's it really. I think for Raine it was a mixture of both', says her good friend Julian Fellowes. [8]

Although her first speech was all her own work, that she could project her voice and confidently string more than a few sentences together, was undoubtedly thanks to BC, who had routinely required that all of her three children 'speechify' after family dinners. She'd seen how practice had helped her darling brother Ronald in his career. Far from being put off by her first tiny audience and a somewhat trepidatious start Raine became ambitious for what she told friends would be a 'proper role' and in May 1954, she took her mother's advice to get a job on the local council, winning a seat on

Westminster City Council for St George's ward in Knightsbridge – the youngest person ever to do so.

Alongside her fledgling political career, Raine was also speedily raising her social profile. Her dinners were known for being packed with the up and coming or the already influential. Not every party went to plan: On one occasion, Raine and her dinner guests sat around the dining table at Chester Street impatiently awaiting the services of her butler, Edward Davies. Davies, it turned out, was otherwise engaged – he was busy attempting to determine whether a syndicate of what the *Yorkshire Observer* termed as 'silent raiders' were still in the building. Jewels and fur coats to the value of £7500 were taken. 'The police found fingerprints on the windowsill of Mrs. Legge's bedroom at the rear. A police dog followed a scent and then picked it up again in the courtyard at the back of the house. The house is a six-storey period building, one of a long terrace. At the end of Chester Street are the walls of Buckingham Palace grounds', reported one paper. This would not be the only time the Legges were targeted. In another incident the reknowned cat burglar, George 'Taters' Chatham, who prided himself on his network of Belgravia informants and researching his targets via *Burke's Peerage, Country Life* and *Tatler*, escaped from the Legge's home, after falling four floors. As a result he would spend the next six weeks in traction. He returned to his chosen line of work with the casts still on his arms.[9]

By luck or judgement Raine also became one of the so called 'set', otherwise known as the court of the young, irrepressible Princess Margaret, who cast Raine in her amateur production of *The Frog* in 1954 (the Princess was directing) in aid of needy children. Here Raine and Anne Glenconner would meet for the first time. 'I remember it very well because Colin was required to capture Raine at a certain point and drag her into a cupboard under the stairs where they would remain for the rest of the play. So I think Colin got to know her incredibly quickly!' Also starring were Lord

Dudley, Lord Porchester (later Earl of Carnarvon)and Billy Wallace – an ex-boyfriend of the Princess. The play caused a rift between Margaret and the Palace but raised £10,000 for the Invalid Children's Aid Society. It was to be the start of an unrequited love affair between Margaret and 'the entertainers' – for the rest of her life she would seek out the company of actors and actresses whenever she could. Subsequently Raine was often seen accompanying the Princess. In October 1954, *The Stage* reported: 'Princess Margaret opened the Pilgrim's School of the Invalid Children's Aid Society also attended by Mrs Gerald Legge, Mr Billy Wallace and other members of the cast of *The Frog*, the society play whose proceeds were largely responsible for the purchase of the new school building.'

In November of that year Raine got her first taste of mass public approval in the infamous coffee cups incident. Rushing through London Airport (later named Heathrow) to catch a flight for Paris she was dismayed to see the tables of the airport café brimming with dirty cups and saucers, rubbish and overflowing ashtrays. Having asked, politely but firmly, for it to be cleared up, she complained to the management, saying loudly 'I have never seen such filth in my life'. She was met not only with sulky, begrudging compliance, but also by a pleasing barrage of approving newspaper headlines the next day. 'I remember my mother reading the newspaper and saying Mrs Gerald Legge was quite right. I'm glad she said something', says Michael Cole.[10] Questions were asked in parliament about hygiene at London Airport.

Raine, now ensconced with Gerald at the Ritz in Paris (always her favourite hotel), issued a press statement proclaiming that untidiness and dirt were not only bad for the health of the public 'but because they inevitably produce a messy and inefficient attitude of mind'. On her return from Paris some days later, she beamed at the assembled press and cameras waiting for her expectantly and pronounced of the café that 'Everything is clean and nice'. She even posed for her picture holding a coffee cup up to her lips, expertly dropping her chin and smiling in three-quarter profile.

If any moment could be pinpointed as the time that Raine really understood the uplift and empowerment that mass media exposure, thanks to the expression of a few pithy words, could engender, it was this. To say that she was not influenced by her mother in this, as in so much else, would be disingenuous. One interviewer described Barbara as a journalist's dream, 'peppering her conversation with a series of quotable soundbites and guaranteed to have an opinion on everything'.[11] She possessed her mother's ability for convenient amnesia too: In the *Birmingham Post* on 14 October 1955, she advised women to put family life first saying, without a hint of irony or a mention of her own full-time nanny, butler, cook and cleaner, that they 'should not leave their children to push their own perambulators'. 'Even the most successful career could not', she opined 'compete with a husband's smile when he returned home or a child's: "Mummy I need you".'

As she began to feature more in the public eye, Raine was presciently and carefully crafting her image with the attentiveness one might associate these days with a teenage Instagram influencer. With some tweaks here (the elevated backcombing) and some teases there (even Raine's hemlines rose in the sixties in inverse proportion to the depth of the plunging necklines of her taffeta evening gowns), she was moving towards what would become her signature 'look'. You could never say that Raine's silhouette of a nipped in waist and a full New Look style skirt, which she continued for the rest of her life (aside from the odd experimental Sixties mini) was not entirely her own.

A criticism that would dog Raine all of her life, was that she was overbearing and deaf and blind to social nuance. 'She was utterly devoid of the common touch', says Sir Roy Strong, a friend of long acquaintance, 'for someone with an analytical mind she often did herself no favours.'[12] There was little better example than the *Weekly Dispatch (London)* report on Sunday 14 August, 1955, which stated that 'Mrs Gerald Legge disappeared when a little girl in the under-fours section of a talent contest she was judging sang "Walking my Baby Back Home". "It seems so ridiculous to see these tiny children get up and sing these emotional love songs" she said. "I personally would not like to hear my two children singing . . . There are hundreds of suitable ones such as 'I saw Three Ships Go Sailing By'".' Few could argue though, that she did have a point.

Raine put in the hours, even if most of her work ostensibly sounded like fun. In May 1955, she was 'at home' with Lady Pamela Berry, president of the Incorporated Society of London Fashion Designers, alongside the Duchess of Gloucester, the American ambassador and Douglas Fairbanks, at the Mansion House. Later that month whilst on the stump in West Bromwich for the Conservatives she told her audience that 'We women of Britain want most of all an era of peace, prosperity and freedom for our families. But that doesn't mean peace at any price . . . We are a terrifyingly small island; we must therefore be strong. Bullies never listen to little boys.' The *Birmingham Gazette* helpfully informed us that Mrs Legge's talking point was a hat – 'a spring confection of royal blue straw adorned with pink moss roses'.

In October of the same year, the *Manchester Evening News*[13] gave us an 'up close and personal' insight into Mrs Legge, with barely a mention of there being a Mr. In response to a feature entitled 'Here's who I'd like to meet' readers had nominated Raine, declaring her 'a woman with the courage of her convictions' and 'a woman with an abundance of courage'. The *Evening News* reporter was almost overcome, describing Raine, in a torrent of lavish praise, as 'seated like Greer Garson in the robes and tricorne hat of a Westminster City Councillor', adding, 'her hat is her own design, she had it remodelled by Erik'. Mrs Gerald Legge, the writer concluded, had made the list because she was the perfect example of 'The Woman Who Will Not Be Pushed Around'. 'I loathe dirt and bad manners', she chirruped, whilst wowing him with her magnificently appointed home with its purple stair carpet, green and gilt regency hall, its Venetian room with hand-painted ceiling (she painted it herself she told him: in gold and white), the dining chairs made in the reign of Charles II and a dining table of rough blackened oak which was 'a good 50 years older'. The bathroom, marvelled the reporter, has 'glazed reproductions of *Vogue* covers instead of tiles', including one, of course, bearing a smiling Raine. A Grinling Gibbons mirror and wall cases of Italian intaglios completed the picture. A cigarette box on a side table displayed what the reporter faithfully reports as an 'affectionate inscription from the Mountbattens' engraved inside the lid.

The article had, like everything else in fifties society, more than a whiff of deference about it. This was still the age wherein so called 'better breeding' – i.e. belonging to the upper classes – allowed one to proselytise on what was 'good' for the rest of the population. The fact that most people doing this were male, made Raine even more exceptional. The old boys' network had rarely been more in evidence. When Churchill was re-elected in 1951, he led a party containing seventy-six old Etonian MPs. In the 1955 Eden government ten out of the eighteen male ministers had been educated at Eton. The notion of a female having pertinent opinions was still almost unthinkable, let alone that a woman might actually give a man a run for his money. There were twenty-eight women MPs by 1958, but that was still less than 5 per cent of the total of 630 MPs. Change was slow in coming, but it was marked by the moment a certain Margaret Hilda Thatcher was appointed to only the third ever female cabinet minister role in 1961 (the first was Margaret Bondfield, Labour 1924, the second was Florence Horsburgh 1954 and the fourth Barbara Castle 1964), taking her seat on the Conservative front benches as Parliamentary Secretary in the Ministry of Pensions and National Insurance in the 1961 Macmillan government.

In an approach which we would now recognise as brand building, Raine began to focus solely on TV. As the *Leicester Evening Mail* reported on 6 March 1956, 'known for her forthright views, Mrs Gerald Legge, daughter of Barbara Cartland, the novelist, and wife of an ex-Coldstreamer, who is now a banker, will be *At Home* to BBC viewers on March 21'. She was on screen again in 1957 in another Pathé segment, letting her audience know what she thought about the crisis in men's fashion. 'Drab clothes mean a drab outlook', she opined, 'and that is the trouble in the world today – we're lacking imagination, inventiveness.'

Her next major campaign would be a mother/daughter co-production when she joined BC in campaigning for the elderly, setting up the *Mrs Gerald Legge Fund for Old People.* She was tireless in her efforts, touring the country to speak on the plight of the elderly. In the first year the fund raised enough to pay for an old people's bus for the elderly of Hendon and beyond. The bus (and subsequent others) was fitted with a toilet and a stretcher so that even the most incapacitated could use it. 'Lavatories are always important', she later told Michael Cole. 'Men forget about them but they are always a woman's first thought.' Raine named the bus Polly, after her grandmother, who was the first woman aboard. She even released a single for the charity with the Duchess of Bedford, featuring the songs 'Lucks in Love with You' and 'I'm in Love'. 'Don't expect two new stars, but if you feel like helping a good cause the record is well worth buying – and listening to' said one critic.[14] It was voted *NME*'s worst record of 1957.

All this media attention was allowing Raine to become more confident politically, and she had an acute eye for what would make a good picture and a story. 'I've always said I don't care what they say behind my back. I just want them to be nice to my face', she told a friend. To another she would say, 'oh I don't worry about what they say about me – nobody reads anything. What really matters is how I look. People will only remember the picture'. On 28 June, 1957, Raine was photographed, perfectly made up and coiffed, climbing down into the sewers of Westminster. 'Wearing a battle-dress blouse, and thigh high boots, Mrs Gerald Legge, socialite and a Westminster City Councillor, spent an hour yesterday wandering around the Westminster City Sewers' the papers faithfully reported. The reason for this unashamed, near perfect photo-opp was, as Raine explained, that she had wanted to see how the £65,000 that the council had allotted for repairs was being spent.[15]

Raine always maintained that she did not wish to be an MP, often using Gerald as her standard excuse and inferring that she was still very much in the subordinate role where the bigger picture was concerned – 'my husband is dead against it'.[16] This was untrue and it would not be the last time she would use Gerald as a foil to mask her own independence and power. Raine wasn't the first female to recognise that she could always get more done by deferring to her partner, but all the while doing exactly as she wished. In reality it's more likely that she recognised that the drudgery of the long hours of being an MP would impinge upon her social life and also, that she could, given her social standing, achieve as much 'outside' the tent as in it. 'Never forget' she once said, 'that the real power of women lies in their power to influence men, and through them, the world around them'.[17]

'Let us be frank about it – most of our people have never had it so good' said Harold Macmillan in July 1957. 'Go around the country, go to the industrial towns, go to the farms and you will see a state of prosperity such as we have never had in my lifetime – nor indeed in the history of this country.' It was undeniable. The 1950s were a time of post-war high employment. In 1954, rationing had ceased, people were buying their own homes, driving their own cars and taking their first package holidays. When Raine opened the Birmingham *Ideal Home* exhibition on 2 October, 1957 – 'opened by Mrs Gerald Legge one of the leaders of London fashion' as a local paper described her – the radical convenience of the new washing machines, telephones and refrigerators was transforming domestic and social life and wall free 'open plan housing' was being hailed as 'the new trend'. The British were earning more and spending more. This age of affluence was to hurl Britain into the 1960s, sweeping away much of the old order with it.[18]

In 1958, writes Katherine Whitehorn, in her memoir, *Selective Memory*, the previously unthinkable would occur, 'family planning was urged on the Lambeth Conference of the Church of England'.[19] Raine's views on family planning were clear, it was not to be taught at schools but 'doctors should do it' she said. She was clearly in favour of birth control though – at some point after Rupert was born in 1951, she must have decided she did not want to give birth again for some time. As a result her next child would not be born for another ten years.

On Saturday 1 March 1958, the death of the 7th Earl of Dartmouth was announced. The Earl had made few headlines, although most of the obituaries noted that he had been president of the MCC during the controversial 'bodyline bowling' England Tour of Australia 1932–33'. Gerald's father became the 8th Earl and Mr and Mrs Gerald Legge became Viscount and Viscountess respectively. This was the era when succession to a title – almost any title – still made the local front pages, in the provinces at least, 'Mrs Gerald Legge becomes a Viscountess' trumpeted the *Belfast Telegraph*.

On 5 March, the week following the announcement, the new Lady Lewisham told the papers of her bid to make it onto the London County Council, standing – appropriately – for Lewisham

West in the upcoming April elections: 'I won't be having meetings and I won't be speechifying' she said. She would, however, she told the reporter from the *Hartlepool Northern Daily Mail*,[20] 'be concentrating on welfare, housing and town planning'. The interviewer wrote in conclusion that she would brighten up the Council chamber with her hats.

The irony of an aristocrat (who was coincidentally the focus of the immensely popular TV show *This is Your Life* at the tender age of twenty-eight) campaigning in one of London's most depressed boroughs was not lost on many. The site of a notorious train crash on 4 December, 1957, when two trains collided head on and ninety people lost their lives, underprivileged Lewisham with its market stalls, Littlewoods discount department store and social housing could not have been further from Raine Spencer's point of reference. You might also expect that Lewisham's residents, a mixture of white working class and immigrants from the Windrush generation, would be the last people to appreciate Lady Lewisham in her furs and diamonds. But this was still a world where reverence and respect for the upper classes prevailed. And in any case, they admired her spirit. 'She did have that extraordinary ability to make people think she was on their side and she was never afraid, she would go into the roughest areas and talk to people on their level. She said that everyone was interested in something, you just had to find out what it was. I admired her terribly for that', says Anne Glenconner.

'Then I became Lady Lewisham – you know – where the buses go to', Raine later told Michael Cole, laughingly referring to the name of the London suburb displayed on the front of the bright red London double deckers travelling to Lewisham. She won the southeast London borough for the Conservatives on 17 April 1958, by just seven votes (12,520) beating her Labour rival Mrs B. D. Vernon (12,513). Her tactics were admirably guileful. 'She got us to help her by driving various elderly ladies to the polls', says Anne Glenconner of Raine's socialite band drafted in to help with voters, 'of course we didn't put the pen in their hands or tell them how to vote'. Raine would never be that clumsy. But she unquestionably had her own way of charming the populace – a case of Noblesse obliging. 'When we asked her "what shall we wear to pick up the voters" she said "Oh darling you must dress up. Put on your hat, gloves and jewels and look splendid"', says Glenconner.

'How in the great LCC battle has the cult of TV personality fared?' the *Kemsley Evening Express* wanted to know. The answer: 'Lady Lewisham last fluttered her eyelashes on the screen a week ago – unlike her fellow candidates who have not appeared for the last month'. The paper added a hint of caution noting that 'the magic of TV as a vote-catcher might be exaggerated'. There had been a tense recount before Raine was duly elected.

Raine was to hold the twin representation of Westminster and West Lewisham until London County Council was abolished in 1965. After the election she gave an interview to London's *Evening Standard* newspaper. 'I know people have been saying: "Why should that flighty empty-headed over-dressed Mrs Gerald Legge be chosen to represent the people"? . . . I believe one must always be honest with oneself and the electorate. It is insulting to people as well as dishonest, so I always deliberately dressed up and wore all my jewellery and furs – after all, everyone knows I have them.' She had studiously ignored a loud disgruntled male detractor who had shouted 'you're nothing but a television box of tricks' over her victory speech. 'She was very much an old pukka Tory', says Sir Simon Jenkins[21] who met Raine at about this time. 'Her mother whom she referenced a great deal, put a lot of pressure on her to behave in a certain way and I'm afraid in the end she did almost become a parody of what her mother thought she should be.'

As the decade was drawing to a close, Raine would put in even more hours giving speeches and representing causes which she felt were in the public good. Amongst the subjects that exercised her were the number of criminal assaults on girls; prostitutes in Mayfair; toffee-nosed shop assistants who 'hoped their customers dropped dead outside the store so they wouldn't have to serve them'; and as President of the National Association for Health – a role she had accepted in 1964, the dangers of a lack of food hygiene, headlined in *The Times* on November 11, 1959 as, 'Lady Lewisham Asks For Clean Food Protests' . . . 'those who prepare and serve food can kill just as surely as dangerous drivers'. Her first speech for West Lewisham focused on giving old people their own small council homes.

And what of her two small children? Because Raine never mentioned either William, by then aged ten, or Rupert, aged six, in any of her press interviews, we must assume that they were both at home being looked after by a nanny. Like BC before her, Raine did not believe in wasting time on her growing children. 'I think she was much better with them when they grew up', says a friend. 'She was hopeless with infants.' Again her standard response to the constant question about whether she was ever going to stand as an MP gave the game away: 'I would love to and have been offered several seats, but my husband is dead against it . . . as MPs always seem to be working between six and midnight *he* would never see me.'[22] There was no mention, and neither would there ever be, of what Raine's children must have felt about their absentee mother.

More than a few would complain that whilst the Conservative Councillor for West Lewisham could dole it out, she couldn't take it, as an incident at the London School of Economics, suggested. She was there to talk to the Conservative Association, only to find that the meeting had been infiltrated by what she later described as 'socialists' who barracked and booed throughout her speech. She lost her head and her temper: 'Often I found that where socialist voters lived there were dirty milk bottles on the doorstep.' she said, rather spitefully, as part of her summing up. She swiftly left the hall and her cat-call marred speech was reported extensively by the papers the following day. 'She could be her own worst enemy', says Sir Roy Strong, 'in a way she was just like Osbert Lancaster's cartoon character, Lady Littlehampton.' Lancaster's fashion plate 'Maudie', married to her distant cousin, 'Viscount Draynefleet', appeared in the *Daily Express* between 1948 and 1981. With her extreme right- and left-wing views she expressed a broad, witty take on the politics of the day. Often politically incorrect and never seen in the same outfit twice, she stood as a Liberal candidate in Lancaster's cartoon strip, losing her deposit on both occasions.

The disruption at the LSE was a precursor of things to come. Change was in the air as the decade began drawing to a close – you could smell it wafting from the 'revolutionary' coffee shops which were opening on the streets of Soho; you could see it in the changing habits of the young who freely embraced on the streets; it was there in the teenage hemlines which began to rise provocatively, and in the increasingly long hair of young men growing their locks as a symbol of rebellion. Even a conservative like Raine could sense that the future really did belong to the young. The traces imposed by the build-back after the Second World War needed loosening. Despite her right-wing allegiances, Raine would always be a champion for honesty and transparency, two issues which underpinned and drove the dominant new political movements of the upcoming decade: civil rights and Vietnam. In February 1960, she spoke out against the proposal to oppose the Public Bodies Bill, giving the press and public access to council meetings saying, 'What is there that goes on behind the closed doors of committees and cannot be revealed to the 3,500,000 people of London?' She went further with a threat, 'I suggest the time is not far off when ordinary men and women will lead a revolution against the suppression and tyranny of County Hall'. Coincidentally (or perhaps not) the Bill was the first to be introduced by another up and coming politician – the MP for Finchley, Margaret Thatcher – who made it the subject of her maiden speech in the House.

In a Pathé newsreel Raine sagely defended Britain's budding youth movement, the latent power of which was becoming all too apparent. 'Sometimes I think young people get rather a raw deal', she said brightly, fixing her interviewer with a glossy smile, in fact, she said, she thought young people were 'splendid', and she was struck by 'their enthusiasm and new ideas, which after all is what we in this country so badly require'.

But whilst the new decade might signal a change in the global zeitgeist, the salutary lesson learned by Raine was the role the media could and would increasingly play in both an individual's success and their downfall. A fact she made only too clear in a newspaper interview given soon after the LSE debacle: 'I have received over the years many thousands of Thank You letters from ordinary people whom I have helped in different ways – but none of this could have been achieved without the press who have underlined my activities and my nuisance value towards authority.' But what she and none of her peers could have comprehended was that in the decades that were to follow there would be a sea-change in the power and influence of the media, which would mean that the press, which had so far maintained a relatively healthy 'respect' for the upper classes, would no longer be prepared to play by the same rules.

4

Left Legge and the
Swinging Sixties Countess

On 17 October 1962, even the *Daily Mirror* was interested in commenting on the quaint titular peculiarities of the British aristocracy:

> The *Countess of Dartmouth* is a new name in this column. She is better known as Lady Lewisham. She became the Countess of D. yesterday when her father-in-law the Earl of Dartmouth died at the age of seventy-four. Her husband, Viscount Lewisham succeeded to the title. Name check: Miss Raine McCorquodale became the Honourable Mrs Gerald Legge when she married. Mrs Gerald Legge became Viscountess Lewisham when her husband succeeded to the title. Now Viscountess Lewisham is the Countess of Dartmouth. Four names with but a single marriage.

And just like that, Raine had become a Countess. Naturally she took it in her stride, she was busy settling the family into the new home they'd moved into the year before in Hill Street, Mayfair. She had employed the services again of interior designer David Hicks who had married her bridesmaid, now one of the Queen's ladies in waiting, Lady Pamela Mountbatten and he was hard at work covering everything in her favourite hues. She described her bedroom and bathroom to an interviewer as 'Pink Camelia in my bedroom with turquoise carpets and turquoise and white in the bathroom . . . frightfully David Hicksy – if you see what I mean'.

She was pregnant again – her first child for a decade which suggested, if not proved, that she and Gerald had reached a better understanding. On 16 July 1963, she gave birth at home to a daughter, Lady Charlotte Legge, christened at the Grosvenor Chapel, South Audley Street. She and Gerald began again to socialise as a couple, but friends acknowledge that the relationship was strained. 'If you had them to dinner then Raine would do 80 per cent of the talking and Gerald possibly 20 per cent', says Frank Partridge, 'that really sums up their relationship.' 'I was terribly fond of Gerald', says Anne Glenconner, 'he was very clever, but he was simply not Raine's equal.'

Gerald, now the 9th Earl of Dartmouth, might have been quiet and reserved but he was no slouch. Unlike many in a similar social position, he worked – as his father had done before him. Having been appointed a Fellow, Institute of Chartered Accountants (FCA) in 1952, he became a director of Rea Brothers in 1958 and would spend the rest of his lucrative working life in the city. Perhaps he didn't move at Raine's speed, but he was united with her in his belief that aristocrats should strive to be useful within society and work for a living.

'I do think that both she and Gerald held similar views about contributing to society. There's also no doubt that her mother was a bit of a role model for her in that she knew that she had to get on and do something, rather than just sit around', says Anne

Glenconner, adding that 'Of course, her mother had Raine on a biscuit tin with her hair all dressed at about the age of six.' Even at that young age BC had put Raine to work in advertising campaigns.

You might expect a traditionalist like Raine to have been at odds with the 1960s and in many ways she found the whole thing a puzzle. The decade of 'peace and love' was a direct affront to many of the values that the upper classes had long held dear. The fifties had dammed the pent-up tide of emotions of a post-war generation, as the UK slowly recovered economically and socially. Economic hardship, unemployment and displacement had the effect of suppressing what might naturally have evolved into a 'youthquake' amongst a disaffected, impatient youth, free for the first time from conscription. But by the early sixties Britain was boiling with an undercurrent of reactionism and ready to party. The arrival in the late fifties of a new kind of American music: rock 'n' roll, and the availability both of drugs (particularly LSD) and the contraceptive pill (available for the first time on the NHS in 1961) was an intoxicating cocktail. Later, the Abortion Act of 1967, would legalise termination for pregnancies up to twenty-eight weeks, underscoring what many detractors regarded as the 'permissive decade'.

Politics was changing in ways that even five years previously would have been unthinkable for a Tory like Raine. With President Kennedy in the White House, America was in protest mode and its amplified voice rolled across the Atlantic, making waves in Britain. Later, together with the Vietnam protests, Civil Rights leader Martin Luther King's messages for change would shake the bedrock of the establishment. The 'grown ups' were no longer in charge. The advent of hippie culture rejected the status quo on both sides of the Atlantic, paving the way for a whole new way of thinking and being – one in which not duty but personal advancement and the cult of the individual began to feature. On 5 October 1962, an unknown Liverpool Boy Band called The Beatles released their first single,

'Love Me Do', which rose to number seventeen in the charts, much to the surprise of their new record label EMI.

A few months before the Liverpool boys began their global ascent a snippet of gossip had appeared in the society magazine *Queen*, kicking off a scandal that would rock both the upper classes and the political classes (often one and the same) to their core. In the column entitled 'sentences I'd like to hear the end of' appeared the following: 'called in MI5 because every time the chauffeur driven Zils drew up at her front door, out of her back door into a chauffeur driven Humber slipped . . . ' This was a sly, prescient reference to the imminent breaking of a political scandal – the Profumo affair – which would topple the government and reveal the Conservative Party, not for the first or the last time, as a hotbed of sleaze and corruption. The scandal revolved around an affair between the War Secretary John Profumo and Christine Keeler, a nineteen-year-old dancer who was also having an affair with Eugene Ivanov, a Russian military attaché. It mattered, not least because it touched the lives of many in Raine's own circle and underscored the uncomfortably intimate links which existed between the social and political classes. Profumo and Keeler had first met at Cliveden, the home of the immensely wealthy Astor family, in July 1961. The story broke in 1963, when Profumo was forced to resign after first having apologised for misleading Parliament.

The event exposed a fissure in the trust held by the British public for the government, which had initially been damaged by post-war unemployment and the Suez Canal debacle in 1956. Raine's Tories were losing their natural constituencies and 'the shires' were falling out of love with them. Macmillan resigned in 1963 because of ill health and the party limped on with Alec Douglas-Home at the helm. They were defeated in 1964 by Harold Wilson's Labour government. Wilson was a newbie. He'd only been party leader for a year, but he had addressed the nation, when, as the leader of the opposition, together with Sir Alec Douglas-Home, he'd broken the news of President Kennedy's assassination.

Wilson adopted a new approach to politics which had surfaced in the Labour Party at around that time – known as 'Butskellism', a conflation of the names of its two progenitors, the former leader of the Labour Party Hugh Gaitskell and the prominent Conservative R. A. Butler. Gaitskill and Butler had been united in forging a new political approach based on moderation, a slightly left-of-centre consensus, recognising the power of the trade unions and the need to address the needs of the working class.[1] The most radical element of Butskellism was the acceptance of the real need for a welfare state to help those less fortunate and an acknowledgement that higher taxation was an inevitable by-product. It was in this new direction that Britain was to move – at least in the short term – and it meant that dyed-in-the-wool Tories like Raine would have to move with it or be left behind and out of a job.

BC pitched in to help the Conservatives, publicly offering the Tory party a mix of her own vitamins whilst campaigning at Conservative meetings in the south west, on a platform of 'Fit Tories Need Vitamins', the Rex North column informed its readers.[2] She also thought that the electorate could use some too. 'A course of pills, Brewer's yeast and honey is guaranteed to put life into any jaded Tory . . . The reason so many Socialists are against everything and are so disagreeable, is because they are not 100 per cent well.' Despite such ridiculous utterances, Cartland was about to become a public servant herself. When her daughter became the first president of the National Association for Health in June 1964 she appointed her mother as deputy. In actual fact this would be one of Raine's most meaningful and effective roles. She was way ahead of the curve with her campaigns against insecticides in food and antibiotics in meats, calling for a registration of pesticides and a set of food standards symbols, so that shoppers could understand what they were buying. If her safer foods campaigns indicated a forward-thinking woman interested in issues of wellbeing and scientific safeguarding, her attitudes to other matters were beginning to sound positively Victorian.

The prevailing zeitgeist – one in which the young finally had status and power – manifesting in a blatant disregard for the old guard, was patently at odds with Raine's conservative upper-class values. Rather than tempering her approach (an impression she had been at pains to give as the fifties drew to a close) she used precisely that moment to double down on her right-wing stance. This worked, as it so often would, to her advantage, and her opinions were constantly sought, more for their sharp contrast to the current modernising political mode than for their relevance. As far as the hungry media were concerned, she could be relied upon to have a noteworthy view on just about anything from smoking[3] to stiletto heels.[4] In short, Raine had become 'a talking head' – the woman to turn to if you wanted an outrageous quote or a beguiling and some-times cringeworthy visual. 'Women are doing a man's job without his physical stamina', she informed the Round Table Annual Conference at Bognor Regis holiday camp. 'Every woman should say, "I will never be too tired to listen to my husband's worries and try to help."'

The canny female, hungry for power but grounded by societal expectations, could have described both BC and Raine. Raine was almost always the only woman in a room full of decision-making men, and there were plenty of times she'd needed to use her feminine wiles and charm to get what she wanted. The old-fashioned view of a 'woman's place is in the home' perhaps belonged more to her mother's generation than to Raine's, but the whiff of antiquated class snobbery which underpinned many of her pronouncements during the sixties, 'I know what's good for the "ordinary people"', spanned both generations.

A voracious reader and an avid news consumer, Raine simply cannot have been insensible to the second wave of emerging feminism from across the Atlantic, with its activists like Gloria Steinem, Betty Friedan and Australia's Germaine Greer, or the newly minted American glossy *Cosmopolitan*, with its kick ass editor Helen Gurley Brown, author of the 1962 blockbuster *Sex and The Single Girl*. As a strong purposeful woman, essentially operating in a man's world, she would certainly not have been blind to the challenges that the newly emerging female workforce faced in taking on the patriarchy. What made Raine successful, though, was femininity rather than feminism and, perhaps even more importantly, her comprehension that reactionism made for better copy and greater coverage. In May 1965, she fretted over the death of romance, under the headline 'Wives with no time for Love', telling the *Daily Mirror* that love was dead and that women had killed it, 'instead we now have sex in its most revolting forms . . . women have sold themselves into slavery comparable with sweatshops.'

There were times during the mid-sixties when Raine was in danger of becoming a parody of herself. Whilst she might not have actually opened an envelope, she opened pretty much everything else: from a Tableware Fair in Belfast in 1964 to a high-profile dinner with the Iranian ambassador, celebrating the Shah's Silver Jubilee in 1965, to an artificial ski slope with the women's Olympic Ski team at Crystal Palace in 1967.

If anyone had taken the time to analyse this near maniacal round of public and media appearances, they might have concluded that at the root of it were two bereavements. On 29 December 1963, Hugh, who had been in all but name her father since she was six years old, died of complications brought about by his wounds from the battle of Passchendaele. Privately, Barbara was devastated but she didn't show it. As she had once infamously chastised Raine, 'We don't have feelings. At least not in public'. A year later, Raine's father, Alexander George McCorquodale, would die from a heart attack at his ancestral seat, Cound Hall, having enjoyed a happy eighteen-year marriage to his second wife, Margaret Theresa Eileen Browne. Whilst she was not close to her father, having looked upon Hugh as a surrogate, Raine was deeply affected by the loss of the two stalwart male figures from her life. And picking up as she always did on her mother's insecurities, they both felt for the first time the emotion expressed by C. S. Lewis, 'No one ever told me that grief felt like fear'. And Raine was fearful: mostly for the future – she knew that her relationship with Gerald would never be the passionate love affair so profitably idealised in her mother's romantic fiction and she could see also that local politics was changing at a rapid pace. The need to secure her place in the public's consciousness had never been more urgent. Her mother would, after all, always be known first and foremost as an author. What was to be Raine's legacy?

She began by perfecting her image. In the early age of television her slightly 'extra' appearance – the big hair, the glossy lips and the manicured nails – worked extremely well, 'It was almost as though she was made for Telly – you needed to be larger than life and she absolutely was' says a friend. She knew too all about the old feminine trick of using your eyes to tell the story even on camera; it was something her stepdaughter, Diana, later also understood only too well. Raine confided her own beauty secret borrowed from her mother to the *Observer* in 1966: 'Instead of mascara I used Meltonian shoe cream in Navy Blue'. Barbara had also provided the young Raine with a manicurist to teach her how to paint her nails. History does not record whether Raine, like BC before her, bought the bristles otherwise used to make small kitchen brushes by the yard from a hardware shop in London's Wardour Street, with which to create her false eyelashes.

Raine's feelings of insecurity and instability were not helped when in 1965 the LCC was superseded by the Greater London Council and her joint representation of Lewisham and Westminster came to an end. She became more determined than ever to remain in the spotlight and embarked on another relentless round of appearances. At the Industrial Society she told her audience that deprived, frustrated women 'of all income groups' used shopping as a means of 'buying friendship, fulfilment and power', in another speech she pontificated on the potential of having 'a cosy computer to do all the chores', and at the opening of a trade fair in Birmingham she spoke movingly about the loneliness of the elderly.

In her determination to make an impact and to say something quoteworthy, she was still occasionally misjudging her audience. On 15 April 1966, she gave what would now be regarded as a howlingly inappropriate interview to the *Daily Mirror*, describing how once, on an official visit and travelling by train, she had eaten a meal and discovered that she had only 10 shillings in her purse to cover a 25 shilling meal: 'So I looked round and saw this simply charming sweet man and to be quite frank I picked him up.' And did he pay asked the *Daily Mirror* journalist? 'But of course.'[5]

It was clear that she needed more distraction and in 1966, despite her former protestations to the contrary, she decided to run for the Conservative candidacy of Richmond, London. Her attempt failed (not through lack of hard work) but it whetted her appetite again for the structure and discipline that local politics required. In 1967, she triumphed in Richmond's local elections, coming first in the Tory poll, becoming a representative on the Greater London Council. 'Everything seemed to be going so badly that I felt that I should come and do my duty', she told Max Hastings, then of the *Evening Standard*, adding a sentence or two guaranteed to disgruntle at least part of the electorate, 'I haven't got an axe to grind. I've got a wonderful husband, beautiful children, a glamorous life, an amusing life and an interesting one.'

She protested too much, but as ever people took notice. On 19 May 1967. the *Daily Mirror* ran a headline, 'Oh, no – not her again!' 'Celebrities come and celebrities go, but Lady Dartmouth/ Lady Lewisham/Mrs Gerald Legge goes on forever', it proclaimed. Headline notwithstanding, the piece was a grudgingly admiring look at Raine's popularity, listing some of her many appearances and utterances, which included her current view on sex: 'someone has to try to stem the tide – people taking drugs, illegitimate babies, people proud of living in sin'. The Countess was listened to concluded the paper, in a manner which today seems jaw-droppingly sexist, 'because however silly the statement may be coming from that pretty rosebud mouth, Lady Dartmouth has a habit of standing up in public and pronouncing on the very subjects other women are currently discussing around the dinner table or over the garden fence'.

The very fact that a paper still could and would publish such a column, which objectified and patronised a member of the opposite sex (and a titled one at that) reflected a new mood brewing in newspapers and the media. It was no accident that the negative press surrounding Raine would begin to ramp-up during a decade of media revolution. There was a new man in town: a certain Rupert Murdoch who breezed into Britain in 1969 and bought the *News of the World*. A year later the *Sun* would be added to his stable, setting the tone for three decades of unrivalled 'kiss and tell' or 'gotcha' journalism, which arguably ended, or at least faltered, with the death of the Princess of Wales in 1997.

Some would argue, as Tina Brown does in *The Diana Chronicles*,[6] that the rot had already set in and that the *Daily Mirror* had set the pace. Brown points to the pivotal moment that Hugh Cudlipp, 'the feisty Welsh editorial director' of the paper, polled his readers over Princess Margaret's love life, asking whether Princess Margaret should marry her lover Group Captain Peter Townsend, a divorcé and a former member of the royal household. When the paper ran a headline on 19 August 1955, 'Come on Margaret! Please Make Up Your Mind!'[7] it prompted the first complaint to the newly formed Press Council. The council upheld the complaint, stating it was 'contrary to the best traditions of British journalism'. It was all downhill from there.

No sooner had Raine been elected onto Richmond's Council then she was in trouble again. As a member of the Licensing Committee she had insinuated herself into a hornet's nest of controversy by very publicly opposing the release of a film based on James Joyce's *Ulysses* – Britain's entry for that year's Cannes Film festival. She later admitted to not having seen the film and additionally having not realised that the British Board of Film Censors had already given permission for the movie to be shown uncensored at a cinema on Oxford Street before the prerequisite twenty-nine portions of dialogue and two scenes were cut for general release. 'There are certain things that can be read but not heard!' she said, before going on to describe them, 'unmentionable sex things (or) picking their noses, spitting or going to the lavatory'. If protest was not made, she went on, 'people will be making love naked in Piccadilly Circus. Passers-by won't even have to pay to watch. They'll just walk by without noticing'. (It was almost as though she was presaging the porn/social media explosion of the past twenty years.) When she wrote to the chairman of the committee, Harold Sebag Montefiore, to complain, she knew full well that she was beaten but she did it anyway. Sebag Montefiore was unmoved, 'the decision was unanimous. Lady Dartmouth is jumping to conclusions without having seen the film'. Lord Willis, the president of the Writer's Guild of Great Britain, demanded her resignation on the grounds that she had neither seen the film nor consulted the committee before speaking out.

A far more successful appointment which allowed for the total eclipse of the 'Joyce incident' was Raine's Chairmanship of the GLC

Historic Buildings Board. The role, likely bestowed on Raine by her old friend from her Westminster Council days, Sir Percy Rugg (by now the chairman of the GLC), might at first have seemed to some to be a lightweight, but appropriate role for a woman who had likely spent more time staying in her friends' historic and listed buildings than visiting them. 'My husband and I travel miles looking at buildings of beauty and historic interest', she claimed, 'it is our hobby.' In fact, Raine's new position would turn out to be one of the most significant and influential roles in local government of the sixties and would underscore her reputation as a powerful woman in her own right.

On 5 April 1968, the *Kensington Post* pictured a beaming Raine attending a dinner with Sir Percy – she was in the very early stages of pregnancy with her fourth child, and it didn't yet show. He was born on 28 December 1968. 'Ancestor's name for Dartmouth baby', announced the *Telegraph*, devoting two pictures and half a page to the announcement of Henry's birth. *Tatler* covered the christening on 27 February 1969: 'here was the Countess of Dartmouth cooing happily over her baby son Henry at his christening in the Grosvenor Chapel Mayfair yesterday'.

Raine didn't stay at home as the dutiful mother for long. She had taken care during her pregnancy not to put on weight, declaring that she had actually eaten less, 'not this nonsense of eating for two which simply blows you up'.[8] Sensible of being an 'older mother', she extolled the virtues: 'Having a baby at almost forty is partly a matter of readjustment . . . it keeps me alert and on my toes'. So much so that she hit the ground running in her new role, giving a speech about GLC provisions in February, less than ten weeks after Henry's birth.

Raine was skilfully crafting her message to reflect that she and no one else was in charge of five hundred historic buildings, listed or preserved by law: 'Beautiful buildings I am convinced, have a calming effect on the mind and soul' she said whilst speaking on the benefits of maintaining London's listed buildings for the general population. On her committee was the architect Sir Hugh Casson, 'she wanted your energy one hundred per cent and if you didn't give it, she knew how to rub you up the wrong way' he said. Few doubted her abilities though. For starters she persuaded the GLC to increase its provision for listed buildings from the £30,000 it had budgeted under a Labour Government in 1965/66 to £75,000 in 1969/70.

In early 1969, the phone of a young reporter rang on his desk at BBC TV News, Television Centre, Shepherd's Bush. 'Hello', said a warm voice with cut glass vowels, 'This is Lady Dartmouth. I am chairman of the GLC Historic Buildings Board. We are saving the Coutts Bank headquarters. It's a good story. Would you be kind enough to bring your cameras down to The Strand?'

'I said "Yes". Of course I did', says Cole. 'In 1969, I was a young BBC television reporter. Politicians didn't ring me. Yet here was one of the most famous women in the country . . . bothering to do her own PR work.'

When the camera crew and Cole arrived, Raine beamed, gave a textbook interview without notes to camera and then confided: 'And when we have stopped them pulling down Coutts' lovely façade, we are going to save Covent Garden.' But first she would take on the government over their plan to demolish the portico and steps of the Tate. She fought doggedly, despite backlash from those in her own party and pushback from 'The Ministry'. 'The Tate was saved by public protest and press campaigns', she later reflected, but there was little doubt who had been the driving force. Prince Charles might have taken inspiration from Raine as she raged through 1969, decrying architectural monstrosities and carbuncles left and right – the new Knightsbridge barracks was a 'monument to Government vandalism' and in a letter to *The Times* in April 1969 she asked 'do we really care about our towns and villages?', the implication being that the government certainly didn't. As if to underline her thesis she published a book: *Do You Care About Historic Buildings?* Headlined as an account of the role of the Historic Buildings Board on behalf of the GLC, there was little doubt but that it was a manifesto for Raine's campaigning and her bid for greater power.

The production of the book was a bravura performance and underlined what made Raine uniquely qualified to operate in what was then still ostensibly 'a man's world': she didn't mind one bit taking on the establishment she was supposed to be part of. In fact, she seemed to rather enjoy it. The list of committee members, aside from Raine, was almost all male – out of twenty-five members there were only three other women and one was the head archivist. She later admitted that the committee had been appalled by the first draft of her book, claiming it was 'absolutely against council policy' and had 'far too many adjectives' – clearly an attempt to diminish her efforts. Instead of giving in, she rewrote the whole thing in a day. In the afterword she sets out her stall: 'Better the old teddy bear with the missing ear than the spiky new model of the space-ship. Better the shabby building which is also part of the landscape than the brash modern construction which seems to shriek "Notice me, I am new."'

The small book, with its fashionably witty cartoons by Osbert Lancaster, ended with a flourish with a poem exclusively written for it by John Betjeman, who Raine had persuaded to contribute:

> 'Before slabs are too tall and our hearts are too few
> Let us keep what is left of the London we knew.'

The book was a best seller, the National Portrait Gallery put it on display and Selfridges gave it an entire window to itself. Later Raine admitted that when they had first seen it the committee members were again aghast – this time at the lavish centre spread of colour photographs of everything from the Painted Room at Spencer House to dinosaurs at Crystal Palace and the newly restored neoclassical Adam Library at Kenwood on Hampstead Heath. The book is well paced and thoughtfully art directed. Raine would have made a good magazine editor.

Raine's involvement in (or rather interference with) the GLC's plans to raze the 'Pepper Pots', was her introduction to the vast planning debacle that was the ominously named: Covent Garden Redevelopment Scheme – part of the Greater London Development Plan of 1969. The colloquially named 'Pepper Pots' were four cylindrical towers, capped by cupolas, which neatly bookended a section of architect John Nash's Strand opposite Charing Cross Station, and incorporated the Edwardian addition which housed the Queen's private bank: Coutts. They were scheduled for demolition by GLC planners to make way for a highway linking Orange Street in Covent Garden to the Strand. Almost before the planners had time to intervene, the strength of public opinion, fanned by Raine's publicity, resulted in the Ministry of Housing slapping them with a preservation order. As buildings of historic and architectural importance the Nash Pepper Pots were from then on protected from the bulldozers.

With her successful defence of the Tate, her book and her victory in the Pepper Pots saga (the plan would finally be rejected after her intervention and a further public inquiry in 1972), Raine was fast building a reputation as someone who meant business where the defence of historic buildings was concerned. She was just getting started. In 1970, the National Gallery announced its trustees' decision to demolish the National Portrait Gallery and expand backwards into that space. The NPG's new young, thrusting director, a certain Mr Roy Strong, thought otherwise and determined to thwart the National Gallery's ambitions – he decided to attempt to get the Portrait Gallery listed. His meeting with Raine is recorded in his diaries:

> At that time the historic buildings orbit of the Greater London Council fell within the domain of the then Lady Dartmouth. My first encounter with her was in some grim cafeteria in County Hall. Raine Dartmouth remains a remarkable apparition but I couldn't at the time reconcile this diamond-bespangled fashion plate with anyone remotely effective. In that I was to be proved immediately wrong. In the middle of our conversation the division bell rang and she got up to vote. Her aide, left at the table with me, said after she had gone: 'You won't believe this but she's absolutely marvellous. If we feed her with the right information she never gives up'. Shortly afterwards the NPG building was listed so that even if the National Gallery did take it over they would not easily be able to demolish it.[9]

'She was from another world', says Sir Roy reflecting on that experience, 'and from then on she would enter my life on and off – I always admired her. Nothing was half measures. Nothing escaped her.'[10]

London was on the cusp of a planning revolution, thanks to the far reaching influence of the Le Corbusier-influenced planning academic Patrick Abercrombie, who in 1945 had been asked by the London City Council to create a new city landscape for post-war London. The blitz had wreaked havoc on the capital, with over fifty thousand buildings destroyed. Over two million more had suffered bomb damage. Abercrombie's vision for London, which influenced the city's planning for decades to come and materialised in part in the 1969 plan, was similar to that of Le Corbusier's for Paris: skyscrapers and canyons. The city would be rebuilt for the motor car, he said, with four new roads including a new covered dual carriageway along Maiden Lane, an upper-level pedestrian walkway linking Trafalgar Square and Leicester Square and a new conference centre in Covent Garden.

Abercrombie thought London a city composed of 'obsolete, bad, unsuitable' buildings. With the exception of some villages – such as Kensington, Hampstead or Hackney – he seemed to think the rest of the metropolis should be flattened, aside from a few significant historic buildings like St Paul's and the Houses of Parliament. He proposed a series of 'ringways' circling London to iron out the traffic flow and reduce congestion. The 1969 plan dismissed parts of his original plan and effectively enclosed the capital within four major road arteries which became known colloquially as 'the London box'. The jewel in the crown of the 1969 plan was to be a new Covent Garden.

Proposals included enclosing the famous Inigo Jones Italianate square – The Piazza, commissioned initially by the 4th Earl of Bedford – and demolishing the Coutts building with what was thought to be a John Nash façade in favour of a major road.[11] Raine had dealt with the intended demolition of Coutts, but the rest was still very much up for grabs. 'The Covent Garden redevelopment plan had the potential to have more impact on the face of the capital than any since the great fire of London', wrote the architectural expert, writer and later director of the National Trust, Sir Simon Jenkins.

The battle for Covent Garden would require far greater levels of the by now infamous Dartmouth stamina. Raine entered the fray having been drafted in by Environment Minister John Plummer, who was chairman of the GLC's Covent Garden Joint Development Committee. The committee had been set up after the GLC had been forced to seize control of the project. Attempts to implement the original 1968 plan by Camden and Westminster Councils had failed spectacularly, dismally and very publicly, thanks to infighting, confusion and protest.

In an article earlier that year Raine had given an indication of what she thought best qualified her for just this sort of role, which would involve her seeing things from the perspective of the man (or more importantly) woman on the street. 'I may not be creative like Mummy, but I can certainly see when a city council shows me high-rise flats for married couples, how some young mother is going to have to climb 15 floors with her baby and her toddler (gosh that might be me with Henry) and her pram and groceries when the lift's not working.'

In reality, the three-hundred-year-old market and almost everything that went with it, aside from the local social housing residents, had no choice but to move. Swelling in size every year, the market was choking the heart of an already crowded city with the pollution and traffic caused by heavy goods vehicles and delivery vans, bringing in the tea, coffee, flowers, fruit and vegetables which were traded daily. By the mid-1960s London was a very different place to the days of Charles II when he first granted a private charter to the Earl of Bedford to hold a market on the site every day but 'Sunday and Christmas Day'. The narrow, cobbled streets and hairpin corners could not accommodate the huge delivery vans which rumbled through daily. The vast old decaying warehouses, which had held the nation's tea and coffee shipped in from India, Kenya and beyond, were a vertiginous health and safety risk. To move the market to a vacant site at Nine Elms seemed like the only option.

But the 1968 plans represented not just a desire to rehouse Covent Garden, but a naked landgrab by Camden and Westminster councils, who saw the opportunity for the rebuilding of 100 acres of central London after the 13 acres of market, which sat stubbornly in the middle, had been removed. There appeared to be a consensus amongst the powers that be that some of London's most expensive real estate was being taken up by social housing and that this effective 'land squat' should be dealt with.

The radical plan called for moving out families and businesses who had lived and worked in 'the garden' for decades, replacing social housing with tower blocks of offices, luxury flats and turning High Holborn and the Strand into a four-lane highway. Most alarming of all was the idea of demolishing Piccadilly Circus, enclosing the Covent Garden Piazza and running elevated walkways above street level, removing pedestrians from the area entirely. A conference centre would be at the heart of the new plan which would see acres of central London, including many historic buildings, demolished.

The plans lit the touchpaper in an area where the disadvantaged felt unheard by a Conservative government used to getting its own way. But Covent Garden was different, as the government would learn to their cost. The area had become renowned for its central location, cheap rents and huge run-down buildings which offered aspiring writers and artists the space to create. Angry mobs of local inhabitants, small business owners, artists, fledgling planners, writers and architects, resistant to what they saw as government and developer greed, filled the streets daily, interrupting public meetings, squatting in vacant buildings and harassing local councillors. In *Private Eye*, Paul Foot wrote 'There is a fire and militancy in Covent Garden not seen in central London for decades'.[12]

Celebrities signed petitions and gave evidence. These included Sir John Betjeman, who protested strongly at the intention to level his favourite restaurant, Rules. Before giving his speech he introduced himself to the enquiry as: 'a Companion of Literature and an Honorary Associate of the Royal Institute of British Architects. Until my extended term of office expired last year. I was a member of the Royal Fine Art Commission. I am an honorary advisor to the Historic Buildings Committee of the GLC and one of her Majesty's Commissioners of Ancient Monuments.'

The protesters were led by two firebrands: Gamekeeper turned poacher, Brian Anson, an ex-GLC official whose letter to the Covent Garden inhabitants expressing doubts against the plan had resulted in him being unceremoniously fired, and a local architect and planning activist, Jim Monahan. There was an unlikely third member of the triumvirate – the vicar of the local church, St Martin in-the-Fields, Austen Williams. All were united in their opposition to the developers, who they felt were driving the planners, and to the Edward Heath-led government, which had approved the plan without taking any account of local feeling or local needs. Many locals were unaware of exactly what the plan, which was first mooted in 1965, actually involved. The GLC was accused of keeping local residents in the dark and attempting to exploit their community for financial gain. 'We were a bit of an anarchist bunch', John Toomey, the head of the Covent Garden Community Association (CGCA), who had grown up and lived in Covent Garden for forty-five years, admitted later, 'and it was the collective effect that worked – the marching and the occupations, we just refused to sell the shop to the GLC.'[13]

At the inaugural meeting of the CGCA, set up to fight the planners and the GLC on 23 April 1971, Toomey had outlined the fundamental problem: most of the residents were not privy to the government's planning process or to the decisions being taken on behalf of their community by the GLC. 'These are not people who can afford £2 for a government report from the Stationery Office and they do not read the announcements in small print in *The Times* and the *Guardian*.'

The best hope for 'the small people of Covent Garden' argued the *New Law Journal*, 'lies with Lady Dartmouth . . . who has proved her grasp of human, architectural and traditional values and her capacity to carry others along with her'.

'The canonisation of Raine Dartmouth was both alarming and funny', writes Brian Anson in his book of the events, *I'll Fight You*

For It: Behind the Struggle for Covent Garden 1966–74. 'Her leadership of the GLC committee had not altered the basic premise of the plan. The GLC valuers were still basing their financial studies – which would subsequently affect rents – on a land value of over £1 million an acre.'[14]

Soon after she was appointed as Covent Garden Committee chairman, a soigné Raine, dressed in a black and white tweed mini-suit, appeared on Thames TV, interviewed in Covent Garden surrounded by locals and answering questions: 'I've always said that it's people who matter', she said brightly, flashing the camera a smile and clutching her black patent handbag in her white gloved hands, 'I want to hear what the people have to say'. *The Times*, calling Raine the GLC's secret weapon, reported on her visit to the Covent Garden Piazza calling it 'delicious My Fair Lady stuff'. The papers reporter described the scene: 'Like some immaculate and huge hatted fairy godmother, she stood in front of the hot dog stall under the portico of Inigo Jones's St Paul's, listening, noting names and addresses, occasionally vouchsafing a dazzling smile for the sake of Thames Television'.[15]

True to her word she set up the Covent Garden Discussion Group with a mission to make it easier for locals to air their grievances. 'Even if the redoubtable Lady Dartmouth – fresh from her experiences on the Historic Buildings Committee is to make any progress in disentangling the GLC from the web of bitterness and resentment woven round its grandiose £140million redevelopment plan, she'll need all the support she can get', wrote Nicholas Wright of the *Illustrated London News*.

On 27 May 1971, Raine introduced the latest GLC proposals 'flanked by a clutch of the Greater London Council and a bunch of artist's impressions that would have done credit to a pupil of Canaletto', reported *The Times*. The performance was vintage Raine as she smilingly handed out glossy brochures, containing the new plans which had made some concession to providing larger amounts of public housing, but had also upped the number of private housing units. Raine's defence was that the increase in private housing, shops, hotels and car parking would allow social housing rents to remain low. Covent Garden community leaders were not impressed. What *The Times* tactfully called 'a dialogue' developed between Raine and Mr Monahan, who was wearing a 'Stuff the GLC Covent Garden Plan' badge, and who later complained that the planned road network would devastate the area. 'We do not want just purely destructive criticism and comment', said the Countess, whose critics, as *The Times* had previously pointed out, 'have been heard to say that the one-time Lady Lewisham runs her politics like a cabaret'.[16]

Privately Raine had at first seen little wrong with the plans and she said so publicly, telling the *Chelsea News and Advertiser* on 11 June 1971, 'fears of a blight are unjustified'. Her line was that the mixed housing would limit the area for further development, therefore preserving the village atmosphere. The CGCA were not impressed: 'Lady Dartmouth says she wants a scheme that makes the people happy', wrote one woman to a local newspaper, 'it's a pity that the planners are so blind and deaf that they don't realise that the way to make people happy is to leave them in their own environment.'

The protests became more heated. During one march an effigy of Raine was paraded through the streets of the Garden, in another, participants marched across London to her home in Mayfair where they were held back by a police cordon. Local celebrities such as DJ David Jacobs and actress Amanda Barry got in on the act, with Jacobs – who had been born and raised in the area – pointing to a woman dressed as Nell Gwynne, pushing a cart selling oranges, claiming 'we used to own that'. Paul Foot, of *Private Eye*, lambasted Raine calling her the 'scourge of *Oh Calcutta!* [A reference to a risqué show playing at London's Round House, to which she had objected] And all things vulgar . . . who is intent on imposing the most hideous vulgarity on London with her obscene Covent Garden plan!'[17]

But the truth was that Raine was beginning to listen, and she was not alone. On Wednesday 7 July, Covent Garden residents festooned part of Charing Cross Road with banners protesting the development. It was day one of the Covent Garden public hearings, with barristers Mr John Taylor and Lord Colville presenting for the development on behalf of the GLC. However, evidence and protest from the CGCA was so compelling that QC John Taylor approached one of the representatives and invited the whole group for dinner, where upon he proceeded to tutor them on how to put up an avid defence, telling John Toomey that he personally did not believe in the redevelopment scheme.

As the forty-two-day public inquiry played out, Raine's sympathies too were moving towards the campaigners and against the GLC, led by Sir Desmond Plummer, who was at the vanguard of an aggressive new planning ethos for the city. 'There was a seismic revolution in London's planning policy in the early 1970s and Raine was in the middle of it', says Sir Simon Jenkins, who was writing for the *Evening Standard* as architecture/planning critic at the time. 'And she certainly had to deal with some very sinister characters on the Covent Garden Residents Committee, but gradually they rather took to her and she to them.'

The planning inspectorate recommended the plans for development to the Secretary of State for the Environment, Geoffrey Rippon. The Labour Party announced a campaign for leadership of the GLC based on a pledge to abolish the existing plan, stating, 'We do not think that Lady Dartmouth's plans of restricting the area of comprehensive development to 15 acres belonging to the market authority would ensure the whole area was adequately dealt with'.

Tensions ran high. 'Apart from anything else the Covent Garden community is nurturing within its bosom some pretty extreme characters. John Toomey told his audience "we are not marchers but ordinary people who want to live. When it comes to the crunch we will fight"', reported Jenkins in the *Evening Standard* on 16 May 1972.

When Raine's home was picketed, she acted decisively. Arguing at town hall meetings was one thing but coming to her home and scaring the children (and possibly more importantly irritating the neighbours) was another. The strength of local feeling over Covent Garden had shocked her to the core and with her appreciation for historic buildings and historic London she had become increasingly concerned about the future of the area. She said as much to Sir Desmond Plummer when, along with her fellow developing committee members, she wrote to ask for a meeting with Peter Walker, the new Secretary of State for the Environment. She wanted the power to act on decisions being made over the 15-acre site, which the Covent Garden Market Authority had agreed to sell. When the committee rejected her case, Raine felt she had no option but to resign. She wrote to Plummer saying that she was: 'unable to work for a project in which I no longer believe and which could do unnecessary and irreparable damage to an historic part of London. I have felt increasingly that our proposals are out of date and out of tune with public opinion, which fears that the area will become a faceless concrete jungle.'

The CGCA felt vindicated, but they also recognised that Raine had done what they never believed that anyone in authority would do: listen. 'It has become increasingly rare for public figures to admit that they have changed their minds', they commented, 'let alone that they may have been seriously wrong. The courage of Lady Dartmouth in making both decisions will not be soon forgotten.'

Six months after Raine's very public resignation had created waves, another public servant was revealed to have been secretly working with her behind the scenes to ensure the authenticity of the Covent Garden area. The minister for Public Works, Geoffrey Rippon quietly listed 250 of the buildings within the area as having 'historical and architectural merit', thereby permanently protecting them from demolition.

By January 1973, the entire Covent Garden redevelopment plan was in tatters. Rippon had effectively come to the same conclusion as Raine: that to rip out the heart of central London would deny its inherent and valuable history and, far more importantly, destroy a community with roots reaching back hundreds of years. Sceptics said that Raine's nose for politics simply meant that she had scented which way the wind was blowing and had changed tack to garner favourable press. Rippon disagreed and paid tribute: 'Lady Dartmouth in the past has been too readily dismissed by some as an attractive but frivolous ornament of London local government. She is in reality an accomplished politician with a transcendent affection for the character of the capital and its people.' The press agreed. Even the normally acerbic columnist Lynda Lee Potter in the *Daily Mail* referred to Raine as a 'titled professional charmer'. 'You've got to admit', she confided to her readers, 'it's only surface gloss on a shrewd, relentless toughie.'

In fact, Raine was already exercising more of that ambitious shrewdness. On 10 February 1971 a headline had appeared in *The Times* announcing, 'Four groups to prepare for environment talks'. The article reported that Peter Walker, Secretary of State for the Environment, had ambitious plans for what would effectively be the world's first Earth Summit – the United Nations Conference on the Environment to be held in Stockholm in 1972. According to Walker it offered 'what could be the widest public participation exercise on environmental matters yet carried out'.

Walker was the world's first Environment minister. His position had been created in response to the growing environmental concerns of the 1960s. The long list included the Torrey Canyon oil spill of 1967, the Aberfan coal waste disaster of 1966, an oil spill off Santa Barbara in 1969 which killed an estimated 3,500 sea birds, a mass fish poisoning in the Rhine, drought and famine in the Sahel and the Minamata Bay accident in Japan which saw 2,265 people die after a chemical company released mercury. He duly announced four working parties to prepare for the United Nations Conference on the Environment in Stockholm in June 1972. The chairperson of the group on Human Habitat, reported *The Times*, would be a certain Lady Dartmouth, chairman of the GLC Historic Buildings Board. 'I chose her because she had terrific energy, was provocative and had strong views on most topics', Walker was quoted as saying. 'I was seeking a lively intelligent mind.'

The UK, alongside France, had been led by the nose to the UN table in 1968, when the possibility of UN action on the environment was first tabled. Notably both countries were concerned that developing countries, particularly those recovering (or not) from colonial oppression, would use the conference to gain greater financial support/reparations. Sweden pushed ahead and in 1968 the UN General Assembly adopted resolution 2398, calling for the inaugural conference on the relationships between environmental, social and economic issues to be convened in 1972 in Stockholm.

Energised by her fresh new mission (whilst still trying to smooth the waters in the very tense Covent Garden stand-off) Raine carried out a whirlwind tour of the country with her committee, from the newly opened Pantechnicon of Knightsbridge to the waterways of Reading, visiting people in their homes and asking questions about the way they lived. She generated headlines wherever she went. Sir Simon Jenkins, who sat alongside her on the working party and accompanied her on some of her countrywide visits, remembers one particular occasion when on a visit to a Kent village to view their conservation area, Raine insisted on seeing the home of a

Citroen-Deux-Chevaux-driving, scruffily attired, left-wing conservationist. The startled rebel who had at first put up an admirable fight against Lady Dartmouth viewing his humble abode finally relented:

> Jumping into his little car he led the way with Raine in her shiny black, chauffer driven Daimler following closely, with the rest of us speeding in convoy behind. The Deux-Chevaux driver took a sharp turn onto an unmade bumpy track and we all followed with clouds of dust billowing. We drew up at a forest clearing at what was obviously a hippy hangout. Raine elegantly got out of the car and disappeared into one of the shacks, telling the man's exceptionally reluctant and rather sulky wife 'I do so want to see your lovely home'. We all expected the worst, but after 20 minutes Raine emerged carrying a tray of tea, with the man's wife, following behind, practically purring.

Jenkins also remembers the cover of the finished report on 'The Human Habitat', entitled 'How do you want to live?', which presented its own set of problems: 'Raine wanted a particular Snowdon picture with a woman in a see through diaphanous gown emerging from a lake. The civil servants practically had a heart attack. The committee kept saying it's simply not done.' She ignored them and pressed on. 'The cover of the report', a scandalised *Coventry Evening Post* duly confirmed, 'has a coloured cover by Lord Snowdon of a scantily clad girl walking out of the mists of a lake'.

Perhaps even more impressive was the fact that Raine had commissioned Phillip Larkin to write a poem specifically for the prologue of the report, entitled, somewhat unimaginatively, 'Prologue' – later better known as 'Going Going' – bemoaning the loss of the English countryside. The poem was not without its controversies. When the commissioning committee censored and then removed Larkin's lines about 'spectacled grins', 'takeover bids' and 'Grey area Grants' because they found them too 'pointed', Larkin uncharacteristically accepted their censure, but later included the poem in full in his best-selling poetry collection *High Windows*.

The UN Conference on the Human Environment, the first ever global UN conference with the word 'environment' in its title, was deemed a success. Amongst the resolutions of the conference, which was attended by two prime ministers (India's Indira Gandhi and Sweden's Olof Palme), was the setting up of UNEP – the United Nations Environment Programme.

Sitting alongside Walker (who would use Raine's report to inform his own) was the glamorous and brilliant ecologist Barbara Ward, author of *Only One Earth: The Care and Maintenance of a Small Planet*, a report specially commissioned by Maurice Strong, Secretary General of the conference. Wearing chic sunglasses, Walker also gave evidence to the UN on behalf of the British. Hansard, 22 June 1972, details exactly what Peter Walker and the rest of the British Delegation had voted upon:

1. a declaration on the human environment;

2. the establishment of an information system under which those needing information on environmental matters would be rapidly referred to all available sources of information: an early meeting of experts is expected to be held in London to develop this concept;

3. the initiation of improved programmes for monitoring pollutants, especially in the air, on a world-wide basis;

4. the selection of London as a site for a Conference to be held in October during which we would hope to get agreement in principle on a Convention on the world-wide control of marine dumping;

5. the establishment of a Governing Council to oversee the environmental responsibilities of the United Nations, with the necessary secretarial support; and

6. the establishment of a United Nations voluntary environmental fund to which substantial contributions have already been pledged, including a contribution by the United Kingdom;

7. a world clean river programme;

8. a world-wide increased programme of technical assistance and co-operation.

Job done, Raine returned to her other work as a board member of the British Tourist Board (later Authority). As 1972 drew to a close, she announced that she had made the decision not to stand again for the GLC. This proved to be sagacious (or simply well timed). In 1973 the London Tories suffered a defeat and the newly Labour run council moved to abandon the entire Covent Garden plan including the notorious 'motorway box'. Raine had other things on her mind. She had agreed to take on another role as chair of the UK Executive Committee preparing for European Architectural Heritage Year in 1975. She had also recently become reacquainted with an old friend – one of Britain's leading aristocrats, Edward John Spencer, styled Viscount Althorp, heir to the earldom and the 13,000-acre Althorp House and Estate in the county of Northamptonshire.

5

When Raine Met Johnnie

———————•◆•———————

Edward John Spencer, distant relative of Henry VII, known as
Johnnie Althorp, was rumoured to be the gloomiest man in
London. His was the sort of despondency normally reserved for
slighted romantic heroes, like Thomas Love Peacock's Scythrop
(modelled on Percy Bysshe Shelley) or more latterly the hopeless,
hapless donkey, Eeyore of Winnie-the-Pooh fame. It had not always
been thus. Before his wife, the Honourable Frances Ruth Roche,
daughter of 4th Baron Fermoy, had publicly deserted him for the
dashing heir to a wallpaper fortune (Peter Shand Kydd) in 1967,
sparking a salacious society scandal, Spencer had been the very model
of a society bon vivant. Not to mention a textbook Earl in waiting.

Educated at Eton, where he had reputedly followed the time-
honoured tradition of occasionally beating his 'fag' for burning his
toast and other even less spectacular misdemeanours, Spencer had
lacked the wit or inclination (or possibly both) for Oxbridge.
Instead, he took a commission at the Royal Military College at
Sandhurst, followed by a spell at the Royal Agricultural College,

Cirencester, to prepare him for the farming of the 13,000 acres, which would come with the inheritance of Althorp, the thirty-one bedroomed stately home and Spencer family seat for over five hundred years.

The Spencer story was and is a history of hard work and fortunate, if flagrant, liaisons. Fifteenth-century sheep farmers in Warwickshire and Northamptonshire who expanded their lands and established Althorp in the 1500s, the Spencer family had many distinctions, not least that at one time they were the richest family in England. From the get-go the Spencers made a name for themselves. After the 2nd Earl had the misfortune of setting himself alight when his tailcoat caught fire, he designed a short jacket named for himself – the Spencer – to avoid further such incidents. The jacket was later adopted by the British military as 'mess dress' and worn widely by men and women alike during the eighteenth and nineteenth centuries. In the 1600s, three Spencer women were mistresses to Charles II (a monarch whose offspring made up at least 25 per cent of the dukedoms of Great Britain and Ireland). In the same century, Arabella, daughter of the first Winston Churchill (the Spencer name was changed to Spencer Churchill by the 5th Duke of Devonshire denoting the connection) bore James II a daughter. The antecedent 'Diana Spencer' – second daughter of Charles Spencer, the 3rd Earl of Sutherland – failed where her descendent would triumph, when her grandmother, Sarah, Duchess of Marlborough (Rachel Weiss in *The Favourite*) attempted to marry her in secret to Frederick Prince of Wales, George II's heir apparent in the 1730s. The plot was foiled by the then Prime Minister, Robert Walpole.

The family achieved notoriety with the antics of eighteenth century society beauty, campaigner and iconoclast Georgiana Cavendish (née Spencer), the Duchess of Devonshire (played by Kiera Knightley in *The Duchess*). Georgiana was notorious as much for her anti-monarchic pro-Whig party campaigning as for her unusual sexual 'arrangements' in which she famously tolerated not only her husband's multifarious affairs, but also his lover, Lady Elizabeth Foster, living as a member of the family. After finally birthing a successor to the Earldom, William George Spencer Cavendish, Georgiana was 'permitted' her own very public love affair with George (later Earl) Grey, British Prime minister, with whom she had an illegitimate child in 1792.

It was said, sometimes in jest and sometimes in all seriousness, that the Spencer family had more royal blue British blood running through their veins than the current reigning monarch Elizabeth II, with all of her Teutonic connections. Johnnie Spencer, the 8th Earl in waiting, had served as a Captain in the Royal Scots Greys during the Second World War and had been mentioned in dispatches after leading a British Army unit to liberate the French towns, La Neuve-Lyre and La Vieille Lyre. Post war he had the distinction of having served both King George VI and then his daughter Elizabeth II, working for them both as equerry in 1950–52 and 1952–54 respectively. It was a measure of the new queen's affection for him that she had allowed Johnnie to cut short a royal commonwealth tour, disembarking the royal tour liner *Gothic* at Tobruk and flying home from Libya to marry the eighteen-year-old Frances. It had been a whirlwind romance, during which there had been an uncomfortable 'breaking off' of his original somewhat unofficial engagement to the daughter of the Earl of Leicester, Anne Coke, now Anne Glenconner.

Johnnie's father, Jack, the 7th Earl, who did not take kindly to his son at the best of times, had warned him off Coke on the grounds of family 'madness'. Rarely his own man and as his former commanding officer in the Grays described him, according to Max Riddington and Gavan Naden in their book *Frances: The Remarkable Story of Princess Diana's Mother*, 'very nice but very stupid',[1] Johnnie conceded defeat and turned his attentions to the not dissimilar looking, blonde, blue-eyed statuesque Frances. The family's royal connections satisfied Jack of his future daughter-in-law's suitability (although it has been suggested that he never liked her and that the feeling was mutual). Frances's mother, Lady Fermoy, was a friend of the Queen and later, on her husband's death, would become extra Lady of the Bedchamber to the Queen Mother. The age difference between Johnnie and Frances was twelve years, exactly the same as would later exist between their daughter Diana and her husband Prince Charles.

By the admission of her own son Charles, now the 9th Earl Spencer, Frances Roche was not cut out for motherhood: 'Our father was a quiet and constant source of love, but our mother wasn't cut out for maternity. Not her fault, she couldn't do it,'[2] he told the *Sunday Times* in an interview to promote his new book in 2020. The question of whether Frances was maternal or not is moot for those not directly involved. Perhaps more contentious is the behaviour of Johnnie over Frances's increasing reluctance to remain in a marriage beset by issues of progeniture, tragedy, apathy and stultifying boredom. After giving birth to two girls and under pressure to produce an heir, Frances finally gave birth to a son, John, born on 1 January 1960. The baby died after only ten hours without Frances being allowed to hold him. She never truly recovered. Magnifying her grief was the fact that she was 'sent' (by whom it is not clear but likely a combination of her mother and the 7th Earl) to a Harley Street gynaecologist for tests and treatment to investigate her inability to produce sons. 'It was a dreadful time for my parents . . . and probably the root of their divorce because I don't think they really ever got over it',[3] concluded Charles Spencer – the much-vaunted heir – finally born to Frances in 1964.

'Johnnie was the best company when he was a young man . . . but then he just became boring, wrapped up in his children and his country life', the jilted (but by then married to Colin Tennant)

Anne Glenconner told Sarah Bradford for her book, *Diana*.[4] Frustrated, dejected and bored, living at Park House on the Sandringham estate in Norfolk, the very house she had grown up in, Frances began to spend more time in London and the marriage began falling apart. 'There was no single circumstance which served as a moment of realisation that we were hitting the marital rocks', she guardedly told Riddington and Naden.

At a friend's dinner party, she was unexpectedly bowled over by a handsome, laid-back bohemian – Peter Shand Kydd, heir to a wallpaper fortune, who arrived in her life with all the refinement of a hurricane. He was fun, fearless and spontaneous. Everything that the plodding Viscount Spencer was not. They began an affair in secret and in the summer of 1967, Shand Kydd left his wife Janet. The pair became increasingly indiscreet and very quickly, Johnnie knew too. Incandescent with rage over what he regarded a very public betrayal, he nonetheless refused to believe that Frances would leave him.

Much has been made of Johnnie's fierce temper and the question of whether or not he subjected Frances to violence. There is no concrete evidence for this save for a comment from his own daughter, Diana, that she'd seen her father slap her mother: 'they were arguing with the doors open and I looked around it and I saw that' she told voice coach Peter Settelen in tapes they made together in 1992.[5]

'In the summer of 1967 Johnnie and I agreed to a trial separation', Frances told Gordon Honeycombe.[6] She took Diana and Charles with her to live in London, where she rented a flat in Cadogan Place. 'I don't know if there will be a reconciliation', she told the reporters who knocked at her door. Johnnie was at a loss, retiring into himself and barely speaking to the children.

'The biggest disruption was when Mummy decided to leg it. That's the vivid memory we have the four of us [including her brother and two sisters] . . . People took sides. Various people didn't speak to each other. For my brother and I, it was a very wish-washy and painful experience', Diana told author Andrew Morton, indirectly, for his book *Diana: Her True Story*.

Johnnie recovered his equilibrium, furious at the very public humiliation Frances was visiting upon him. During Christmas 1967, which the couple spent together at Park House for the sake of the children, Johnnie wreaked revenge by refusing to allow Frances to take the children with her back to London, insisting that they be schooled locally and live with him. The elder two, Sarah and Jane, were away at school, so it was Diana and Charles who would bear the brunt of remaining in Norfolk without their mother. A devastated Frances lodged a petition to the High Court for custody of her four children, which should have been a foregone conclusion. For as much as she naively failed to factor in the wealth, influence and societal power of the future Earl, she could also not possibly have imagined that her mother Lady Fermoy would take the stand against her.

Later many would speculate on Fermoy's motivation for speaking out against her daughter's childrearing abilities, suggesting that Peter Shand Kydd's lack of a title had provided the impetus, together with a desperation to remain close to the Spencers and thus the Crown. 'I did it because Charles had to be brought up at Althorp', she is said to have told a friend, referring to the stately home Johnnie was due to inherit. It was also well known that Fermoy's best friend, the Queen Mother, abhorred scandal and divorce and that Fermoy had always been slavishly in her thrall. The trump card was played without Spencer's influence, but much to his benefit, when three days into the custody hearing, Peter's wife Janet Shand Kydd was granted a divorce from him. Frances had been cited as co-respondent. She didn't stand a chance.

When the appeal was denied, Frances sued for divorce citing cruelty as grounds. There were more rumblings about Johnnie's behaviour (the divorce file and papers for the case remain sealed and

Frances's biographers Max Riddington and Gavan Naden's attempts to access them in 2002 were thwarted by a legal judgement) which only served to raise suspicions about what they contained. Johnnie counter-sued, citing Frances's admission of adultery. The judge ruled once again in Johnnie's favour.

That Frances had already been cited as a co-respondent in a divorce case made things easy for the judge and for Johnnie – most other divorcing couples still had to jump through hoops to prove their incompatibility and most simply lacked the money or the emotional fortitude to go through with it. The law was as ever weighted heavily in favour of the man. In A. P. Herbert's satirical novel on divorce, *Holy Deadlock,* a fictional solicitor tells his client, 'If you violently knock your wife about every night the ordinary person will conclude that you have not much affection for her, but the law requires you to prove it by sleeping with another woman.' The novel was published in 1937 and not much had changed since. The sixties were still seeing a good number of 'Brighton Quickies' – a set up wherein the plaintiff and his lover visit a hotel, checking in as 'Mr and Mrs', with the sole intention of providing legal evidence of infidelity. The bill for the night was then duly sent to the plaintiff's actual wife who sued for divorce. When, as the law required, enquiries were made at the hotel, a chambermaid was 'produced' who 'brought the couple morning tea in bed' and thus acted as witness to the fact that the husband was committing adultery.

It's hard to imagine now the stigma surrounding divorce in 1968 and the societal pressures to 'conform' to the prevailing ideal of a 'happy marriage'. In that sense the birth control pill and the subsequent 'free love' ethos of the sixties had done little to alter society's received view that a broken home equated to personal failure. To make things worse, until the 1969 Divorce Reform Act, the onus was on the ability of the correspondents to 'shame' each other by proving adultery, cruelty or desertion. Most upper-class marriages remained intact. It wasn't that the upper classes didn't have affairs, rather they preferred to come to an 'arrangement', with each party pursuing their own interests and coming together for family occasions and official events. The stigma attached to a divorcee was weighty and whilst it might not have troubled Barbara Cartland that divorcees were not permitted in the Royal Enclosure at Ascot, there were plenty who viewed that sort of prohibition as social death. Frances was without her children and faced social ostracism, but she would not lose the man she loved: she and Peter married at Westminster Registry Office, three days after the decree absolute was issued on 29 April 1969.

By 1972, Johnnie Spencer's life had settled into what many (and indeed he, himself) might have described as a quiet monotony. 'He was really miserable after the divorce, basically shell shocked. He used to sit in his study the whole time,' recalled Charles Spencer.[7] A nanny – Mary Clarke – had been brought in to care for the children – who were now, with the exception of Charles, all away at boarding school – during the holidays. Frances made one more attempt to gain custody in 1971, calling into question both Johnnie and Mary's competence, but again she was thwarted in court by Johnnie's lawyers. 'I wanted no share of the despair of the mother or the jubilation of the father', Mary told Riddington and Naden, of her own experiences of having been called upon to testify.

'It was a hot day and everyone was in the garden', recalled Raine of the Kensington charity lunch party, where she and Johnnie Spencer became reacquainted. As anyone who knew her would attest, on no account would the Countess of Dartmouth ever expose her skin to the sun, insisting on taking a parasol or hat wherever she went, or better still on being in the shade – at least literally speaking. This day would be no different. As the sun blazed, Raine headed indoors out of the heat. 'There was only one person there – John.

"I haven't seen you for twenty years" he said. We just sort of hit it off.' The pair bonded over a love of historic buildings and before long, as part of her mission to cheer the gloomy Viscount, Raine had elected Johnnie as chairman of the Youth Panel for the European Architectural Heritage Year. Was this a ruse to allow them to spend more time together? Possibly. But there's little doubt that his very obvious sadness and loneliness stirred Raine's maternal instincts. 'I suspect that from the beginning there might have been an element of mothering', said a friend.

So what attracted forty-three-year-old Raine to the forty-eight-year-old divorced Viscount, heir to an Earldom and one of the grandest stately homes in the UK, with ties to the royal family and enough Gainsboroughs, Rubens and Van Dykes to rival the world's greatest art galleries? It was easy to draw the obvious conclusions and many did. Barbara Cartland compounded the rumours by offering an ill-advised comment after their affair became public and defending Raine against criticisms that she was a social climber, 'she gave up a sixteenth Earl for an eighth Earl – hardly social climbing. Everything gives the impression she came out of the gutter. It is not true'. The statement of course said more about Cartland than her daughter. Ever the snob she was anxious to underline the family's existing social standing. It would not do for anyone to think they came from the 'lower classes'. 'The McCorquodales were a perfectly well established Scottish upper class family', says Julian Fellowes, 'so it was a little harsh to suggest that she was moving up a ladder.'

In reality the attraction was simpler and deeper than status: they were simply mad about one another. 'Raine loved men and she loved sex. She simply found Johnnie irresistible', says a friend. 'And the feeling was mutual.' 'Johnnie was besotted by her', says Frank Partridge, 'absolutely besotted'. There were other rumours too, 'Lots of stories were flying about relating to her being great in bed', says biographer Anne de Courcy, 'apparently they were always nipping into lay-bys and hotels and leaving the chauffeur waiting outside.' One story – apocryphal or not – is related by a friend who tells of a budget hotel alongside a motorway filling station where another friend to whom they had offered a lift, was required to wait in the Rolls with the chauffeur whilst the couple made use of a room.

'I really don't think Raine had any intention of falling in love with Johnnie Spencer, it simply happened. It was real love, they adored each other, you could be sitting with them at a dinner and there they would be talking to each other, laughing and having fun. They were very much in love and got on like a house on fire' says Raine's half-brother Ian McCorquodale, 'I think my mother was a bit bemused by the whole thing.'

Raine meanwhile was on a high professionally – she was on the board of the British Tourist Authority and had just been appointed as Chair of the United Kingdom Executive Committee for European Architectural Heritage 1975, with the Duke of Edinburgh as president. When she announced a £1 million fund to save Britain's most historic buildings, she raised eyebrows, in the same way that the Duke's son Charles later would, by calling modern architecture 'a new form of pornography'. In private, friends and relatives noted that all was not well between Raine and Gerald, although she publicly stated he was 'the Rock of Gibraltar and divine; so steady and strong and yet such humour'. 'She was beastly to him and so dismissive', Angela Levin quotes a friend as saying in *Raine and Johnnie*. 'I loved Gerald', says Anne Glenconner, 'but he was not her equal.' 'She had such a nice first husband: an incredibly kind and modest man. It was never going to last', concludes Sir Roy Strong.

But there were signs that Gerald might become the mouse that roared. It seemed he was becoming increasingly tired of Raine's singleton outings and of being generally excluded. 'She'd been giving dinner parties without him for years', said another 'friend', 'he would just slink in the back door'. Simon Jenkins remembers going for a drink with the couple at Raine's request to assuage Gerald's suspicions and 'to calm things down a bit'. 'He was terribly nice', he says of Gerald, 'but she was firing on all cylinders and it was perfectly obvious that he was never going to excite her.'

'I've fallen in love just like in one of your novels', Raine told Barbara Cartland, 'and there's nothing I can do about it.' Her proclamation was genuine. By Raine's nature she was flirtatious – more of a 'man's woman' as the old-fashioned saying went. 'She liked a good brain, power and looks', said a friend, 'of the male variety'. Constantly surrounded by men – and very often the only woman in the room or around the board table – she had never wanted for admirers and had had every opportunity to take an appropriate lover, had she so chosen. But all along she had remained faithful to Gerald, with whom she had found love and companionship. She liked his intelligence, his wit and his kindness, something which hadn't been much in evidence in her own childhood, at least where her mother was concerned. 'We were all very fond of Gerald indeed. He was a fine sportsman, liked his shooting and fishing. He was a good husband' says Ian McCorquodale. There were those who posited that Raine had married a father figure of whom she was growing tired, something upon which she never commented or confided.

Raine famously kept her own council on pretty much everything – she thought female friends were dangerous: 'if you absolutely must have a best friend, make it your husband or your mother', she once said to author Angela Huth,[8] adding, 'but even with them there should be some reservations'. She was against 'close and absorbing friendships with women' she said, because, 'One: She'll always steal your husband or try. Two: The best friend is the only person who can make a dangerous enemy. Three: Best friends nearly always become jealous of some aspect of your life – perhaps you are cleverer or prettier or have more money in which case, due to jealously, the best friend cannot help but be disloyal.'

Close friends or not, it was absolutely obvious to anyone who saw them together that there was something more than friendship between Raine and Johnnie, although she tried her best to hide it. 'It was a coup de foudre when Raine met Johnnie', says the wife of an old acquaintance of Raine's, 'of this at least I am completely sure.'

But Raine's trump card was not her sexual allure, her wit, intelligence or beauty, it was Johnnie's father, the 7th Earl, Albert Edward John or 'Jolly Jack', so nicknamed because he was anything but. An embittered, frosty, eighty-something widower, whose first love was his stately home, he despaired of his son Johnnie from whom he was all but estranged, viewing him as weak and rather hopeless. He was immediately captivated by Raine, seeing in her an intelligent, dynamic female who appreciated architecture and the historical provenance of Althorp's paintings and antiques. Raine, who was, and always would be, a sucker for an old aristocrat with a twinkle in his eye, took to Jack, spending hours walking Althorp with him, discussing its many merits and treasures. She made it her mission to broker a reconciliation between father and son in a genuine desire to heal the rift. Was there a teensy bit of self-interest in there too? Probably.

Jack Spencer's loyalty to Althorp and his fierce desire to keep it in the family famously knew no bounds. His one great error where the house was concerned, writes Charles Althorp the current Earl, was in selling Holbein's only portrait from life of Henry VIII in order to find enough cash to pay for his children's education. The painting was sold for £10,000 to the Thyssen family in the 1930s,[9] was valued at £30 million in the 1980s and is 'now one of the masterpieces of the Thyssen collection in Madrid, where I visited it four years ago with a pang of regret',[10] writes Charles Spencer. 'It [Althorp] was the one true passion of Jack Spencer's life. He was in love with it', said the Duke of Devonshire of Jack.

Jack's ingenuity meant that Althorp was better appointed architecturally than at any time since its genesis. The family's London

over girl: Raine's first magazine cover which mittedly she shared with her mother, novelist rbara Cartland, August 1930. Photographed by ciety photographer Madame Yevonde.
vonde Portrait Archive/ILN/Mary Evans Picture Library)

The Bystander, August 13, 1930

the IBYSTANIDEIR

No. 1391. Vol. CVII

An attractive studio portrait of Mrs. A. McCorquodale, whose novels, published under the pen-name of Barbara Cartland, have enjoyed considerable popularity, with her little daughter, Raine. She is now at Strabisher House in the Orkney Islands, where she is busy putting the finishing touches to her fourth novel, "For What?"

Stage left: performing at a charity matinée at the Hippodrome for Madame Vacani's dancing school, June 1937.
(Illustrated London News/Mary Evans Picture Library)

Vartime London, 18
nuary 1944: Raine with
other Barbara, Ian (far
ft) and Glen.
Keystone/Stringer/Getty Images)

'We had to improvise': the 'Winterhalter' dress with Barbara's ribbon 'improvements', 1947. *(Little/Daily Mail/Shutterstock)*

(above) Outed: *Tatler* reports on the traditional 'coming out' celebration – Queen Charlotte's Ball – with Raine dominating the coverage. *(Illustrated London News/Mary Evans Picture Library)*

(left) Dressed for success: fake flowers and silk – a newly engaged Raine McCorquodale at Royal Ascot, 1948. *(Dave Bagnall Collection/Alamy Stock Photo)*

The TATLER
TWO SHILLINGS & BYSTANDER MAY 6 · 1953

Spring Number

MRS. GERALD LEGGE

Off the shoulder: Raine sports a rather outré number on the cover of *Tatler*, May 1953.
(Illustrated London News/Mary Evans Picture Library)

Glamour queen: a newly married Raine at a Givenchy fashion show. *(Little/Daily Mail/Shutterstock)*

'It Girl': defying convention with a 'grass muff' at Ascot, 16 June 1953.
(Douglas Miller/Keystone/Getty Images)

Sweet charity: Raine has her hair dressed by legendary stylist, Steiner, before performing in a charity show at the Scala Theatre, London, May 1953. *(Ron burton/Keystone/Getty Images)*

Storm in a teacup: Raine photographed after the Infamous 'café episode' at London Airport, 1954. *(Ray Warhurst/Sendtoppo/Shutterstock)*

(above) And the children . . . :
William's christening, 1949.
(Superstock/Alamy Stock Photo)

(left) With William aged thirteen
(left) and Rupert aged twelve (right)
(Ann Ward/ANL/Shutterstock)

With Charlotte after her christening at the Grosvenor Chapel, 1963. *(Frank Apthorp/ANL/Shutterstock)*

Raine and Henry, 1969. *(Tony Prime/ANL/Shutterstock)*

With Charlotte (right) and Henry (left) being photographed for the *Evening Standard*, 1962. *(Evening Standard/Hulton Archive/Getty Images)*

Presented: meeting Queen Elizabeth II for the first time at a party hosted by the Mayor of Westmins
at the Royal Academy London, 29 November 1956. Queen Elizabeth The Queen Mother, is seen far
right. *(Monty Fresco/PNA Rota/Getty Images)*

Silver spoon: Raine, now Lady Lewisham, arrive
at Foyles Literary luncheon to celebrate the Duk
of Bedford's book: *A Silver Plated Spoon*, 15 May
1959. *(Derek Berwin/Fox Photos/Hulton Archive/Getty Image*

seat, the splendid Spencer House, located at 27 St James's Place, designed by John Vardy and James 'Athenian' Stuart, had been tenanted since the 1920s. Before he let the place, Jack had personally overseen the removal of anything of merit from the house. This would include eighteenth-century chimney pieces, marble busts, skirting boards and even the decorated panels from the so-called Painted Room. During the war he rented the place to Christie's the auction house, whose offices had been destroyed by bombs. The tenancy of Spencer House continues. It is currently let to Jacob Rothschild's company, RIT Capital partners, which spent millions on renovations. In the 2021 RIT Capital half yearly financial report, 30 June 2021, the value of investment into Spencer house was quoted at £30.5 million.

Althorp, which had been in the family since 1508, when prodigious sheep farmer John Spencer acquired the land and had it built, is spectacular if a little cold in appearance thanks to Henry Holland's remodelling in 1787, when a new façade of white brick was added. At this point the house was in the hands of the 2nd Earl who amassed the greatest private library in the world. In Simon Jenkins's book, *England's Thousand Best Houses*, he quotes Sacheverell Sitwell on the unprepossessing exterior: 'we may feel that architecture is nearly at an end. So little less and it will have gone'.[11] As Jenkins points out, inside is another story entirely where an astonishing entrance hall of two storeys rises to a coffered ceiling and a Restoration staircase rises in a single flight to a gallery. 'The picture gallery is converted from the Elizabethan version and the stables flanking the entrance drive are a superb composition of 1732 by Roger Morris. Their portico is a copy of St Paul's Covent Garden by Inigo Jones.' In all, the parkland, woodland, farms and cottages surrounding the house run to 13,000 acres of verdant Northamptonshire countryside.

So onerous and expensive was the running of the vast estate that in 1942 Jack had attempted to give Althorp over to the National

Trust. The Trust's local agent James Lees Milne recalled his visit: 'Lord Spencer was huffy at first because of my lateness and because of the depreciation of Althorp by the agent whom the Trust had employed to make a report on the property . . . In the end I liked Lord Spencer for not being crosser than he was. He said I was the first National Trust person who had talked sense.' Lees Milne stayed to lunch, 'poached eggs with maize and cabbage – which we ate in a little panelled room. Lady Spencer, like a goddess distilled charm and gentleness around her'. He was less complimentary about the house itself which the local agent had reported was suffering from, amongst other things, wet rot, dry rot and the death watch beetle: 'Certainly I appreciated Althorp. But the difficulties will be infinite before we get it'.[12] In fact, the Trust required an endowment before they took the house off Jack's hands, which he most certainly did not plan to give. Jack took the whole thing personally and from then on would work to restore and maintain the house himself, earning the title of 'the Curator Earl'.

The war had seen Jack at his most irascible and intransigent where his beloved house was concerned. He complained so vociferously at the army's use of the grounds, that the powers that be decided against pushing their luck any farther and attempting to commandeer the house. Jack also tirelessly grumbled that the soldiers passing his study spoiled his view of the parkland. As a result, they were ordered by their commanding officer to break into a run every time they passed the Earl's study window. The result, a steady, endless stream of soldiers jogging noisily past Jack's window, breathing heavily, was not much of an improvement.

Jack applied for a series of government loans that had recently become available for the upkeep of 'national heritage'. The trade-off was that he had to accede to the government's requirement for him to open the house for sixty days a year. He would do practically anything to preserve his home – including researching and choosing the paint colours for every wall and embroidering his own chairs, which led to him becoming chairman of the Royal School of Needlework. But his pièce de résistance was his decision to install the Spencer House treasures at Althorp rather than returning them to Spencer House.

Sadly, Jack never succeeded in establishing the same warm regard for his son Johnnie as he had for his stately home, even when Raine was in tow. Where Jack had an active and involved interest in the arts – he was a trustee of the Wallace Collection, a fellow of both the Society of Antiquaries of London and the Royal Society of Arts and Chair of the Advisory Council of the Victoria and Albert Museum (1961–69), his son had an interest in photography and a vague interest in collecting wine. 'My father and Grandfather had a difficult relationship, which had enjoyed intermittent periods of under-standing and mutual appreciation', writes Charles Spencer.[13] Johnnie, like so many other people, seems to have been terrified of his father, hiding in a false ceiling in the nursery bathroom with his terrier dogs for company when things got too stressful as a child. One of Jack's chief complaints and resentments of later years was that Johnnie had demolished a home he had given him at North Creake in Norfolk. The Shooting Box had housed land girls during the war and to Johnnie's eyes it could not be saved. Jack found this approach almost unforgivable but it didn't stop him giving Johnnie some 8,000 acres of the Althorp estate to avoid death duties. Notably, Johnnie was left very little in the way of 'liquid' funds, a matter which would become significant once he succeeded to the Earldom. Instead Jack chose to leave much of his estate in trust to Johnnie's son, Charles, thereby skipping a generation. His will reads: 'I devise and bequeath all my real and the residue of my personal estate . . . UPON TRUST for my grandson the Honourable Charles Edward Maurice Spencer absolutely if he shall survive me and shall attain or shall have attained the age of Twenty Five'.[14] 'When I married Johnnie he was so hard up he had only three Turnbull & Asser shirts to his name, all with frayed cuffs. At night he would cry his eyes out over the cruelty of his father's treatment which had left him in virtual penury,' Raine told her friend Michael Cole.

Johnnie was everything that Jack was not – or so it may have seemed to his father. Jack was a tireless workhorse, publicly as well as privately, serving as Lord Lieutenant of Northamptonshire, in addition to his trusteeships and chairmanships, and he was also a member of the county council and on Northampton Hospital Committee. It wasn't that Johnnie didn't see active 'service' in the charity sector – he was Chairman of the National Association of Boys Clubs, he served as a JP, and was Honorary Colonel of the Northamptonshire Territorials, amongst other roles. His attitude though was of diffidence, rather than dynamism. Neither Earl would make their mark in the House of Lords with Johnnie never giving a speech and Jack speaking on just one occasion on 9 September 1924, when Hansard records that as a second response to the King's speech (the first was offered by the Earl of Plymouth) he 'craved your Lordships' indulgence . . . I come from a family which has never produced a good speaker in your Lordships' House'. The bad run of Spencer family speakers would end with Charles Spencer who sat in the Lords until the House of Lord's repeal act of 1999 and spoke three times. His most memorable speech (arguably one of the most iconic of all time) was the eulogy he gave at his sister's funeral service in Westminster Abbey on 6 September 1997.

In retrospect, Jack may have viewed his son's marriage to Frances as a mistake and the publicity that Johnnie's divorce attracted was almost as unwelcome as the hordes of visitors who were now tramping the halls.

To her credit, Raine seems to have been one of the few women willing to spend time with the irascible Jack after his wife Lady Cynthia died of a brain tumour in 1972. On Cynthia's death, the Queen had personally visited Johnnie at Park House to offer her condolences for the loss of her friend. As a mark of that friendship, she offered a memorial service at the Chapel Royal, St James's Palace. 'Although he rarely showed his feelings, Lord Althorp was delighted about the Queen's visit. He was devoted to his mother', Johnnie's former butler recalled. Raine spent countless hours with the 7th Earl, listening to his stories about the great house and his ancestors. She was genuinely interested in what Jack had to say and her interest flattered him. She nurtured their friendship – adding to his collection of antique walking sticks and bringing him his favourite chocolates from London every time she visited.

Things did not go as smoothly when Raine first met the Spencer children at their Park House home in Norfolk. Nanny, Mary Clarke set the scene:

Betts [the butler] had placed Lady Dartmouth on Lord Althorp's right and Sarah opposite her on his left. Charles sat next to Sarah with Jane on his left. I sat opposite Jane with Diana between me and Lady Dartmouth . . . I knew her mother was Barbara Cartland, the romantic novelist who always dressed in pink, so I suspected her daughter might also be a bit different. However, nothing prepared me for the woman who appeared in the dining room that day and who was later to become a permanent fixture in the lives of the children and their father.[15]

One can only imagine the entrance of the immaculately attired and tonsorially teased Raine, in a draughty, comfort free, Norfolk country mansion, sitting awkwardly with the children in jeans and sweaters, dogs in the grate and Johnnie in his shy, diffident way, trying to smooth her path. The lunch was not a success. The children seemed determined not to like Raine. It was not surprising. They had never had a competitor for their mother before and they had never come across anyone like Raine. Johnnie had done nothing to prepare them for her visit and he was powerless against their united front. Meanwhile Raine, with her customary mixture of aplomb and thick skin, ploughed on regardless, trying but failing to make conversation with the children. 'They were at this stage still mourning the loss of their mother', says Simon Jenkins, who could see both sides of the story, 'in came Raine, very much her mother's daughter and here was this quiet, restrained, very private family, whatever she did would not have worked'.

Raine's first instinct was to make herself indispensable to the children, who she recognised had had a very tough time. 'She tried very hard with them' says Michael Cole, 'but they simply did not want any competition for their father's love.' She plied Diana with her favourite romantic fiction (which happened to have been written by her mother Barbara Cartland) and went out of her way to help Sarah prepare for the eighteenth birthday party Johnnie threw for her at Castle Rising, an old Norman castle in Norfolk, suggesting Sarah and Johnnie attend as Henry VIII and Anne Boleyn. Not content with just any old costume for Sarah and wanting to please both father and daughter, Raine set about using her not inconsiderable powers of persuasion to bag Sarah one of the dresses worn by Geneviève Bujold in the movie *Anne of the Thousand Days*.

The dress was worn and the party was a success, but it cut no ice with Sarah or the other children, who refused to speak with Raine and began putting up a spirited and united fight against her and trying to persuade their father to see sense. Raine (now known to them as Acid Raine) pretended not to notice, 'I could have them all for breakfast if I wanted to' she told friend, interior designer David Laws.[16] Inwardly she was concerned that the children's 'war' against her would sway their mild-mannered father. When the calm, persuasive reasoning of his eldest two daughters failed with Johnnie, all four children turned to overt warfare and the much written about (and possibly apocryphal) chanting of 'Raine, Raine go away' began.

But Johnnie was insensible to their pleas. The undivided attentions of the woman he loved were far too valuable for him to be swayed by his offspring. He'd been lonely and hopeless in divorce and he recognised in Raine a woman who could provide companionship, organisation and affection. Raised in a household where emotions were suppressed, with a loving but distant mother and a cold, detached father, the attentions and ministrations of a dynamo like Raine to whom he was both physically and intellectually attracted, were all but overwhelming. Raine had given him a purpose too – a year after she'd put him to work on the Youth Panel for European Architectural Heritage Year he would take the photographs to illustrate her book created for the GLC: *What is our Heritage?* It was yet another excuse for the two to spend time together.

By 1975, Raine found herself in an invidious position. She was increasingly recognised within social circles as 'the companion' of Johnnie Spencer and the negativity with which she was being greeted was beginning to irritate, in spite of her self-professed thick skin. She was married to a man she no longer loved, but shared a strong companionship with, who provided her with many of the social and economic 'niceties' she craved – money, a mansion and a title. If she put a foot wrong, she could end up with neither man. The press had wind of the story and whilst she had thus far politely corrected them and nothing extensive had surfaced in the papers, she knew that it was only a matter of time.

On 9 June 1975, Jack Spencer died of pneumonia and the Spencers moved from Park House, Sandringham into Althorp, the home Johnnie had for so long desired. The children, (whose prefix titles had been 'the Honourable' were now 'Lady' and 'Viscount' respectively) had been reluctant to leave Park House, which had been the family home with their mother, and move from Norfolk to Northamptonshire, where they knew no one. It didn't matter that a 100,000 square foot stately home awaited them – they had barely ever been there. Charles, then eleven, and Diana, thirteen, were the only two of Johnnie's children who would really spend any time 'growing up' at Althorp, with the other two, Sarah, twenty and Jane, eighteen, already having partially left home. Charles records that during his childhood he had found Althorp a 'a terrifying house to stay in: the vastness of the place was somehow even more pronounced at night, with the sound of footsteps outside the room and the opening and closing of doors discernible . . . our short candles never lasted the whole night'.[17] It would be Diana, who used to practise her tap dancing on the black-and-white chequered floor of the Palladian entrance – 'Wootton Hall' – who would benefit most from her association with Althorp, when it became very much the backdrop, both literally and metaphorically, to her engagement to the heir to the throne. If anything would underline Diana's suitability for her position as future queen it would be the infamous post-engagement photoshoot of her and Prince Charles walking in the grounds of Althorp – the first glimpse the world had of what they mistakenly took to be Diana's 'childhood home'.

It is unlikely that the family move could have been achieved quite so smoothly without Raine at the helm. Johnnie had put himself entirely in her hands and with her consummate organisational skills, Raine set to work. She overlooked Johnnie's feeble attempt at explaining away her constant presence to the children by saying that Raine was simply there to organise things. As Diana remembered it for Andrew Morton, 'that was a terrible wrench, leaving Norfolk, because that's where everybody who I'd grown up with lived. We had to move because Grandfather died and life took a very big turn because my stepmother, Raine, appeared on the scene, supposedly incognito'.

The press were getting wind of what was going on. The situation had undoubtedly not been helped by Sarah, who answering the phone to reporters had once related that her father could not be disturbed as he was still in bed . . . 'with Lady Dartmouth'. On another occasion she told a reporter 'Since my grandfather died last June and we moved from Sandringham to Althorp, Lady Dartmouth has been an all too frequent visitor'.[18] Lady Colin Campbell recalled how Barbara Cartland used to confide that the Spencer children would tell Johnnie, 'You can marry anyone but Raine'.

Perhaps it was the publicity, or maybe the normally mild-mannered, scrupulously polite Gerald was simply tired of being cuckolded. Either way, he finally sued Raine for divorce on 29 May 1976, naming Earl Spencer as co-respondent. The petition, which included a signed affidavit from Raine, admitting adultery, appeared to have been agreed by both of them in mutual acknowledgement of the disintegration of their marriage.

Raine knew she was facing a very public humiliation, but she was also too proud to push Johnnie into marrying her. On the day that her divorce went through she confided to David Laws, whom she had already employed for Johnnie at Althorp to redecorate the late Earl's suite of rooms and who would later play a significant role in the re-vamping of Althorp, 'I am not saying anything to Johnnie. I know he loves me, but I have told him he must not feel because of the divorce he was committed in any way'.[19] Anne Glenconner was all too familiar with Raine's plight: 'She used to ring up all the time to discuss Johnnie. She just couldn't get him to commit. I didn't know what to tell her because obviously I'd had the same problem. That was Johnnie's weakness – an inability to commit.'

Gerald gained custody of his two younger children, Charlotte and Henry, and somewhat predictably the judge did not find 'against' Earl Spencer, 'a man against whom the charge has not been proved' said Judge Everett, referring to Raine's confession.

The hypocrisy of both Raine and Johnnie was lost on few. Here was a man who had relentlessly pursued his own wife through the divorce courts for custody of his children, claiming her an unfit mother, taking up with a woman who was leaving her own children.

And as for Raine, if she was devastated at losing custody of her younger two children – Charlotte, aged thirteen, and Henry, seven – she didn't let it show publicly. 'Raine left the family home [Chipperfield Manor in Hertfordshire] taking very little with her. I believe what she took were literally the contents of a horsebox which she towed behind her car to Althorp', says friend Michael Cole. She left behind a broken family who, in stark contrast to everyone else involved in the Spencer/Dartmouth/Windsor saga, have retained a dignified silence to this day.

According to Lady Colin Campbell, it was William, Raine's eldest son, who counselled his mother to seek an invitation to someone's yacht and go cruising for two weeks in order to cut ties with Johnnie and make him realise what he was missing. The 8th Earl Spencer was still refusing to commit and Raine was losing hope. Whether or not she followed William's advice is unclear, but something certainly moved Johnnie. Possibly it was the memory of his gloomy few years post his divorce with Frances and his recognition of how much better his life was with Raine on board. 'Along came Raine who said "lets have some fun. What's the point of having this great estate and this great house without enjoying it? Let's get cracking Johnnie"', says Julian Fellowes.

Two months later, on 16 July 1976, *The Times* carried a simple announcement in its marriages section:

> The Earl Spencer and Raine, Countess of Dartmouth.
> The marriage took place in London on July 14 between
> Earl Spencer of Althorp and Raine, Countess of Dartmouth,
> of 48 Grosvenor Square, W1.

The couple had married in secret at Caxton Hall registry office with Raine's half-brother Glen as witness. 'It was such a quiet wedding that even I didn't go', said Barbara Cartland, eager as ever to give a quote to the press. 'They rang me immediately afterwards and said "hello, we're married".' The children were livid, as Diana later related in a videotaped session with Peter Settelen, her voice coach in 1992. 'Sarah rang me up, she said. "Have you seen the newspapers?" So I said "what?", "Daddy married Raine" – "My god how do you know that?" "It's in the *Express*." We were so angry but Sarah said "Right Duch" – my nickname was Duch, "you go in and sort him out."' According to Diana, her remonstrations with her father who said of Raine, 'you'll grow to love her as I have', ended with Diana slapping him around the face 'if I remember rightly'. The acerbic Sarah talked directly to the press with her normal understated pithy sarcasm. 'We weren't invited' she told a reporter of her father's second wedding ceremony, 'not grand enough'. Some said twelve-year-old Charles was left to hear the news of his new stepmother from his prep school headmaster.

6

Saving Althorp, Saving Johnnie

———————— •◆• ————————

We are both very different but we compromise. My wife is a very forceful personality, but easy to get on with once you know her . . . She's a town woman. I'm a country man. She's a saver, I'm a spender – I suppose good champagne, brandy and port are my biggest extravagances. She has beauty and brains and she came to me an older and wiser woman.' Johnnie Spencer on his marriage to Raine.[1]

The pair celebrated their marriage with an opulent ball that September, with Raine and Johnnie seated next to each other at the long table in the State Dining Room. 'They looked like the king and queen at a medieval feast' David Hicks told Angela Levin. They may as well have been Marie Antoinette and Louis XIV for as much as they seemed in touch with Labour run 'recession Britain', which would soon suffer an embarrassing IMF bailout after strikes, the oil crisis and skyrocketing inflation threatened to disable the entire country. No wonder the rebellious fervour of a new musical movement – punk – was emerging. But the couple and their friends were untroubled. They were floating in the Tory bubble of landowners, bankers and the business elite, for whom an economic crisis simply presented the opportunity for a change of British leadership, which would arrive soon enough in the form of Margaret Thatcher in 1979.

The Spencer children were apparently not invited to the hedonistic party. And if they had been, they would probably have declined. They were a resentful brood, and Raine took care to keep the Spencer children and her own apart. As Barbara Cartland explained to Lady Colin Campbell. 'It was always arranged that they would visit Althorp at different times to Johnnie's children and therefore they were never particularly good friends'.

Raine was less restrained around the Spencer children now that she was married to their father, but she never lost her veneer of calm politeness. BC had taught her always to respond with unfailing civility, no matter what one felt – it was a 1930s upper middle-class approach to life (as typified by the monarch) and it would constantly pay dividends.

The Spencer children's ring leader was, according to Raine, Sarah, who, possibly bruised from a breakup with the man who was soon to become Britain's richest and most eligible bachelor, Gerald Grosvenor, later the Duke of Westminster, was spiralling downwards into anorexia, which would become so severe that she would need hospitalisation and specialist treatment. 'Sarah resented me even my place at the table and gave orders to the servants over my head. Jane didn't speak to me for two years, even if we bumped in a passageway', Raine would later tell columnist and so-called queen of Fleet Street Jean Rook.'[2] A friend of Diana's was less than impressed by her behaviour when she visited from West Heath School where the two were boarders (Diana's family home took her by surprise and she was so overwhelmed by her surroundings that she curtsied to Earl Spencer). 'For Diana what was absolutely unforgivable was the fact that her father clearly loved her [Raine].

For me there were no baddies in this story, I think they all had a right to the position they took', says Julian Fellowes.

In any case, the new Countess Spencer had plenty of other issues to occupy her. She was certainly not under any illusions. 'She knew what she was getting into and she knew the state of the finances which were parlous', says a friend, 'and I think she relished the challenge.' Another friend remembers the shock of the debt, 'from what I remember the death duties were around £2 million and there was no money washing about with which to pay them. I don't think people understood that many of the assets which generated significant cash – Spencer House in London for example – were in trust to Charles Spencer, which meant Johnnie could not touch them. Johnnie later admitted in an interview, 'I inherited £1.5 million in death duties and another £2 million in estate debt.'[3]

'We got the show on the road right away, no hanging about', said the new chatelaine to a friend. She needed to. The entire house was in a state of extreme dilapidation. 'When I first stayed there it was like any country house', wrote Kenneth Rose, the celebrated social and *Sunday Telegraph* diarist, who wrote a column called 'The Albany' for the newspaper, 'A footman brought you a can of tepid water. There was some primitive central heating that gurgled all night.'

Raine needed to think on her feet and she did. While the 7th Earl had first opened the house to the public in 1957, what Raine did was make the whole thing more attractive to the visiting public. She opened a gift shop and a café; it wasn't a matter of choice; it was a matter of necessity. Frank Partridge, then of Partridge Fine Arts who were involved in the renovations, remembers the scenario the newlyweds were faced with:

First they tried selling the paintings in lieu of taxes to the nation but when that didn't work Raine realised she would actively have to make the house pay, that's why she opened the gift shop and began to work there herself. She was incredibly passionate and an incredibly hard worker, she saw it as her duty really. And then there was Johnnie, who, by his own admission liked spending money – it had to come from somewhere and Althorp was simply a money pit.'

For all of his possessions, his land and his titles, the 8th Earl Spencer was not cash rich.

'Johnnie Spencer was left no liquid to run the estate, so they had to make the house work 24/7 just to keep the roof on',[4] says Peter Constandinos – Raine's long-term hairdresser and friend. Rory Clark, deputy land agent for Althorp from 1987 to 1991, bore witness to the problems: 'They were definitely asset rich and cash poor, things simply had to be sold and these things were valuable. I'm not so sure, despite everything that was said, that they had particularly sentimental value to the family at that point.'[5]

And then there were the servants, lots of them – many of whom had been around for decades and were coasting to put it mildly. Raine, who expected those around her to work as hard as she did, acted accordingly. She first persuaded Johnnie to sack his land agent – essentially the individual in charge of running the estate – and install the experienced Richard Stanley, who ran the estate for fifteen years thereafter. Once in post, Stanley made changes, the negative effects of which were, in what was to become an increasingly common narrative, blamed on Raine. In other words, the minute that Raine married Johnnie Spencer any of the problems related to the estate, employees, fractured familial relationships, even Johnnie's fading personal friendships were blamed upon her.

In terms of the staff, many had been at Althorp for decades: 'I'm afraid I had to blow the whistle', Stanley told John Pearson, of some of the old retainers who were no longer pulling their weight, 'they ran to Johnnie, but Raine made him do what was necessary. She was a ruthless woman and I say that admiringly'.[6]

Raine undeniably loved having staff – she'd become accustomed to a certain way of life almost from birth, but the difference was that initially it had been thanks to her mother's hard work that she had people to wait upon her. Since her first marriage it had been thanks to her husband's birthright: 'she lived in a world of white gloves and servants. It had never once occurred to her that there would be no one around to pick up after her', says Roy Strong. In her second marriage, the number of staff required to run a great house the size of Althorp was punishing both in terms of wage bills and oversight. About forty full time staff worked at Althorp in various states of employ. Raine ran her own team hard by everyone's account, promoting her cook Betty Andrews to also act as lady's maid. 'Countess Spencer had some jolly good points and was kind in her way. If she shouted at me I used to shout back', said the redoubtable Andrews.[7]

Rory Clark found his own way to deal with the Countess: 'You had to stand your ground. A lot of the staff were afraid of her but I think her fierce approach was simply a way to get people to do what she wanted and quickly. Often she'd ask me to do things and I'd say "that's barmy". I could see from the expression on her face that she actually agreed!' It didn't help that many of the new staff were extremely young. 'There was a huge turnover of staff, mainly because they were always employing young people with little experience who could not or would not stay the course', says Clark, who contends that much of Raine's bluster was an act. 'In a funny way she was very much like Margaret Thatcher. A huge presence who had concocted a persona which worked. This involved being immaculately turned out and very forthright verbally. You did not want to get on her wrong side.' Raine's 'persona' would often extend to dramatic gestures guaranteed to get her noticed – something her mother had also specialised in. 'She would insist on being chauffeured from the front door of Althorp to the gift shop in her Rolls-Royce', says Clark, 'of course, she knew as well as we did that this was utterly ridiculous, but it made a statement which was what she intended.'

Accounts of Raine's treatment of her staff, apocryphal or not, abound, from her specificity about foods (not crème caramel apparently) to the confidentiality agreements she had her employees sign. Clark recounts a number of stories in his humorous fictionalised account of working at Althorp and other estates: 'You Did What My Lord?', including Raine's battle with a ewe who insisted on navigating the cattle grids and defecating on the manicured front lawn of the house and later, her insistence that staff protect her ornamental bay trees from the Princess of Wales' helicopter downdraft, by wrapping each one in bedsheets.

Pearson's accusations in his book, *Blood Royal*, are less humorous and forgiving, likewise those of Angela Levin in *Raine and Johnnie*. Other writers, including the biographers Sarah Bradford and Tina Brown, follow suit, piling on the criticism of Raine: she was difficult, she was a profligate, she was indulgent, she was waspish, she was grand and she had a temper. The same critical eye was never applied in the same way to Johnnie. As an aristocrat and later father of the Princess of Wales, he could do no ill in the eyes of a forelock-tugging world, where the greatest crime seems still to be the audacity of marrying into a grand family without coming from one yourself. 'Of course the great question is how would Raine have been treated and what would she have been able to achieve had she been a man', says Jeffrey Archer.[8] 'I think you'll find things would have been very different for her – from her days as a Westminster councillor onwards.'

In marrying Johnnie, Raine became fair game in a way that she never had been before. Gone were the glowing headlines of the sixties and seventies about Raine 'the powerhouse political operator'. The narrative of 'wicked stepmother' was so speedily and eagerly crafted by the tabloids that by the mid-eighties, it would be hard to remember Raine as anyone other than the impossibly demanding, overly coiffed wife of Johnnie Spencer and wicked stepmother of the future queen. No details were too tiny – from Raine's predilection for using talcum powder post-bathe, to her desire to have her monogrammed sheets changed daily and her habit, presumably inherited from her mother, and hardly a crime, of being served breakfast in bed, whilst making her morning calls, propped up on her pillows in her silk negligee.

It's hard not to cite an element of class snobbery when it comes to the developing narrative around Raine, once she became 'Countess Spencer'. Had Raine come from a different family, how much fuss would have been made of the way she behaved or what she did? Many had, have and will behave much worse. But a particularly nasty kind of class-conscious malevolence attached itself to Raine. Those who considered themselves 'better bred' than her saw fit to damn her actions as those of a 'parvenue', whilst onlookers – newspaper readers, columnists and social commentators – ravenously marvelled at her insouciance and her refusal to apologise for who she was, what she did or said or how she looked. Had she been male, her actions, 'landed gentry' or not, would have been roundly lauded. But a woman who came from a family of Scottish printers . . . to perch this high up in the social tree and not be a humble apologist for her less than blue-blooded upbringing? It just wasn't done. Well not in Britain anyway. 'To say Raine didn't care about what the press said would be wrong. I think she did wish that they would be a little bit kinder to her. She wasn't prepared to give up just because some journalist said that she was an entitled fiend', says Julian Fellowes.

Raine's agenda was never entirely clear. It seems likely though, that given her upbringing and her strength of personality, she was simply determined to plough her own furrow rather than to launch a one-woman assault on the social barricades of late-twentieth-century Britain. That said, it would be remiss not to note at this point that

Raine seemed to suffer the kind of negative malice which is attached these days to the Duchess of Sussex and her much maligned extended family (save her mother, Dora). In other words, British society has a long way to go before it 'levels up' from the top down.

If Raine's treatment at the hands of society and the press was a bright and shining example of class snobbery and misogyny in action, she not only turned the other cheek, she went out of her way to act very differently to those pointing the finger: 'Raine was absolutely not a snob', says Michael Cole, 'she literally could and would talk to anyone, she had a very different approach from that of a lot of other people with whom she mixed socially'. According to Cole and many others, Raine never minded the negative publicity or the catty comments from those in her social sphere, 'she always said "never mind what they write or say – is the picture good? That's all people remember"' laughs Cole. 'Her attitude to nastiness was pity – she thought "poor them" and not "poor me"' says her half-brother Ian.

Where Althorp was concerned, Raine was going to need a very thick skin. She had learned from her political career the necessity of putting the right staff in place to achieve the changes required and to ensure things ran smoothly. 'Raine set to and began the process of restoring it to its former glory, this was her goal and although it took a long time, she achieved it' says Partridge, who recounts the process of the renovation in which his firm, Partridge Fine Arts, participated. 'Raine was direct and clear about what she wanted and was always a pleasure to deal with', he says. The same might not have been said for David Laws from society decorator Colefax and Fowler, who was advising on the 'soft' elements – carpets, curtains and paint colours. Colefax, started in the 1930s by socialite and friend of the Duke of Westminster, Lady Sibyl Colefax, were, in the 1970s, the last word in chic, understated, comfortable, if somewhat floral, country house interior design. Laws himself was a theatre designer by trade and known for his design 'flourish', which broadly speaking seemed to be composed of as many and as much floral cushions, curtains, pelmets and 'swagging' as was humanly possible, with some serious luxury carpeting thrown in for equal measure. Described by Wendy Nicholls, the current president of Colefax, as 'a very ebullient sweet man with a filthy temper'[9], it was Laws who installed the vast, heavy curtains at Althorp, which were to be the source of much derision, and advised on the much maligned 'orange dralon' chairs in the Great Room.

'The whole renovation of Althorp took seven years. There was always a bloody big bill to pay. Of course they needed to sell some items like paintings and furniture to pay for it, but I want to emphasise that it was Johnnie who did the selling and not Raine, he liked to have cash in his pocket and there was not much about', says Partridge.

At this point, though some might dispute it, Raine likely knew a lot more about the house than Johnnie or any of the Spencer children. Her innate curiosity and her avid interest in historical design had meant that she'd actually paid attention to what Jack had told her on their walks together around the grand house. She knew for example what needed to be saved and what renovated. 'The children have a lot to thank Raine for. She deserves their praise for saving a lot of things – for example Althorp has one of the most important pairs of globes in existence, and if we hadn't restored them they would be ruined by now', says Partridge.

The couple were getting into the swing of their life together and were by all accounts radiantly happy. There was no more talk of or time for Raine's political career and she seems to have been content to leave it behind, instead concentrating solely on Johnnie, and Althorp. Raine certainly enjoyed being the chatelaine and her parties and dinners were legendary: 'she sent their chefs to the Ritz in Paris to learn how to cook like Auguste Escoffier' (the legendary French chef) reports Cole. Shooting weekends and house parties meant that the children were often asked to move upstairs into the old servants' quarters to make room, something they somewhat understandably never forgave Raine for. Her houseguests on the other hand were full of praise: 'She was a wonderful entertainer – my abiding memory of our visits was of always having a terrific time. There were always interesting and very clever people around the table and she and Johnnie were terrific fun' says an old friend who dined regularly with the Spencers. 'It was always very lavish' says another, 'lovely food and wine, very good conversation, people always left saying they'd had a great time.' Not for nothing had BC schooled Raine in the art of entertaining – in any case she'd had plenty of practice as the Countess of Dartmouth. 'It was all white gloves and butlers' says Sir Roy Strong, who remembers 'Raine once came to lunch with me wearing a hat! I mean, who wears a hat these days? Nobody!'

It was at one of these lavish shooting parties overseen by Raine, that Earl Spencer's youngest daughter was formally introduced to the Prince of Wales. She'd been allowed home from school for the occasion and was introduced to Charles, who was at that time seeing her sister Sarah, who was still reeling from her breakup with Gerald Grosvenor. The heir to the throne remembers little if anything of their fated meeting in a field between drives. All he could offer when quizzed on the day of the couple's official engagement was that he recalled Diana as 'bouncy' and 'jolly'.

On the other hand, Diana, who may or may not have had pictures of the Prince on her wall in the school dorm as is claimed (a similar claim has been made about the now Duchess of Cambridge, having pictures of Prince William above her school bed), was energised by her meeting with the Prince. Her piano teacher and form mistress at West Heath told Sarah Bradford that on Diana's return to school: 'Her only talk was of him and meeting him. I'm not sure there was any talk about marrying, but she just seemed completely besotted, dreaming of escape, I should think, into a fairy tale'.[10] Diana's relations with Raine did not improve despite the fulfilment of Diana's dream meeting, although Mary Clarke acknowledged in her tell all, *Diana: Once Upon A Time*, that Diana was the only one of the Spencer children who was ever effectively prepared to give Raine the time of day.

Despite the fact that she put on a poised front, Raine was struggling to find any way of connecting with the children. Angela Levin recounts what she was told from a 'senior employee', 'With the exception of Jane who wasn't too bad, the children could not have been more difficult and colder to Raine. There was open hostility, not just to her as a person. They also disliked the way she dominated and became so possessive of their father which made them feel they had to compete with her for his attention.' If this rankled with Raine she never let it show. In private she put pressure on Johnnie to act. Instead of talking to the children himself, Johnnie, who was by anyone's standards a somewhat lax and indulgent parent, detailed various friends to mediate. When Kenneth Rose went to stay at Althorp he described the atmosphere:

> You could cut the atmosphere with a knife between Raine and the children. They joined us for a meal. I said to Jane, 'Do you come here often?' and she said 'When I am asked'. They never addressed a word to Raine. Johnnie was obviously uncomfortable. He'd lived in a turmoil of family conflict – almost disinherited by his father, banished to Norfolk, then all the Frances acrimony.[11]

Soon though, two of the children would be permanently off their hands – Jane married distant relative Robert Fellowes, son of the Queen's Sandringham land agent, Sir William Fellowes, in April 1978. (Robert Fellowes would go on to become the Queen's private secretary.) 'We'd been trying to trap him for years', confided

Sarah to the press. Two years later, in 1980 Sarah would marry a distant relative on Raine's side, Lincolnshire farmer Neil McCorquodale. Sarah's budding relationship with Prince Charles had dwindled into oblivion, after she'd blotted her copybook by giving a candid interview to the downmarket magazine, *Women's Own*, about their 'platonic' relationship, famously and disastrously stating 'I wouldn't marry anyone I didn't love whether it was the dustman or the King of England. If he asked me I would turn him down'. This unguarded quote was enough to ensure that Charles would definitely not be popping the question, leaving the field open for her younger sister.

A few months after he'd walked Jane down the aisle and after just two years of marriage to Raine, on 19 September 1978, Johnnie Spencer's life was to change utterly when he collapsed in his study at Althorp – he'd suffered a cerebral haemorrhage. 'He went over like a felled oak', recounted Charles Spencer in his book *Althorp: The Story of an English House*. Raine, who had been having one of her regular lunches with her mother at Claridge's, roared back up the motorway in the chauffeur driven Rolls-Royce. She was first at the scene at Northampton General Hospital. She was distraught but collected. 'Raine was always at her very best in a crisis' says an old friend 'and this was a monumental crisis. But she decided there and then Johnnie was not going to die'. 'Raine told me her thoughts were, I've only just married the man I truly love – this simply can't be it after only two years', says Peter Constandinos.

Even before the children arrived, Raine learned that Johnnie's condition was life threatening. He held on overnight but on the second day he developed pneumonia. It became swiftly obvious to Raine that Johnnie needed immediate expert care that Northampton General Hospital could not provide. She took it upon herself to organise a private ambulance to transfer him to the National Hospital for Nervous Diseases. It was a big risk. Johnnie could have died at any moment during the transfer, for which Raine would have had to shoulder the blame. 'I knew what I was doing', she later told a friend, 'I did my research.'

Once Johnnie arrived he almost immediately underwent a risky four-hour operation at Raine's insistence. When it was over Johnnie was on life support and fighting for his life. Raine hardly left his side for the two weeks that he was in an induced coma: 'I willed my life force into him', she later told Margaret Duchess of Argyll.[12] She determined also that having the recalcitrant children around, arguing with her over Johnnie's welfare, would not help his recovery. As a result, she instructed the nurses to bar access to the children. This did not have the desired effect. Naturally the children wanted to see their father and arguments ensued in the corridor outside his room. 'The fights were terrible', John Walsh (one of the doctor's responsible for Johnnie's care when he was moved to the Brompton in Chelsea) told Lady Colin Campbell for her book *The Real Diana,* 'I overheard several'. 'We saw another side of Raine which we hadn't anticipated', Diana later recalled for Andrew Morton, 'as she basically blocked us out of the hospital, she wouldn't let us see daddy.' According to Charles Spencer, his sister and Raine took turns, 'Raine and my sister Sarah, separately sat for hour after hour by his bedside'.[13]

Either way, Raine, had far more to worry about than Johnnie's angry children. She was busy researching new drugs and alternative therapies. The stroke had hit Spencer hard: on top of the massive cerebral haemorrhage, he'd contracted pseudomonas – a bacteria resistant to antibiotics. There seemed to be no solution and little hope. But Raine would not give up the latter and she found the former in a drug called Azlocillin, which was not yet approved for use in the UK. As ever, her weighty contact book came in handy. Her friend Lord William Cavendish-Bentinck was on the board of the German pharmaceutical company, Bayer, which supplied the drug and Raine persuaded Johnnie's doctors to give it a try. 'I'd rather he died my way, doing something, than your way, doing nothing', a friend relates that she told them with her typical mix of bravado and pragmatism.

Meanwhile Raine was continuing with her alternative plan of attack – like her mother she also had a belief in less conventional therapies. 'Don't say "Johnnie please get well", say "Johnnie, you *will get well*"', counselled BC, a devout believer in positive thinking. Raine prayed every day for Johnnie's recovery and asked everyone she knew to do the same. According to hearsay, she also asked the Reverend Victor Malan, Vicar of All Saints Church, Northampton, to exorcise the ghost of Johnnie's father from Althorp, as she believed that the continued presence at the house of the 7th Earl was hindering Johnnie's recovery.

Both BC and Raine also believed in the redemptive power of music and Raine would play over and over Johnnie's favourite aria from Madame Butterfly, carefully placing the headphones onto his head and turning the Walkman up to full volume. When she wasn't playing music, she would be holding his hand and talking to him, dressed as she always was, immaculately, in full makeup and jewellery, in the hope that he might open his eyes and she would be the first thing he saw.

In astonishing storybook fashion, Raine's determination paid off and the 8th Earl Spencer started slowly to recover. He was not and never would be the same man – unsteady on his feet, slurred of speech and slow to react – but he had not lost any of his wit or sense of humour. 'Raine took a suite at the Dorchester for Johnnie to recover in once he left hospital and there she literally set up a private hospital room, with staff coming in and out. I remember going in to visit him and passing a nurse on the way out adjusting her apron, he was laying there with a huge smile on his face "oh Peter he said, I've just had one of those bed baths it was marvellous – I've never had so much fun in all my life!"' says Constandinos.

'He got better and he basically changed character. He was one person before and another person after. He's remained estranged but adoring since' said Diana in the Morton tapes. Nicolas Norton, who became a long-time family friend of the couple and director of the antique jewellery dealers S. J. Phillips, confirms that 'Johnnie became a much nicer, kinder and more interested person after the stroke. Beforehand he had been rather cold and aloof'.[14]

Post recovery, the couple would grant an interview to the *Daily Express*'s Jean Rook. According to Johnnie: 'I couldn't talk to Raine, but I knew she was there, holding my hand. She just sat there week after week, holding my hand and talking about our holidays and my photography, things she knew I liked . . . I could feel her great strength, her determination that I should live even when the doctors said she must lose me. Raine won . . . She stops at nothing.'[15] Simon Jenkins remembers that time well: 'She literally willed Johnnie to live, she was relentless, she did absolutely everything she could to ensure he would pull through. It was hugely impressive and it was also typical Raine.'

In all likelihood it was the drugs rather than the arias and Raine's attention that had had the desired effect; but without the drug obtained by Raine, Johnnie would almost certainly have died. A lesser individual could not have pulled it off. Saving Johnnie had taken all of Raine's resources – the same resources she had applied to her earlier life and her political career. It would not be an exaggeration to say that the 8th Earl Spencer was forever in his wife's debt, a fact of which he was only too well aware and she, with good manners and rather atypical delicacy, never felt the need to remind him. For the remainder of his life, Johnnie would tell anyone who would listen that it was only thanks to Raine that he was alive. For Raine's part, friends observed that her relief that Johnnie had lived gave her life an intense focus on just two things: a determination to protect Johnnie from anything stressful and an even greater desire for them both to seize life and live it to the full.

With that in mind the couple created a trust to run the estate with Raine, the family lawyer Hugo Southern, and the estate manager Richard Stanley making the decisions. A service of thanksgiving for Johnnie was held at All Saints Church, Northampton, with Norman St John-Stevas giving a speech to the invited throng – a mix of friends, locals, estate workers and the medical teams who had saved Johnnie's life. After the service the couple set off for a celebratory recuperative vacation in Monte Carlo, thinking that the biggest challenge of their lives was behind them. Little did they know that another epic event was just around the corner – one which would catapult them both onto the world stage – a location from which Raine, in particular, would never be entirely able to retreat.

On the couple's return, Raine became even more focused on the business of running the estate. A cursory glance at the figures told her all she needed to know. 'I do remember her telling me that it was going to cost half a million to replace the roof' remembers Jeffrey Archer, 'and I remember thinking how is that possible? But then I saw the size of the roof. You could play cricket up there.'[16] She stepped up the renovations at Althorp with the intention of re-creating the house as it had been when first built, convinced this would increase its tourist potential. But first she had to find the money to carry out the next stage.

Johnnie was cash poor and Raine quite rightly had no intention of pouring more of her own money into a home from which she knew she would be ejected when Johnnie died. Whilst the trustees had oversight of the land, they had no say in what happened to the house or its contents – Johnnie could do as he pleased. Their inability to raise cash left the couple with few options and so, as had happened at Althorp in decades past, they began selling things.

If there was a new female boss breaking the mould at Althorp, there was another first in the British parliament – a female running the country. When Margaret Thatcher came to power on 4 May

1979, the Conservatives under her leadership had garnered the largest electoral swing of support since 1945. Comparisons between Raine and Thatcher were often made – one the educated daughter of a Grantham grocer, the other the uneducated offspring of a self-made society maven, both with a similar will of iron. 'The difference', says Jeffrey Archer, 'was that Margaret had the education and the charm and you could say to some extent, that Raine was missing both. But there was no doubt that the pair had similarities of approach, although Raine's appearance belied her abilities. Raine had the contacts and the determination. Margaret had the real power.'

Nonetheless, the eighties would usher in an era that a self-confessed Conservative like Raine could 'get behind'. Privatisation, neoliberalism underscored by self-reliance and a free market economy fermented the 'greed is good' eighties so beloved of Gordon Gecko, Michael Douglas's award-winning character from the movie *Wall Street*. Alongside bling, boom and bust and the domineering patriarchy of the 'Big Swinging Dicks' on the Trading Floors of Michael Lewis's book *Liar's Poker*, came the 'new romantic' music so beloved of the pearl wearing future Princess of Wales: Duran Duran, Spandau Ballet, Human League, Wham and Culture Club. If the seventies was the decade for better or worse of the Labour Party, the 1980s would be 'True Blue', to borrow a song title from another woman who dominated that decade – Madonna.

Charles Spencer would later characterise the eighties as the decade of loss at Althorp: 'The 1980s saw the exodus of the bulk of the religious paintings from Althorp . . . The saddest loss was of individual portraits of four of the Apostles by Van Dyck', he later wrote in *Althorp: The Story of an English House*, blaming his stepmother of selling 'many dozens of other works, collected by 500 years of my family and now dispersed around the world, having sometimes been sent to London art dealers in laundry baskets from

Althorp's back door to guarantee the anonymity of the sale. Since my family was basically being taken to the cleaners by the art world at the time, the laundry basket was perhaps the most appropriate mode of transport . . . ' 'My stepson thinks Botticelli is a pop group', Raine once famously remarked in response to one of Charles's outbursts at the time.[17]

In 1993, by then the 9th Earl, Charles would give an interview to the magazine *Antique Collector,* blaming the resentment his late father Johnnie had felt for his grandfather as the motivation for the sale of an estimated two hundred artworks, including eleven Van Dycks and paintings by masters as varied as Guercino, Reynolds, Reni, Avercamp and Teniers. 'I believe that my grandfather's compulsive devotion to this house caused great resentment in my father', he said. 'By selling off the art, my father derived great pleasure in the knowledge that the seventh Earl would be spinning in his grave.'[18]

Charles also took the opportunity to criticise his stepmother's taste, which he described as 'more London high society than English country house'. 'Some rooms were successful', he concedes, 'others had the wedding-cake vulgarity of a five-star hotel in Monaco'.

The proceeds of the sales, the Earl advised readers (again), had been used by Raine to fund the renovations at Althorp. Raine's renovations, which continued throughout most of the eighties, provided yet another excuse for the media and society to exercise the kind of snobbery and judgement they seemed to reserve for those who were 'above themselves'. In Angela Levin's book she quotes 'neighbours' from Northamptonshire, making claims that Raine was amongst other things an 'arriviste'. In other words, they believed her decorative style reflected what one termed as 'new rich'. That they lacked enough courage to put their names to the quotes, tells you all you need to know about the tiresome upper class 'closed shop' that Raine had to deal with on a daily basis.

The newspapers were not as reticent as the Spencer's neighbours: 'The rate at which art treasures are being sold from the historic Spencer collection – at Althorp, Northamptonshire – and the lack of reliable information on what is being sold is causing consternation in heritage circles' reported *The Times*, sniffily. The paper went on to qualify its criticism, 'The present Lady Spencer, daughter of Barbara Cartland and stepmother of the Princess of Wales, has had charge of the sales since her marriage to the Earl in 1976, though her husband who has been ill, backs her.'[19]

Much of the direct criticism was directed at the 'Gordon furniture suite', a set of John Gordon, carved mahogany furniture of immense historical importance, which had been commissioned in the 1760s by John Spencer, the 1st Earl, which detractors suggested should have been left as it was. 'That suite was full of moth and all of its joints were loose, there was no way we could have ignored that', argues Partridge. There was criticism, too, about the bright gilding. According to Partridge, the couple had specifically agreed that they were to renovate to 'future proof' the house for the next two hundred years – which meant giving the gilt time to age. 'The question became how much should we age the gilt once it was applied. Of course it would have looked bright when it was originally done, so we re-gilded so that it would appear as it had originally and allowed that it would "wear" over time. This is the mindset with which we approached the whole renovation and of course Raine was quite right to do so.'

The renovation of the 100,000 square feet of interior space was an enormous task. It would take seven years. According to Partridge, Raine approached the renovation as she approached everything in her life 'with rigour and thoroughness. We emptied one room, we renovated, we replaced the furniture then we began on another. She was incredibly organised and systematic. I think she thought of it as her duty really to leave the house in a better state than she found it.'

'She really did have the feeling that it was her duty to take care of the house and to preserve it for others' agrees Jeffrey Archer. Like Roy Strong he was at first dismissive of her, 'I thought, she's exactly the reason I've joined the Conservative Party – to get rid of people like her. Little did I understand her tremendous influence.'

Raine's half-brother Ian remembers his sister's response to the press furore concerning the renovations: 'She was bemused by all the press. All she was doing was restoring it to its former glory. But Raine would always rise above – she never retaliated, she just got on with things.'

'I didn't know Althorp before Raine was there and yes there was much talk of it being "overdone", but to me it seemed a glitzy house, but without being bling', remembers Nadine Bonsor, who, with her husband Sir Nicholas, was a frequent dinner guest. Lady Bonsor recalls Johnnie's response to the criticism surrounding the renovations: 'He seemed very happy with it all. He used to say "well it's rather bright now, but it will be perfect in a hundred years' time".'

'What I think nobody understood about Raine's renovations was that she knew that all of these big houses were initially built as "pleasure palaces". The furnishings were luxurious, the gilding was bright and the whole place was hung with opulent paintings', says Michael Cole, 'and this is the direction that Raine intended – to return the place to its original state.' The same criticisms, of course, have not been levelled at Jacob Rothschild, who holds the lease on Spencer House in London and has also renovated opulently, as Frank Partridge points out: 'It was always double standards as far as anything to do with Raine was concerned.'

It was the inference that Raine had taken advantage of Johnnie's illness and the confusion that it had wreaked to sell the art for her own gain that infuriated her. 'You would think we were selling off all the family treasures to keep me in my old age', she told the *Daily*

Mail exasperatedly. According to Levin, it is 'difficult to judge to what extent his [Johnnie's] stroke affected his judgement and decision making at Althorp, because, although the haemorrhage itself had not damaged the intellectual part of his brain, many felt he was never quite the same afterwards, mentally as well as physically'. The writer Lynn Barber came away from her interview with the couple with a very clear picture of who was in charge: 'Lady Spencer has found her lord and master', she pronounced. Charles Spencer writes of his father's different perspective on life post-stroke, in his book, *Althorp: The Story of an English House*, 'my father, for so long extremely cautious with money, began to enjoy his inheritance to the full, while handing over all responsibility for running Althorp to Raine'.

There's little doubt that after the fractured, difficult childhood he'd had, having Raine arrive on the ancestral doorstep would not have been a walk in the park (no matter how large) for the current Earl Spencer. What is at question is whether it is fair that the blame for Althorp's renovations should have been placed so squarely at Raine's door. 'I would have minded very much if my father had re-married and that person had tried to change everything in my home' says Anne Glenconner, 'one grows up with everything and there are the memories – so I did understand the children's position.' By Charles Spencer's own acknowledgement, he had not entirely grown up at Althorp. He had been eleven when his father inherited Althorp, a home, which thanks to his father's strained relationship from his grandfather, he had rarely visited. When he did inherit at the age of twenty-seven, he estimates that he had 'only spent three or four hundred nights of my life at Althorp'.[20]

Neither had Raine been responsible for the sale of some of the most important pieces at Althorp, such as the Van Dyck, *Lady Andover and Lady Thimbleby*, sold to the National Gallery in 1976 by Johnnie, or the sale of the family archive, collated so painstakingly by the 7th Earl in what was known as the Muniment Room and sold to the British Library during renovations, again instigated by Johnnie in lieu of death duties. The archive was valued by Messrs Quaritch at £570,500, but despite the Public Records Act and the Freedom of Information Act, which requires the Library to make public the full amount when a large scale purchase is made involving public money, it was unable to 'locate' the total amount paid to Johnnie Spencer in its records.[21]

Charles Spencer does not give a breakdown for his guestimate of the 20 per cent of losses from the family collection at Althorp, for which he holds Raine accountable. Nor does he explain how he came by the linen basket anecdote. But then none of the journalists faithfully reporting these matters seem to be too troubled by this. Perhaps it doesn't matter – but it certainly serves to illustrate just how willing reporters were to maintain the negative narrative about 'wicked stepmother Raine'. In fact, aristocrats lucky enough to be blessed with major art collections and vast homes sell work and antiques all the time and no one raises an eyebrow, nor wastes a column inch. Male aristocrats that is.

To wit in 2010, a post sale report on the works of art sold from the Spencer collection at Charles Spencer's behest revealed a realised amount of £21.1 million, according to the auction house Christies,[22] and proceeds from a further 'attic sale' raised £2.2m. Charles Spencer had explained to the magazine *Country Life*, in an exclusive interview on 15 April 2010, that he was selling the art and antiques to renovate Althorp. He fretted over his responsibilities, his words effectively echoing those of his late father and former stepmother: 'Visitors pass through the place and "ooh" and "ah" over what it must be like to live in such magnificent surroundings. They fail to realise that it is a full-time job just to keep one's head above water.' The sale included a portrait by Sir Peter Paul Rubens, called *A Commander Being Armed For Battle*, which raised just over £9 million, and a painting by Giovanni Francesco Barbieri broke a record for the artist at the time, selling for £5,193,250. The Earl explained to *Country Life* readers that the Guernico painting, *King David*, was being sold because Althorp did not have room to 'show off' the classical study because: 'our ceilings are too low for such a piece'.[23]

7

The Diana Effect

——————•◆•——————

Had it not been for Lady Diana Spencer, the wholly unedifying
business of a privileged family sniping over who had sold the
'family silver' and gussied up the ancestral home would have been
relegated to a few column inches on the social pages of middle
market British newspapers. As it was, the entire Spencer family were
about to experience the mega-watt glare of the media spotlight, the
likes of which the world has never experienced before or since.

The initial signs that the family were about to become globally
famous were not entirely writ large. The woman in question was at
that point a listless but quintessential pie crust collar sporting 'Sloane
Ranger'. Not being particularly clever, or, thanks to their privilege,
desperately in need of a nine-to-five job, so called 'Sloanes' spent
their days idling around the Sloane Square area of Chelsea (hence
the name), wearing dowdy print skirts or garish corduroys, braying
their own kind of self-congratulatory 'rah' lingo, spending daddy's
money and drinking at The White Horse (or Sloaney Pony) in
Parsons Green, all the while searching for a potential mate hailing

from a similar lineage. Employment for Sloanes meant taking a 'pocket money' job to fill the days between country house parties at each other's Stately Homes or London DPs (dinner parties) at the weekend, where 'hilarious' games like Ibble Dibble or Are You There, Moriarty? were considered the ultimate entertainment. Diana had all of the attributes required for 'Sloanedom': after failing her O levels ('thick as a plank I am' she once famously intoned) she had attended the pre-requisite Swiss finishing school and was now working in London holding down a couple of part-time cleaning and nannying jobs. Her entitled approach to life and her very evident lack of intellect, not to mention her possessiveness over her 'daddy', meant that she had been at war with Raine since they'd first met around the lunch table seven years previously. You could see the problem. Lady Diana Spencer was about as far removed from her new bouclé-suited stepmother as it might be possible to be. Restless and anxious to leave the nest, which she now regarded as having been 'invaded' by Raine, Diana had campaigned mercilessly to be allowed to live in London since her arrival back in the country from Switzerland. Her motives were entirely self-centred – to have fun and find a rich husband, that is, if Prince Andrew didn't materialise and go down on bended knee first.

It was a family joke that Diana had intentions towards the queen's second son – they had, after all, played together as children when the royal family had been in residence at Sandringham. The light-hearted teasing around this topic had even given rise to Diana's childhood nickname of 'Duch' – a shortened version of Duchess, a nod to the 'grand' behaviour her siblings joked that she exhibited as a child, but also the title that would be bestowed upon her were she to marry Andrew.

On the matter of finding a suitably titled husband, Diana, it seems, was entirely serious. She was certainly more focused upon this than she had been upon her studies. 'My wedding will be in

Westminster Abbey', she ambitiously informed a friend during her sister Jane's wedding at the Guard's Chapel, where she was chief bridesmaid.

When she attended Prince Charles's thirtieth birthday party at Buckingham Palace on 14 November 1978, the seventeen-year-old Diana was still painfully shy and in awe of the heir to the throne. The invitation, which had arrived much to her sister Sarah's annoyance, had taken them both by surprise. Neither can have really considered that the young teenager had been invited out of anything other than politeness. By the time the night was over, there was little doubt that Diana was smitten. For his part, the Prince appeared bowled over by the radical change in her appearance since they had first met on Harbottle Field, between drives in 1977. 'You've grown up', he is said to have exclaimed upon their re-introduction. She did not disappoint, responding cheekily 'oh I hope not, Sir' – you can almost hear and see her saying it with that characteristic droop of her swanlike neck, her eyes cast down as she giggles, extends her hand towards the future king in greeting and bobs a flirtatious curtsey.

She wasn't part of the 'in crowd' though – women of the Prince's retinue who flattered, flirted, hung on his every word and vied for the chance to dance with him, whilst Diana looked on in fascination as the Three Degrees, the Prince's favourite group, performed (at one point the Prince climbed up onto the stage to groove with his 'crush', lead singer Sheila Ferguson). Meanwhile, a retinue of women including Dale Tryon, actress Susan George and, inevitably, a blonde chain smoker with a hearty laugh and a suggestive line in dance moves, a certain Mrs Parker Bowles, all revolved around the Prince, jealously guarding him as he moved from one to the other.

Should Diana have twigged that there was already a dominant blonde in the Prince's life? How could she? A young, curvaceous brunette, fresh up from the country with a brand-new London life, a flat in groovy South Kensington, a gaggle of fun 'flatties' (flatmates) and a blue Renault 5, in which she nipped around the city streets with an abandonment of caution, 'pranking' her male friends by attaching cans to their cars or worse covering them with flour and water. Life was fun. And whilst she was not in the slightest bit overawed by the Palace or the company, she must also have instinctively recognised that were she to play her cards right and tread cautiously, there was far more mileage to be had here.

Like everyone else at the time, she will not have been unaware of the pressures upon the thirty-year-old prince to find a mate. This was after all the end of a decade notorious both for its economic distress, strikes and division, and for the rise of the immensely powerful 'Red Tops' who followed the prince's every move, speculating daily on his inability to find 'Miss Right'. With millions of readers, the tabloids were arguably calling the shots. Not for nothing was the *Sun* able to signal the beginning of the end of the Callaghan Labour government, with its headline underscoring the current Prime Minister's 'ostrich approach'. 'Crisis? What Crisis? Rail, lorry, jobs chaos and Jim blames the press' it screamed, establishing itself as the paper of dubious record, whilst *The Times*, frozen by a strike between management and printing unions, had failed to publish for a year. With a young Conservative leader called Margaret Thatcher warning that the dystopian world of *A Clockwork Orange* loomed ever closer, Britain and the tabloids were looking for some good news. It looked as though charting the progress of Prince Charles as he sought to find a mate might be as close as they were going to get.

Back at Althorp, the children's continued animosity towards Raine and their refusal to regard her as mistress of the house was all too apparent at Sarah's wedding in May of 1980. Raine managed with aplomb to manage the presence of Frances Shand Kydd who, in addition to paying for the wedding, as she had done for Jane, wanted top billing. Raine maintained a dignified distance, although she had overseen much of the organisation for the event. The two women's disdain for each other was legendary, although Frances unaccountably seemed to have the upper hand. As one observer tactfully put it, 'it was all about breeding'. Put another way, it was all about snobbery and Raine, rather uncharacteristically, seemed to accept this. She was never anything but gracious in her dealings with Shand Kydd, who after all had experienced more than her own fair share of negative press and misogyny. 'There were only two people I ever saw Raine afraid of', says Peter Constandinos, 'one was her mother and the other was Frances Shand Kydd.'

Charles, who was now away at Eton, was the only one of the Spencer children still ostensibly living at home and his resistance to the changes his father and stepmother were making was by now palpable. Old friends of Johnnie's thought he had reason: 'Imagine you are a young man and you see what you perceive to be your inheritance being sold off. You cannot imagine your father, the man through whom your title and your great house passes, would do such a thing and in any case you cannot fathom the reasons why. Of course you would demonise and blame your stepmother. And Johnnie did very little to oppose this,' says one.

'Just as "good" marriages through the ages have been responsible for building up fortunes in prominent families, it seems that bad ones with their attendant divorces and short-termist stepmothers have made massive inroads into once secure inheritances', Charles later writes pragmatically.[1] Lady Colin Campbell acknowledges that mistakes were made by both Raine and Johnnie during Althorp's renovation: 'The way they went about it was ill advised. Given that everything had been effectively left to Charles the heir, there should have been consultation – I know how expensive it is to run a stately and one sometimes does need to sell things, but not in secret.'

What would have happened had everyone's attention not been suddenly diverted by momentous events, which were to change the course of the family's history, can only be imagined. As it was the entire nation was rocked by the brutal IRA murder of the Prince of Wales' beloved mentor and great-uncle, Louis 'Dickie' Mountbatten, 1st Earl Mountbatten of Burma, on 27 August 1979. To say that the Prince idolised Louis would be an understatement. A surrogate father in all but name, his was the ear that the Prince bent and the man whose opinion the Prince sought throughout his early adult life, in the place of his real father, the Duke of Edinburgh (and Dickie's nephew), who by all accounts he found remorselessly unsympathetic. It had been Dickie who had encouraged the Prince to 'sow his wild oats' whilst young and then to settle down with a 'suitable and sweet charactered girl before she meets anyone else she might fall for'. If Mrs Parker Bowles qualified as one of Charles's many fertile fields, then it was well known that Dickie's own granddaughter, Amanda Knatchbull, was being lined up as his permanent 'sweet spot'.

Amongst those who disapproved of Dickie, his liberal lifestyle (he reputedly had lovers from both sexes and was in an open marriage with Edwina Ashley, one of America's richest women and former lover of Jawaharlal Nehru) and his machinations, were the Queen who thought him too interfering and the Queen Mother who, it is said, considered him a terrible social climber. The fact that Mountbatten, a great grandson of Queen Victoria, might have any further to climb might seem implausible, but the fact was that being a Windsor would count for so much more than being on an appendant arm of the family tree, which is why Mountbatten continued to push the potential liaison between Charles and Amanda.

Queen Elizabeth and the Queen Mother were wise to Mountbatten's intentions, both believing that he wanted to grow his own dynasty from inside the Windsor camp. He nearly managed it. In fact, Amanda Knatchbull turned down the Prince's offer of marriage. Some say this was before the IRA blew up Earl Mountbatten's fishing boat, *Shadow V*, off the coast of Mullaghmore, in the Irish Republic. The remote-controlled bomb also killed his fourteen-year-old grandson Nicholas, Nicholas's grandmother Dowager Lady Brabourne, and a fifteen-year-old boat hand named Paul Maxwell. Others say that the murder of their beloved Dickie forced either the Prince, Knatchbull, or possibly both, to reassess their lives and decide to move on. (The attack on *Shadow V* was not the only atrocity committed that day. Eighteen British soldiers were also killed in two bomb attacks in Northern Ireland in what were later acknowledged by the IRA as a warning after the violence of 1972's 'Bloody Sunday' when British soldiers killed thirteen Catholic protesters.)

Somewhat ironically, it was to be Mountbatten's murder which provided the opportunity for Diana to make that all important connection with Prince Charles. 'I have lost someone infinitely special in my life', Charles wrote, 'Life will never be the same again.' It wasn't. It was as if, with his late Uncle's advice ringing in his ears to choose a 'suitable and sweet-charactered girl', the heir to the throne suddenly switched course. He'd been playing the field for a while, dallying with Amanda and plenty of other blondes, all the while with Mrs Parker Bowles in the background. Now, to the relief of his parents and advisors, he appeared more focused on the task at hand.

Since their initial re-introduction at his birthday party Diana had not gone unnoticed by the royal family or by Charles. She'd stayed, with her sister Jane, on the Sandringham estate for a weekend shooting party in January 1979 when he'd been present and she had chatted to the Queen, who had, according to Max Riddington and Gavan Naden, given Diana the royal nod of approval. This was later re-enforced when, having been invited to Balmoral in August 1979 as a guest of Prince Andrew, Diana had charmed the rest of the family, although Prince Charles was not present.

Behind the scenes the Queen Mother and one of her closest friends, Ruth Fermoy (Diana's maternal grandmother), had been moving the players around the chess board. The Queen Mother had first spotted Diana's potential at her sister Jane's wedding to Robert Fellowes. 'You must think about her future settlement in life', she is said to have commented to a beaming Johnnie Spencer at the reception, after commending him for doing such a good job in raising Diana.

Much has been made of the two matriarchs of the Windsor and Spencer families lending their immense weights towards constructing an arranged marriage, without the knowledge of the two participants. There is some evidence to corroborate this theory. On 9 November 1979, before the press had begun to report on Diana, Kenneth Rose records in his diary that: 'Jack Plumb [aka Sir Harold Plumb, Master of Christ's College Cambridge 1978–82] tells me he thinks Diana Spencer will marry the Prince of Wales. I wonder whether Johnnie's divorce, not to mention Raine's would be an obstacle. But Jack is very emphatic. Perhaps I shall hear more when I stay at Althorp next month.'[2]

What more Rose hears about the potential engagement from Johnnie, Raine or anyone else is not included in his diaries; it seems likely however that a great deal more went on behind the scenes regarding the 'spontaneous liaison' between the heir to the throne and his 'virgin' bride than either the couple or the public were aware of. To read Rose's comments (he was a friend of the QM) is to conclude that the much speculated upon 'arranged marriage' as constructed by the Queen Mother and Ruth Fermoy (or even the Queen herself who it was said took comfort from the fact that Cynthia Spencer, Diana's paternal grandmother, had been a friend of the family) is almost certainly true.

As far as the received narrative is concerned, Diana and Charles met again in July 1980 at the home of Commander Robert de Pass (a friend of Prince Philip) and his wife Philippa, a lady-in-waiting to the Queen. Their son Philip was a friend of Diana's, and she, by now working as a nanny and a part-time kindergarten assistant, eagerly accepted his invitation, 'you're a young blood, you might amuse him',[3] he apparently said of the Prince who was staying for the weekend to play polo. It was on this weekend, during a quiet moment with Charles, that Diana famously invoked Mountbatten's funeral, telling Charles what he needed to hear – that he was lonely and needed someone to look after him.

For a man with a 'mummy complex' the future Princess had gone direct to the issue at hand. Could a man whose role in life was to remain inert, waiting for his mother's death before he could assume the mantle, really have a fully functioning relationship with another woman? It seemed, given the Prince's romantic history, unlikely. In fact, were it not for the pressure of his parents and his grandmother, it is possible that the Prince would not have married at all. From what we know now, he had everything he needed – an affair with a woman he had long loved, who was deemed inappropriate by the crown but tolerated for the sake of the Prince's happiness and thus without marital pressure, a life of socialising, painting and polo playing padded out with the pre-requisite duties of the heir to the throne. His loyal valet, Michael Fawcett, the man who had allegedly and notoriously squeezed the royal toothpaste onto the royal brush when Charles once broke his arm playing polo (and overseen the extraction of the infamous morning boiled egg – one of seven – at precisely the right moment) effectively played the subservient domestic female role.

But Charles was never going to escape the family pressures to, as Prince Philip later urged him in a letter, 'get on with it'. Given her background and the Spencer's royal connections, Diana was undoubtedly cognisant enough of the workings of the monarchy to understand this. By the time she left the de Pass's she would also have had a pretty good idea that she was not only in the running, but out ahead of the pack.

Later, the recorded tapes which were passed to Andrew Morton by her friend Dr James Colthurst, and contributed to Morton's book, would cast doubt upon the received acceptance that Diana had been a virgin when she married Prince Charles. Rather that she had, as Lady Colin Campbell would conjecture in her own book, *The Real Diana*, made sure that any sexual liaisons had been with men who would, in Lady C's words: 'Keep their mouths shut'. 'Frigid wasn't the word. Big F when it comes to that', she says after Charles first kisses her. There were two implications: either that she was savvy and drawing back or that she knew what a red-hot sexual advance felt like and Charles's was most certainly not satisfactory.

She was smart enough not to accept the Prince's invitation to 'come back with me to London', seeing it for what it was – a probable invitation to at least spend a night in the royal bed. The fact that a girl who seemed so young, sweet and easy going refused to do as he asked must have registered more strongly with the Prince than any night between the sheets. His interest was well and truly piqued. He invited Diana to Cowes and then to Balmoral, 'I was shitting bricks, I was terrified because I had never stayed at Balmoral and I wanted to get it right', she recorded. 'Mr and Mrs Parker Bowles were there at all my visits.'[4]

By now Johnnie (still recovering at home) and Raine were in on the badly kept secret, as were the press. Nigel Dempster, the celebrated gossip columnist for the *Daily Mail*, broke the story in September 1980, and other columnists followed suit. The party line was that Charlie's new squeeze was perfect in every way – in other words still a virgin as royal etiquette dictated. Using words like 'fragrant', 'abundant innocence' and 'delightful charm' the papers hinted at what every prurient reader wanted confirmation on. And then Nigel Dempster came out and said it, 'she's been pronounced physically sound to have children'. Whether Diana had been forced to suffer a similar indignity to her mother at the hands of a Harley Street gynaecologist was never actually revealed. In any case it didn't seem to matter – 'Diana mania' had hit and her shared flat was besieged. The press pack (who were not yet badly behaved enough to be called the Paparazzi as they later were, after the Walter Santesso character Paparazzo in the 1960 Fellini film *La Dolce Vita* – Paparazzi is Italian for 'buzzing insects') had hired the flat opposite Diana's and were following her every move. Despite illicit meetings with the Prince for suppers, dinners and even a drive down to view Highgrove, the Prince's new home in Gloucestershire, no proposal was forthcoming.

Privately, both Johnnie and Raine were sceptical: Johnnie because having been in close proximity to the royals he knew only too well what Diana faced and Raine because she worried about the couple's suitability – 'he'll soon grow bored', she told a friend. She also doubted her stepdaughter's virginity: she'd heard Diana, aged seventeen, speaking passionately to her then boyfriend James Gilbey on the telephone at Althorp. The conversations sounded a lot more worldly than Diana had ever let on. And there was the rumour (never proven) of some topless pictures of Diana, supposedly snapped whilst she'd been staying in Switzerland. Raine knew what this would do to a girl who, as far as everyone else was concerned, had a spotless reputation. She consulted a lawyer and was told that an injunction could be granted if necessary.

It was at about this time that Raine and Johnnie, inspired by his recuperative holiday in Monte Carlo, purchased a flat in Brighton where they would spend weekends and Johnnie would develop an affection for the south coast which lasted until his death. He viewed the sea air as rejuvenating and the couple were convinced that this would aid his recovery. That they would often spend weekends together down on the coast, 200 miles from Althorp, spoke volumes about Raine's dedication to her husband. She would far rather have been back in London at the flat they had bought in Grosvenor

Square, which as it happened, was in exactly the same block as the flat she had lived in with Gerald.

It had become apparent that Johnnie would never be able to attend to anything in the same way as he had before his stroke. His powers of concentration were entirely shot and Raine became increasingly protective of his time and energies. Angela Levin quotes Rupert Hambro, a colleague of Johnnie's from the time he'd spent as chairman of the National Association of Boy's Clubs where Hambro had become treasurer in 1973, as saying that Johnnie's recovery – such as it was – was driven by his strong sexual attraction to Raine. 'She was able to give him physical enjoyment which got him mentally up and going', he told Levin. 'Raine was a very sexual being', agrees Michael Cole, 'she was very open about that. "The physical side of things", she would say, "is most important"'.

The only association Johnnie maintained after his stroke was the Schoolmistresses' and Governesses' Benevolent Institution, where he would strike up conversations with old ladies in the SGBI residential home, telling eighty-four-year-old Grace Randall that Raine had saved his life and when she would next appear on TV. 'He always said he thought Raine had looked so beautiful and her hair was so lovely.' The couple were still very much in love, and Johnnie even more dependent on Raine than before. For her part, she was focused on running the estate, fearful of the day when she might have to break it to her husband that there simply were not enough funds to keep the house and estate running. Johnnie, who could cope with less, had a simple mantra now to live by, 'I always look for the lighter side of life . . . find something that makes me laugh. There is quite a lot you know'. He looked to Raine to make the arrangements for just about everything.

For her own part, Raine had become much more acutely aware of the fact that her life and lifestyle was predicated on Johnnie's ability to stay alive. This sounds predatory, but in Raine's case was simply practical. She had contributed a good deal of her own money to the initial renovations and brought with her to Althorp her own collection of art and furniture. As if to imprint her stake in Althorp she installed a large romantic Carlos Luis Sancha portrait of herself, which she had commissioned at Johnnie's request, in The Saloon at the top of the great stairs next to the entrance hall. It hung in prime position amongst the gallery of portraits of other illustrious Spencer ancestors. It was impossible to miss. The gesture only served to increase the ire of the Spencer children but Johnnie loved it. At about this time and in recognition of the role Raine had played in his life and her fundamental role in keeping him alive, Johnnie would change his will to ensure that Raine would be taken care of after his death. He would also buy her a house in Farm Street which the couple used, but with the understanding that it would be the place to which Raine would repair after his death. 'He did not trust the children to look after her', says a close friend.

As for the unfolding drama surrounding Johnnie's youngest daughter and the heir to the throne, it was an uncharacteristic slip-up on the part of the Prince of Wales in maintaining the subterfuge surrounding his long-time affair with Camilla Parker Bowles which ultimately forced his hand. By now Diana was accepted enough as Charles's 'partner' to be invited to Princess Margaret's official fiftieth birthday party at the Ritz on 4 November 1980 – by all accounts a raucous affair, which ended with the Queen's sister dancing with a balloon tied to her tiara. The then Lady Diana was photographed arriving and leaving with her sister Jane, wearing a pink silk halter neck evening gown, cloaked in a green woollen man's style coat, grinning broadly from underneath her long mousey brown fringe.

On 16 November 1980, the *Sunday Mirror* trumpeted a royal exclusive from its front page, splashing 'Royal Love Train!' across six pages inside, claiming that Diana had 'visited' the Prince on the royal train as it sat overnight in a railway siding. The implication was obvious and potentially damaging: that the potential Queen to be was not a virgin, if she even had been before the alleged incident. The palace sprung into defensive action with Michael Shea, the Queen's press secretary, protesting in a letter to the *Sunday Mirror*'s editor, Robert Edwards, which was later published in full as a form of royal defence. The lady in question protested that she had never been near the royal train, having gone to bed early suffering from a hangover after Princess Margaret's party.

The Spencer family rallied round. Public opinion was all important. The public would need reassurance that Diana was, in her own words, 'tidy', and still perfect material for a monarch to be. Diana's mother wrote to *The Times* protesting against the lies and harassment Diana had endured since her relationship with Prince Charles had become public: 'She has also denied with justifiable indignation, her reported presence on the Royal Train', she wrote, her words bristling with rage. Questions were raised in parliament with sixty MPs drafting a motion 'deploring the manner in which Lady Diana is being treated by the media'. Diana's uncle, Frances's brother, Lord Fermoy, encouraged by Raine, also went on the record: 'Diana I can assure you has never had a lover.' Did they protest too much? Most royal observers think so. Tina Brown[5] suggests that Prince Charles was concerned less for his potential bride's reputation and more for the public's response to what could easily be perceived as an abuse of public funds, since the royal train was funded by the British taxpayer through the civil list. Furthermore, she posits, why did Diana not include this story in her 'confessional gut spilling' for Andrew Morton and Martin Bashir?

But this speculation is all with the benefit of hindsight. For six years, editor Robert Edwards believed he had been wrong about the Royal Train incident and his paper's subsequent 'Splash', which he also conjectured had cost him his anticipated knighthood. And then, in the January that he was named a CBE (and not a knight) in the Queen's New Year's Honours list, a card arrived for him from the diarist and political insider Woodrow Wyatt, bearing just seven words: 'I think you'll find it was Camilla.'

Whoever it was on the royal train is of little consequence, but the response it evoked changed the course of royal history. Without this incident, either one of the two key players in this drama – Charles or Diana – might have come, in time, to see that they were not right for each other as Raine had predicted. Had that been the case, the Spencers would have remained a noteworthy ancient English family, whose most famous spawn was a certain Winston Churchill.

If Diana's life was about to change beyond all recognition so were those of Raine and Johnnie, who had just about gained some sense of equilibrium after Johnnie's stroke. During the machinations and the highly publicised 'would he or wouldn't he?' dilemma (He's in Love Again' blared one tabloid headline) Raine told the press that she and Johnnie had tried to 'provide a refuge from all the personal problems. She had to think over a very momentous decision'. If only. For months the Prince of Wales had been dithering, to the infuriation of both his own family and that of his girlfriend. Diana spent that Christmas in 1980 at Althorp and, as was her way, pretty soon the whole family were embroiled in the drama. Sally Bedell Smith[6] quotes Lady Bowker, a friend of the Spencers': 'I rang up and spoke to Raine. I said "How is Diana?" Raine said, "She is very sad. She is in the park and she is walking alone and she is crying because Charles is not proposing".'

It would be disingenuous to suggest that at this stage of the proceedings neither Johnnie nor Raine had a vested interest in the outcome. Having had initial reservations, they were certainly swiftly coming around to the positive aspects of marrying 'into' the royal family. Ruth, Lady Fermoy, the woman who had taken her son-in-law's side against her daughter in the divorce court to ensure the good favour of the royal family, must have been keeping everything crossed. 'The Spencers were middle class aristocracy, if I can put it like that' says Lady Colin Campbell, 'I mean, they were a good family, but they were not right at the top. Diana's marriage to Charles would change everything. This much they certainly knew.'

The only person to whom this potential marriage of, if not convenience, then 'suitability', did not seem an obvious solution, was the groom-to-be himself. After the Royal Train incident, the pressure on Charles from within the court and the media became almost untenable. The Queen Mother is said to have counselled her grandson: 'There's Diana Spencer – that's the girl you should marry. But don't marry her if you don't love her.' His father was not so delicate, issuing the Prince with an ultimatum either to propose to Diana or stop seeing her. His anger reached boiling point when the press besieged Sandringham over New Year 1981, searching for Diana and ruining the Duke's shooting party in the process. Prince Philip seemed to have swallowed the notion, which was being seeded throughout the court by Ruth Fermoy, that Diana's reputation, damaged by the Royal Train incident, would be forever ruined if the Prince did not propose. The idea of being 'damaged goods' seems so utterly Victorian as to be preposterous in the last two decades of the twentieth century. On the other hand, perhaps it gives a better insight into the way that the Royal Court at that point was operating (and to an extent still seems to – given the recent accusations of racism and elitism).

In Diana's words 'The feeling was I wish Prince Charles would hurry up and get on with it. The Queen was fed up. He wrote to me from Klosters and then he rang me up and said, "I've got something very important to ask you". An instinct in a female tells you what it is. I sat up all night with my girls [friends], saying: "Christ, what am I going to do?"'[7] Of course, the nineteen-year-old Lady Diana

Spencer knew exactly what she was going to do. She had known what she wanted the moment she met the Prince again aged sixteen. The fly in the ointment was that as she notes, 'By that time I'd realised there was someone else around.'[8]

Apparently, the Prince proposed in what had been his nursery at Windsor Castle, which in itself should have been a warning sign. After Charles had telephoned his mother, he rang Johnnie. The next day the princess-to-be rang her parents: 'Daddy was thrilled. "How wonderful". Mummy was thrilled. I remember telling my brother and he said:"Who to?"' Three weeks later, after Diana had holidayed with her mother in Australia to avoid the prurient press interest, the engagement was officially announced on 24 February 1981. The night before, Raine and Johnnie were invited to Prince Charles's apartment for a celebratory drink. It was the first time they had met with the Prince since the courtship began. As the Prince was helping Raine on with her floor length mink at the close of the evening he paid his future stepmother-in-law a compliment: 'This is a very nice fur coat.' Raine didn't miss a beat: 'Yes', she replied, 'it's a little present – from me to me.'[9]

The crowds thronging outside the gates of Buckingham Palace on the morning of 24 February (tipped off by a *Times* headline that morning) were all vying to spot the bride-to-be and read the proclamation, 'It is with the greatest pleasure that the Queen and the Duke of Edinburgh announce the betrothal of their beloved son the Prince of Wales to the Lady Diana Spencer, daughter of the Earl Spencer and the Honourable Mrs Shand Kydd'. The happy couple were sequestered inside giving *that* interview to the TV cameras (the one where Charles's response to the question which effectively amounted to, 'are you in love?' was famously 'whatever in love means'). When the throng of well wishers outside the gates realised they had in their midst the next best thing to the bride – her father Johnnie accompanied by Raine (in white mink and pearls) and

Henry, her youngest, snapping pictures of the crowd on the great day – they went wild. 'I've taken pictures of all the big events in her life', Johnnie told them, 'I'm not going to miss this one.' By this time, the reporters stationed outside had caught on: 'I'm so happy about all this I could burst', said Johnnie. Raine was equally effervescent – in public at least. 'I feel on top of the world', she proclaimed. Privately, knowing Diana as she did, she was sceptical. 'She didn't think it would last long', reported one insider. Johnnie was more positive, 'she loves him all right', he said.

Others were less diplomatic. Penny Junor, the royal commentator, quotes a senior courtier with whom Johnnie's family solicitor had been staying as a weekend guest when the engagement was announced. 'I don't know this one', the courtier commented. 'Well', came the response, 'you know Sarah. This one's got a quarter of the brains and twice the determination and I smell trouble.'[10] Diarist Kenneth Rose was kinder but no less sagacious, 'Watch the Prince of Wales and Lady Diana Spencer being interviewed on TV. She comes over with much charm yet strength of character. Yet there is something sad about a girl of nineteen being led into Royal Captivity.' Two days later Rose would lunch at Claridge's with Martin Charteris who told him that he was delighted by the Prince of Wales's engagement to Diana Spencer: 'It solves a lot of problems.'[11]

For Raine, the wedding, and the long-term implications of her stepdaughter becoming the wife of the heir to the throne, were to prove a test of her well-honed patient, polite public persona. Whilst it would be disingenuous to suggest that she wouldn't enjoy and maximise the unique position that being so close to the throne would confer, she found the whole experience trying, particularly where the media were concerned. With the spotlight intensely focused on the home of the royal bride the negative press ramped up as the wedding date approached. Famously, the *Daily Express* coined the term 'The Di Trippers', reporting that rubberneckers were thronging through the gates of Althorp searching for the ever elusive 'Lady Di'. 'The tills are ringing at Althorp' commented the paper peevishly, with a barely veiled dig at Raine's commercial acumen, quoting her: 'People expect to see us as well as the house'.

There were problems too with press intrusion, something which Raine, like her stepdaughter, would welcome one day and reject the next. Raine and Johnnie were persistently accused of exploiting Diana's fame, which came to a head when several newspapers ran pieces accusing Johnnie of charging photographers to shoot inside the house and selling personal photographs and even a school report of Diana's. Raine banned all unofficial photography, hoping to stymie any further coverage. This caused further problems. The *Belfast Telegraph* reported that a local photographer had had his camera firmly removed from his grasp by the angry Countess: 'Mr Paul Martin (23) said yesterday that after he took pictures of Countess Spencer serving trippers with tea at Althorp on Easter Sunday, she took his camera and removed the film. "She told me no cameras were allowed in the house anymore and said I would have it back when I was ready to leave."'

Shortly after the engagement, more trouble erupted. The papers got hold of a story that BC and Raine had between them cooked up the 'Barbara Cartland Romantic Tour of England', which involved lunch with Johnnie and Raine at Althorp and tea with Dame Barbara at Camfield Place. According to Angela Levin, the cost of the holiday was $1,399 (airfare not included). Raine protested hotly at the inference from the press: 'All this business of mummy and I charging Americans millions to tour Charles and Diana's honeymoon route is so ridiculous. The trips were arranged two years before Charles even thought about marrying Diana.'

We now know that Charles had only considered marrying Diana in the few months before their engagement was announced, so it was almost certain that Raine and BC had indeed put together their moneymaking tour long before Raine had any indication she was to be related, via marriage, to the monarch. But that didn't stop the haters: 'Let's make no mistake' says one social observer, 'Raine probably couldn't believe her luck when *that* engagement was announced, in fact I think she always viewed herself as Royal. Now she would almost be one.'

Frances Shand Kydd took the opportunity to capitalise on the accusations, positioning herself as blameless in that particular arena: 'I feel very strongly that it's not a time for any members of our family to consider making money out of the wedding. I have been asked to sell pictures of Lady Diana, but the answer is a very firm No' she said defiantly. Later, in the gift shop she owned in Oban, she too would sell royal paraphernalia.

In any case, it wasn't a crime to capitalise upon one's circumstances. The Marquis of Bath opened a safari park at Longleat as did the Duke of Bedford at Woburn after selling many valuable paintings and books to raise the funds for renovations and then transferring Hardwick Hall to the National Trust in lieu of tax. The Duke and Duchess of Devonshire (particularly Debo Devonshire) had famously helped to make Chatsworth a magnet for visitors and businesses alike with the Duchess's books, shop and corporate events. Castle Howard, home of the Howard family, has long been the venue for corporate events and a location for films and TV programmes including *Brideshead Revisited*, *Bridgerton*, *Victoria* and *Death Comes to Pemberley*; even more recently, Highclere Castle, home of the Earl and Countess of Carnarvon, was famously saved by *Downton Abbey's* location fees, attendant publicity and subsequent tourism.

But the media and the public held their royalty and their royalty-to-be to different standards. The narrative around Lady Diana's wicked stepmother was beginning to build nicely in terms of column inches. The dichotomy between the beautiful, innocent princess-to-be, her wronged mother and the vengeful 'step' was straight out of a Disney script. Of course, had Raine been perceived to have been 'high born' herself, that story would have been more difficult to sell, though it's fair to say that neither of Johnnie's wives received a fair press. If Raine was the wicked 'nouveau' tearing apart Althorp and dominating Diana's father, then Frances was perpetually known as 'the bolter' by the tabloids who never failed to tell the story of 'Lady Di' being abandoned by her mother as a child, her car wheels scrunching on the gravel as she fled, whether it was relevant to the story, or even true, didn't matter.

Undoubtedly, the Princess of Wales-to-be played a large part in proceedings where the media were concerned. At the beginning she could do no wrong and she knew it. She also began to exert the kind of social pressure that even she could not have dreamt of wielding where her stepmother was concerned. The wedding invitation list and seating plans for the 2,700 guests were cases in point and revealed something of the merciless nature of Diana and the inherent snobbery of the royal family. The Spencer family were allotted only fifty seats. When Earl Spencer showed Diana the list he had drawn up of guests from his side of the family, his daughter fastidiously crossed off the names of everyone who had failed to attend her sisters' weddings. Later, if more evidence were needed about the so-called Fairy Tale Princess's levels of determination, Kenneth Rose writes in his diary: 'Johnnie Spencer tells me that he wanted to wear his Greys uniform when Diana marries the Prince of Wales, but that Diana herself objected. She thought it would detract from her own appearance. This is most extraordinary, like something from *King Lear*.'

He wasn't far wrong. Preparations for the wedding would provoke untold levels of poor behaviour amongst the prevailing cast of characters – not least the bride. As far as Diana and some close family members were concerned, there were two immediate problems to attend to regarding the guests – one was Raine and the other was her mother. At one point, members of the Spencer family apparently threatened to boycott the wedding if Barbara Cartland, was invited. They were not alone: Princess Margaret was also very vocal about BC's unsuitability. Was this snobbery or a worry that the lady in pink would upstage the royals? We'll never know for sure (though we could probably hazard a guess) because some time after the press got hold of the story, BC claimed to have asked Johnnie to give her invitation to 'a youngster'. 'There were hundreds of people at the wedding who had no filial connection to Diana. BC was after all her step-grandmother. It was quite wrong that she was not invited', says Michael Cole. BC had the last word. Dressed up in her St John Ambulance uniform she gave a celebratory party for the ambulance brigade at her home in Camfield Place. As a result, pictures of the party (complete with bunting, teapots and cake) were featured amongst the Royal Wedding press coverage in almost all of the national newspapers.

There was no question but that Raine, as Diana's stepmother, would need to be invited to the wedding and reception. But there was also no reason, as far as Diana was concerned, that Raine should be seated anywhere prominent and certainly nowhere near Johnnie. Certainly, it was right that Diana's mother, Frances, should have had top billing, but to seat Raine four rows back in the congregation – not close enough to matter, but not far enough away for the snub to have gone unnoticed – seems to have been unnecessarily unkind.

Diana was not on her own when it came to foot stamping. At one point, Johnnie offered an explicit example of where his daughter might have learned her behaviour. At a meeting at Buckingham Palace to discuss the wedding protocols he discovered that he would be expected to take his place in a carriage with his ex-wife Frances on the drive from St Paul's back to the Palace. 'Johnnie pulled such a long face that the Queen said "Oh all right then, you can drive with me" which much to his delight he did', records Rose, who it should be noted refers throughout his diary entries on the subject to 'The Prince of Wales's wedding' in the singular.

If the Princess did catch sight of Raine as she walked up the aisle on 29 July 1981 (when she wasn't looking for Camilla Parker Bowles – a fact which she later admitted) she would have been disappointed. Her spiteful actions had, on the face of it at least, made little difference. Looking immaculate in a pale blue outfit with a jaunty hat perched atop 'a sea of curls which would have made Nelson seasick' as one gossip columnist noted, Raine chatted animatedly and excitedly to her fellow guests, looking every inch the regal stepmother of the royal bride-to-be and enjoying every minute. She does not appear in the family photographs which were taken during the wedding luncheon, but then neither does Peter Shand Kydd. Instead, it is Frances, serene in royal purple, who stands smiling politely beside her ex-husband (the papers noted that the two, who rarely spoke, briefly conferred as the service began). Later Diana would record for Andrew Morton, that her mother 'drove me mad when I was engaged – mad, mad. It was me that was being strong and her sobbing the whole time'. 'My mum was very good-looking', she said, 'but when I didn't include her [in wedding preparations] she got hurt, so out came the Valium. She's been on Valium ever since.'[12]

As for Raine, she was simply relieved once the strain of the wedding was over – her main concern had been Johnnie, would he make it up the aisle of St Paul's, the longest in the world? His recovery had thus far not extended to him walking that far and she had noticed that he was soon out of breath and prone to stumbling. Privately she was desperately worried for him, although her outward appearance betrayed nothing of the sort: 'If I was nervous, Raine was shaking worse than I was, especially since she couldn't be anywhere near me when I might have tripped on all those cathedral steps', Johnnie later told *Woman's Own* magazine. Sixty million television viewers held their breath when Johnnie appeared to falter on the top red carpeted step leading up to the cathedral entrance and then let out a collective sigh of relief when the Princess, in cream taffeta with her twenty-five-foot train still being unfurled from the carriage behind her, offered him her arm to steady himself. 'I had to get my father basically up the aisle and that's what I concentrated on' remembered Diana later for Andrew Morton, 'and I remember being terribly worried about curtseying to the Queen.'

8

Tipping Point

———————•◆•———————

Once the wedding was out of the way the couple returned to Althorp. For Johnnie, buoyant with the happiness and pride of his daughter's wedding and its attendant press, pomp and circumstance: this was one of the happiest periods of his life. He was 'still here, thanks to Raine' as he liked to tell everyone he met and he contented himself with the two things he seemed to like best: pottering on the estate and spending money, particularly at his favourite store: Harrods. He'd been visiting the store since he was a teenager and liked to tell people that he knew the staff (and they him) by name.

For Raine, the couple's situation was much more fraught with difficulty. For starters, the estate was still losing money despite the glut of tourists; the renovations were by no means finished and Johnnie had developed a penchant for buying things. Over the next few years his purchases would include three homes in Bognor, a Silver Spur Rolls-Royce, a flat in Grosvenor Square and the house in Farm Street. The added bonus of rubberneckers flocking to view the home of the future Queen, the place they mistakenly believed that she had 'grown up', did not make up the shortfall. The pressure made itself felt when Raine, interviewed by the *Daily Mail* expostulated that 'Of course we have had a bit of luck with Diana . . . but all the extra visitors have cracked the Library ceiling.'

As for the Diana connection, whilst Raine's detractors carped that she was 'cashing in', friends saw it differently: 'She never once lorded it over us in relation to Diana' says a friend, 'but you could quite see how people would interpret her actions as self-interest.' In his book, *Blood Royal: The Story of the Spencers and the Royals,* John Pearson recounts how once firmly in charge of 'double-glazed and tourist friendly Althorp', Raine would refer to the extra income the increase in visitors produced dismissively as 'my Di money'. Art consultant John Somerville offered an insight into the aristocracy's view of Raine when he recounted meeting Mary Roxburghe, granddaughter of Lord Rosebery (who was briefly British Prime Minister) at a Sotheby's luncheon: 'I was on Mary's right and, during the pudding she said to me sotto voce, "My dear if I suddenly get up to go it is not because you are boring me, but I am not having her (indicating Lady Spencer with her spoon) do her usual and try – as she thinks she can, as the stepmother of our future Queen – to be the first to leave and pull rank on me". Although she was not prepared to give so much as an inch when it came to who she was', notes Somerville, 'she travelled to and from Bond Street by bus, whereas Countess Spencer arrived and departed in a chauffeured Rolls.'[1]

It was Johnnie who had captured the public's hearts though and the press never tired of relating the antics of the Earl, who would occasionally let a little of his infamous temper break through the smiling veneer. In April 1983 one newspaper reported on his remarkable show of speed in chasing a photographer who he deemed to be invading the couple's privacy whilst they were on a lunch and shopping trip in the West End. 'Passers-by were astonished to behold the sight of the father of the future Queen of England doing a curious hop-skipperty lope during which – at every few paces – he attempted to kick the photographer in the bottom' relayed the reporter.

Johnnie rarely went out alone but when he did it was noted. When the Earl emerged from the private Lindo Wing at St Mary's Hospital, Paddington, after the birth of the Princess's first child, William, on 21 June 1982, he was solo. 'He's a beautiful baby', he assured the press, who were all gathered patiently in drizzling rain, before getting into his chauffeur-driven car and being whisked away. It was assumed that the Princess had warned her father not to bring Raine. Both her mother and the Queen were visiting on that day.

Later that year the Queen would make a personal visit to see Johnnie and Raine, a particular honour, which they both hoped would put an end to the negative press. After visiting Northampton (and being presented to the Spencers at the Guildhall during the tour) the Queen made a private visit to Althorp, during which she sipped tea and supped on cucumber sandwiches and chocolate cake, all served by the chatelaine herself in the library. The visit was widely reported in the press, 'Queen Elizabeth meets her In-Laws' read one caption, and it seemed to underscore that the monarch herself had no problem with Raine, who she was said to prefer to Frances, nor with the interior renovations in which she had professed an interest to Raine, at a previous function.

Unfortunately, the bestowal of royal favour did not halt the reports that Althorp was being ransacked. The apogee of the selling spree, at least in intellectual and historical terms, was the previously mentioned sale of the vast Spencer archive from the Muniment Room to the British Library. Payment was made by what the Library itself described as 'generous grants from the National Heritage Memorial Fund (£128,398) and the Friends of the National Libraries

(£5,000) which supplement a major allocation from The British Library'. (There was speculation that the total figure had been as high as £1 million.) The archive, which was sold at Johnnie's behest, in lieu of capital gains tax, had been collected by various Earls and painstakingly collated by Jack Spencer, the previous Earl, and contained over five hundred years of Spencer family history. The documents included everything from medieval household accounts to latter day accounts of art sales, shooting parties and extensive personal family records. 'My father had sold the family's records to the British Library in the 80's, leaving the Muniment Room empty', confirms Charles, in *Althorp: The Story of an English House*.

The truth was that much had been sold to fund the enormous bills for Johnnie's hospital care and the remaining death duties which ran into the millions, a fact which he later confirmed: 'I'm afraid you must blame the country's tax laws and not me . . . Running this place which I love dearly is eating into my private funds, but from the sales that have gone through, by opening to the public and by having Americans and Germans to dinner and holding musical evenings we are holding our heads above water.' Even greater opprobrium was heaped upon the couple when it was discovered that they had been breaking up important sets of antique furniture, fine china and ancient family silver and selling them separately and quietly without giving major dealers or institutions the chance to bid. 'I think it was Raine who brokered these deals and she would ring up a dealer and say "I want to get rid of these quietly – can you help?" The reasons were not malicious but simply that she didn't want people to know that they were running out of money', says Lady Colin Campbell. After Johnnie's death the National Audit Office[2] announced that the sales would be the subject of an investigation into retrospective taxes due.

The question of how and why the press were so involved and well informed on what went out of Althorp during the 1980s, has rarely been asked and never answered. The simple response seems to be that in some cases, at least, Diana was beginning to make her feelings and resentments heard to members of the press pack and they in turn gleefully reported on them, happy to have yet another hook for a royal story. Paul Burrell, Diana's former butler, confirmed in a television interview that for years Raine was very much the Princess's 'fall guy' for everything that was going on at Althorp: 'Diana said what is she doing? She's ruining Althorp, she's selling everything', he told the cameras for a Firecrest Films documentary on Raine entitled *Princess Diana's 'Wicked' Stepmother.*[3] 'She did rather get in the clutches of the art dealers with the sales of the art, but I know that Johnnie was very much on board with everything' says Anne Glenconner of the selling spree. After the press furore the Spencers began selling things more publicly – in 1982, they sold a pair of exceptionally rare 22ct gold seventeenth-century wine coolers, supposedly given to the Duke of Marlborough by Queen Anne after his victory at Blenheim, via the London jewellers S. J. Phillips, who sealed a deal worth about £1 million with the British Museum.

By 1982, Raine had already begun working again – having been on the board of the British Tourist Authority she also agreed to sit on the advisory council at the Victoria and Albert Museum. According to friends, she was keen to re-engage her brain and utilise the skills she had honed after many years in local government. She was also slightly bored. Whereas before his stroke she had been happy to be with Johnnie and spend her time overseeing the running of the estate, the new post-stroke Johnnie was quite a different person. His attention span was limited, he no longer read or listened to much music and he was in bed every evening by 9.30. 'Gone was the robust brute with the easy charm; in its place was a shambling, tetchy but essentially kinder person', said Lady Colin Campbell. 'Raine was marvellous with Johnnie', said Lady Fryberg, 'she displayed commendable patience in dealing with a man who had become slow but remained as demanding as ever.'[4] 'He was still charming', says an acquaintance who sat with them at Glyndebourne, 'but he was almost childlike and his slurred speech could often make him sound as though he was drunk. For a woman with Raine's intellect that must have been terribly frustrating.'

For Raine, sitting on the boards of two organisations she had personal interests in – Great Britain and art/history – came as a welcome relief. Johnnie hated her to be out of his sight but equally did not want to leave Althorp. The boards offered Raine the perfect excuse for a mini-escape and she was meticulous in her preparations. 'She was very professional, very intelligent and very hardworking', says Adele Biss who was head of the BTA at the time. 'She always made extremely good contributions – there was a lot more substance to her than you might at first think – she was no rouged social flibbertijibbet, despite first impressions. I had a very soft spot for her.'[5]

Sir Roy Strong, who was running the Victoria and Albert Museum at the time, felt much the same. 'Raine always knew exactly what was going on, she had read the footnotes beforehand and made intelligent suggestions. She was damned clever.' Strong also understood what it took to look after Johnnie: 'Nothing with Raine was half measures – not her style of dressing, not her interiors at Althorp and not her protectiveness over Johnnie. She did everything she could to help him recover – they were devoted to each other. Raine was almost American in her approach to life – and she'd have fitted in well in New York, which has much more of a "pelmets and swags approach" – at least where the rich are concerned.'

Raine had not taken her eye off the ball at Althorp either. In 1982, she had introduced '*special evenings*' which included musical evenings, dinners and dances where she and Johnnie entertained paying guests who flocked to Northampton from North America, Scandinavia and South Korea. 'There were parts of this that I really didn't enjoy', Raine told the *Mail on Sunday*: 'two shops and a café . . . it's a lot of work.' Sometimes it all became too much. After all they were neither of them in their salad days and entertaining at this level was exhausting. 'They would have these huge dinners and they'd slip away half way through and you'd find them in their private sitting room all snuggled up together in their pjs watching television', says Peter Constandinos, 'they really were so in love.'

No matter how she felt about Johnnie, Raine was still not doing herself any favours with the general public. A report in the *Mirror* stated that she had banned wheelchairs from touring the house, for fear of them damaging the floors, something which seems unthinkable today. 'Unfortunately she was tone deaf sometimes and just unable to read people or situations', says Roy Strong, 'I've always said that this was one of her great weaknesses.'

As time went on and the bills rose ever upwards Raine turned to big business to keep the lights on. She knew full well that these were the people with fat cheque books and a hunger to impress on a grand scale. As Angela Levin notes, the couple entertained more commercial entities including Estée Lauder brand Aramis and even (shock horror) car dealers for the launch of a new brand. Today, similar events are the lifeblood of stately homes across the land. At Althorp over the past few years, as a member of the public, you would have been able to take a tour of the home (adult entry: £20), attend a literary festival, marvel at the latest exhibition, sample delights at the food and drinks festival or buy your stocking fillers at the Christmas fair. In 2020, Auto Royal Althorp was launched with the picture of a Shark Nose Ferrari 196 in front of the house (the event was eventually cancelled because of the pandemic). OK, so Charles Spencer was not entertaining car *salesmen* (or if he was they were likely of a certain 'quality') but that doesn't change the point that today Althorp is as commercial, if not more so, than when Raine was at the wheel.

If the passage of time has proved anything it is that in spite of her many and varied critics, Raine was certainly ahead of the game in recognising that to survive the owner of a stately home needed to be financially savvy. Admittedly, some of her projects were not a success, but others paved the way for homes across the country to convert stable blocks into shops, gardens into tourist attractions and house tours into 'events'. Her friends and admirers agreed. Sir Henry Marking told the *Daily Express* that Raine had made the house and its contents 'safe for the next 200 years of existence'. Lord Fawsley went one better saying, 'she should be canonised'. Raine's other skill was in her recognition of the stately home as a vital, totemic reminder of social standing and class division – and whilst the received wisdom might be that things in that arena have changed, one only need look at the social media accounts of the young aristocracy today, to recognise that they most certainly have not.

Noël Coward had it about right when he wrote:

> The stately homes of England,
> How beautiful they stand,
> To prove the upper classes,
> Have still the upper hand.

One place Johnnie loved more than Althorp and perhaps even Harrods, was the seaside. Raine went along with this perhaps because she had come to realise how happy it made him, but also possibly because she understood that simply spending time at Althorp was not good for Johnnie's state of mind. Raine had her own reasons for wanting to get out of Althorp: she had a stalker – 'an intruder obsessed with Countess Spencer has twice been caught at the family home, Althorp near Northampton' reported the *Daily Mail* on 22 December 1983. On neither occasion did the twenty-one-year-old intruder and Raine come into contact, but parallels were drawn between the incidents and Michael Fagan's break-in at Buckingham Palace, which resulted in him sitting on the monarch's bed and chatting with her, whilst she attempted to ring for help.

But Johnnie was not entirely satisfied with apartment living. A spontaneous Saturday afternoon drive along the coast in the Rolls, led to the purchase of a four-bedroomed Spanish style villa called Trade Winds in the deeply unfashionable Sussex seaside town of Bognor Regis – best known for Butlins and George V's likely apocryphal utterance 'Bugger Bognor'. Trade Winds had a large garden, a swimming pool and dynamite sea views. The Earl was hooked, although history does not record his wife's verdict. The Spencer property portfolio was quickly swelled by two more adjoining houses in the next couple of years – with one being used by the servants and one bought for guests, specifically the Princess of Wales and her children. (When one of the properties was sold it was claimed that the new owner had found pictures of the Princess and the Princes in the pool left behind in the attic.)

Much of the publicity surrounding the Althorp art sales had focused on the fact that on the one hand the Spencers were crying poverty, but on the other purchasing more homes. This seems an indefensible position, except when you consider again that the paintings and other items were Johnnie's to sell. They did not belong to the nation, nor to his children. Johnnie's attitude to money had unquestionably softened since his illness and since meeting Raine. He liked fine wines, Rolls-Royces, luxury travel and he liked buying Raine jewellery from S. J. Phillips. As Nicolas Norton says, 'Raine had good pieces but Johnnie was not a regular buyer'. He couldn't afford to be. Their lifestyle included extensive first class travel with luxury hotels – and was costly. 'They really did live high on the hog', says a friend, 'it certainly wasn't the pared back, considered style in which Johnnie had lived earlier in his life.'

Raine was swiftly at work with the renovations in Bognor again bringing in David Laws to advise until they fell out and she turned to a local builder. Beach front weekends were most certainly not her métier, and whilst Johnnie spent the time pottering in the gardens, Raine continued her habit of making her daily phone calls and appointments from her bed. Angela Levin interviewed a member of her staff who happily provided details on Raine's beach trousseau: 'Some weekends she would bring twelve nightdresses and negligees in silk and antique lace and just a couple of outfits, usually from Hardy Amies in case she went out . . . she would have her lunch negligee, her tea negligee, her evening negligee and so on.' The one thing the staff member had disliked was Raine's potty, which she had apparently used because she was unhappy with using the ensuite bathroom at night because it woke Johnnie.

In 1984, Raine threw a spectacular party at Althorp to celebrate Johnnie's sixtieth birthday. Alan Clark, the Conservative MP, self-confessed snob, womaniser and notoriously candid diarist was present:

> Althorp itself was beautifully floodlit and looked perfect in scale, almost tiny . . . endless fleets of (Rolls-Royce Silver) Shadows . . . When we went into the Hall a magnificent sight presented itself: Barbara Cartland wearing an electric pink chiffon dress with false eyelashes as thick as those caterpillars that give you a rash if you handle them, was draped on the central staircase . . . making stylised conversation with the Bishop of Southwark wearing various pendant charms and crucifixes . . . some mature ladies could hardly move so encrusted were they . . . and the Princess of Wales looked absolutely radiantly beautiful and not wearing one single piece of jewellery. All of the minor royals were there. A smattering too of fashionable dons . . . Everything has been restored . . . the overall effect is slightly that of the Schloss of Pontresina.[6]

Clark's reference to the grand Swiss hotel (sometimes cited as one of the inspirations for the film *Grand Budapest Hotel*) is somewhat predictable. As a man with his own stately home (the ancient Saltwood Castle in Kent) his candid diary charts – alongside his hobnobbing with fellow grandees and infamous female 'conquests' – an adulthood spent permanently in fear of bankruptcy, brought about by his attempt to live in the custom he thought Saltwood and his own status demanded. His days are peppered with sales of the ancestral antiques and pictures he is constantly forced to sell in order to keep himself and his family afloat. This, and his much-repeated resentment at never being offered a title, made it unlikely he would ever visit Althorp without it giving rise to a level of waspishly expressed envious regret.

In any case Raine would not have been the sort of person to bear grudges, even if she did read Clark's acerbic comments when part one of his diary was published in 1993: 'I never heard her say a bad word about anyone' confirms Frank Partridge, 'no matter who they were or what they had said or done regarding her.' In any case, Raine and Johnnie were too busy enjoying themselves to worry about other people. In 1985, Raine threw a party at Althorp for her son William, Viscount Dartmouth, who had returned to the UK after working in the USA for almost a decade. Raine was delighted to have William back in the UK. 'She really did worry about her children', says another friend, 'and I remember her concern about William not being married.' (William, later an MEP and party spokesman for UKIP, would go on to have a son with his then partner, producer Claire Cavanagh, in 2005, and marry Australian model Fiona Campbell in 2009 – they are now divorced.)

Nothing made Johnnie happier than visits from his grandchildren. Between 1983 and 1990 he and Raine would be grandparents/step grandparents eleven times over. In addition to Princes William and Harry who diplomatically called Raine 'Aunt', there were Lady Jane

Fellowes's Laura (born 1980), Alexander (born 1983) and Eleanor (1985), and Sarah McCorquodale's Emily Jane (1983), George Edmund (1984) and Celia Rose (1989). Raine's own son Rupert married Victoria Otley in 1984, who gave birth to a son, Edward Peregrine (1986), and a daughter, Claudia Rose (1989), and Charles Spencer's daughter Kitty was born in 1990. Raine reluctantly embraced the role of 'grandmother' although she had never over-come her reticence where small children were concerned. She did her best because she could see that the children made Johnnie incandescently happy. 'I know very well that Raine was an excellent grandmother, she worked very hard at it and always made sure the children had a lovely time when they visited' says Anne Glenconner. Glenconner had an inside track. The nanny who had looked after her own children, Barbara Barnes, was now nanny to William and Harry and often accompanied the Princes to Althorp.

Prince Harry was a particular favourite of Johnnie's. On 15 September 1984, when Prince Charles rang to tell Johnnie that he had another grandson, third in line to the throne, Johnnie flew the Spencer personal standard at Althorp for the week. After he and Raine had greeted the press and photographers clustered around the gates, Johnnie used the 'royal we' in the proclamation: 'We have had a boy!' He righted himself with, 'It will be lovely for him [William] to have a companion, a playmate and someone to fight with.' And then the couple, who were beaming and arm in arm, uncharacteristically invited the press in for a glass of sherry to celebrate the royal birth.

Meanwhile on the polo field where he headed after the birth, the future King of England celebrated by giving a spontaneous drinks party out of the back of his Land Rover, serving champagne in plastic cups to his teammates. In later years, the Princess of Wales would characterise the birth of Harry as (the time) 'our marriage, the whole thing went down the drain'.[7] It seems unlikely that Raine and Johnnie were unaware of the tensions in the marriage. According to some reports, the Princess would often take refuge at Althorp from the palace mandarins, her husband and the press when she found it all too much. Detractors claimed she was still on exceptionally terse terms with her stepmother, in spite of Raine's assiduous attentions to the royal Princes.

With the benefit of hindsight, the Spencers' comments in the run up to the wedding of Diana and Charles suggest that they were all too aware of the fragility of the princess-to-be: 'Diana won't break down because she never breaks down. She is strong like me', Johnnie told the press at the time of the engagement, 'she's not a girl who suffers from depression' added Raine. These were rather odd comments to make on the occasion of an engagement (especially *this* engagement). It was almost as if they were already acting to deny the rumours that they knew would inevitably surface and presaging the couple's deeply troubled relationship.

Relations between Raine and Diana were equally marred by strife during the mid to late eighties, although Raine went to lengths in the press to insist that this was not the case: 'We don't live in each other's pockets' she told one paper and 'She's always been terribly sweet' to another. The young Princes would often visit with just their nanny and their detective present, to Johnnie's delight. He would let them roam the grounds or race pedal cars around the house. 'There's no sibling rivalry between them . . . they lead fairly normal lives really as Diana has lots of girlfriends her own age all of whom have children.'

In 1986, when Raine and Johnnie had begun to travel again, they took a trip to Paris, staying, as usual, at the Ritz, as guests of Mohamed Al Fayed. The friendship was mutually beneficial, 'They were very close friends – it was a special relationship and meant a lot on both sides', says Michael Cole, director of communications at Harrods at the time. When Al Fayed launched his book, *Harrods:*

A Palace in Mayfair, it was Johnnie who asked whether he might make a speech at the launch party. Despite difficulties with his own diction since the stroke, the Earl managed the speech adroitly, with Raine holding his arm for support.

Grandchildren notwithstanding, Johnnie and Raine were on increasingly shaky ground with their commercial activities and their royal connections. Again, it was their closeness to Harrods and Al Fayed which inspired them, at some point during 1986/87, to begin actively courting the Japanese in the hope of creating a mutually beneficial partnership. Raine had first-hand experience of the power of the Japanese Yen from her time spent at the British Tourist Authority, where she had chaired a committee called '*Britain Welcomes Japan*'. The couple decided on a ten-day trip to Tokyo to promote Althorp, where they were feted, and both immediately smitten by the country's beauty and its ancient customs. On their return, Al Fayed invited the couple to open the first Japanese information booth at Harrods, staffed by Japanese women in kimonos. The booth was an inspired addition on the part of Britain's ritziest store owner, who had realised before anyone else the vital role the Japanese would continue to play in British tourism and commerce over the next few decades. (The store would soon open another Japanese Information booth at Heathrow.) With the Japanese ambassador and a raft of Japanese dignitaries present, the couple had cut short a holiday in America to attend, arrived promptly and Raine gave an opening speech in fluent Japanese. 'I could not believe it', says Michael Cole, 'and neither could anyone else, she'd learned the whole thing phonetically and it went on for at least two minutes. Afterwards the whole delegation burst into applause.'

Hoping to cement a connection between the Japanese and Althorp, the Spencers decided to produce a book on Japan, hoping to mirror the success of their first book, *The Spencers on Spas*, published in 1983. For *Spas* the couple had toured, photographed and written about British spa towns. That book included some of Raine's own personal recollections: 'The first time I went to Cheltenham was with Granny Cartland', did creditably well. The couple had vastly enjoyed the publicity and attention despite a snippy review in the *Guardian*. The process had marked a milestone in Johnnie's recovery – that he could take photographs and undertake a fairly hefty tour of Britain was proof that he was recovered enough for Raine to worry less and undertake her own projects.

Entitled *Japan and the East*, and containing glossy large format photographs, the couple's second book flopped. That did not dampen the burgeoning ardour of Johnnie and Raine for all things oriental. They began conversations about licensing the Spencer name for the Royal Spencer Golf Club. 'Raine was very serious about leveraging her tourism contacts into a Japanese deal', says a former business acquaintance of the Spencers, 'and she wasn't afraid of the language.' 'I once heard her converse in fluent French to the man on her right at dinner and then turn to her left and address her guest from Japan in Japanese', says Nadine Bonsor, 'she was very impressive.'

In 1988, Raine decided to sell twelve of her oldest ballgowns at a Sotheby's auction. 'If she had any decorum she would have sold her cast-offs for charity', sniped John Knight of the *Mirror*. In fact, Raine's actions reflected the modus operandi which had dictated her entire life path: 'if something is redundant then get rid of it'. This sentiment underlined her approach to her friends too, although by her own admission she had very few of the female variety, preferring the company of men. Her confidants tended to be people she saw frequently – her decorator, her hairdresser or her PA. Interestingly, most of her close girlfriends were not English – she preferred the company of 'continentals' like Anne Pozatek, wife of the shoe baron Jerome Fisher and later Countess Milly Flamburiari of Corfu with whom she stayed after the death of Diana.

Although the Spencer children and the Dartmouth children rarely met or mixed, they would all attend Raine's sixtieth birthday bash in May 1989. This time the Princess of Wales was present *without* her husband. Also on the guest list – at Diana's request – was a certain Major James Hewitt. Hewitt had also been present at Charles's fortieth birthday in 1988, although the couple had only managed one dance together. According to Sally Bedell Smith, the Princess was much less discreet at the Althorp party. She danced and drank with the major, gave him a tour of the house and then, at the end of the evening, led him out to the pool house where they made love.[8] If anyone noticed (and they had to have done for Bedell Smith to garner this information) there was nothing in the press about it. The complicit silence from the guests, including Raine and Johnnie, suggests that the Princess's unhappiness and the breakdown of the royal marriage were by then an open secret. That Prince Charles did not accompany the Princess gives credence to the rumour that he encouraged the Hewitt liaison because it made his own relationship with Mrs Parker Bowles easier.

Raine had taken charge of the organisation of her own party from the start. And, deploying a tactic she had employed for Johnnie's sixtieth, she asked several of her closest friends and neighbours to host dinners for the invitees, who all then arrived at Althorp en-masse, ready to party. Instead of buying gifts, guests were asked to contribute money towards a present she had chosen in advance from S. J. Phillips – a pair of diamond earrings. 'We couldn't believe it', said one invitee of the request, 'it was either extremely bad manners or the work of a genius. We preferred to think the latter.' You couldn't argue that Raine was not, as ever, ahead of the game. Her party planning was admirable. After all, who wouldn't rather their guests arrived fully fed and watered, and have the ability to choose their own birthday gift rather than receiving an avalanche of questionable tchotchkes?

The Spencers might have turned a blind eye to Diana's behaviour at Raine's party but that didn't prevent them – Raine in particular – from continuing their friendship with Prince Charles. Raine and Charles had a close bond forged by years of discussing the merits of architectural and historical heritage and she was privately sympathetic to his problems with Diana. On a visit to Althorp by Charles and Diana after the Princess had been granted the freedom of the city of Northampton, Diana nudged her equerry Patrick Jephson as they progressed into her ancestral home: 'you watch' she said of her stepmother, 'she does the lowest curtsy in England'. Jephson notes that the Princess 'was denied her fun. That afternoon Raine's curtsies and conversation were all for the Prince'.[9]

Unlike his wife, Johnnie was said to find spending time with the Prince somewhat more enervating. In Kenneth Rose's diary, dated 21 December 1992, he relates that:

> Raine Spencer told me how tiresome Johnnie found the Prince of Wales when he came to Althorp. After two hours talking about rainforests and other environmental themes, he showed no sign of stopping. So Johnnie said he had to telephone and went out. Raine found him lying on his bed and he said: 'I'm not down to dinner for two more hours of rainforest.'

But the tension in the Wales's relationship was leaking out into other areas of their lives. There were reports that both were terse with their staff, difficult to please and ceaselessly irritable. It was in this frame of mind that Diana arrived at Althorp for the rehearsal for her brother Charles's wedding to model Victoria Lockwood, at which Prince Harry would be a pageboy, on 16 September 1989. According to the Princess herself, neither Raine nor Johnnie spoke to Diana's mother, Frances, 'even sitting next to her on a pew'.[10] What happened next was predictable. Diana vented years of frustrations over both Raine and her own failing marriage at the one person she could be pretty sure would not answer back: Raine herself. The infamous row took place on the landing at the top of grand oak staircase which runs adjacent to the spectacular two storey black-and-white chequered entrance hall, to The Saloon gallery around which the Spencer family portraits were hung.

In the Princess's own words (in transcripts of the tapes she prepared for Andrew Morton, and the videos she and Peter Settelen her voice coach made together) Diana takes up the story: 'I took it upon myself to air everyone's grievances in my family . . . my mother said that was the first time in 22 years anyone had ever stuck up for her. I said everything I possibly could . . . I was so angry. I said: I hate you so much, if only you knew how much we all hated you for what you've done, you've ruined the house, you spend Daddy's money and what for?' To her credit, Raine retained her legendary self-control and her Cartland manners: 'You have no idea how much pain your mother has put your father through', was her restrained rebuttal to the incandescently raging Princess. By that point Diana was uncontrollable. In a gesture of unalloyed spite, she shoved her stepmother who toppled down the first set of carpeted steps onto the wide landing. 'I pushed her down the stairs', she told Settelen, 'which gave me enormous satisfaction.'[11] 'She was badly bruised and dreadfully upset', recalled Raine's personal assistant Sue Howe, 'It was not justified and it was a cruel and heartless thing to do'.[12]

Diana's row with Raine, set the scene for what was to be an uneasy marriage celebration for her young brother and his bride. The attendant publicity reflected the mood: a fawn like, nervy, Victoria Lockwood, cloaked in an ivory Tomasz Starzewski tapestried wedding gown, with a Russian sable trimmed dropped waist, the Spencer tiara balanced precariously on her long brunette locks, dodged the rain and puddles as she made her way out of the church, on her groom's arm. Following behind were the bridesmaids and pages – the pages dressed in an outfit inspired by the portrait of John Charles, later Third Earl Spencer, aged four by Joshua Reynolds, which hung at Althorp. At one point, Prince Harry took off his cumbersome wide-brimmed brown velvet hat, fiddled with the enormous sash encircling his tiny waist and stuck his tongue out at the cameras – as if to speak for the entire party. In fact, the whole day took on a rather dark, jaded baroque feel with Raine, recovered from the previous afternoon's trauma, resplendent in cardinal red, accented by white gloves, tights and pearls almost as large as her red pillbox hat, overseeing the entire event, studiously ignoring the Princess of Wales and Frances Shand Kydd. And there was Johnnie trying to mend fences in his characteristically good-natured, slightly bumbling fashion. The best man, Darius Guppy, disappeared before making his speech, leaving a stand-in to make it on his behalf: 'Let's just say he was indisposed', says a guest, 'and leave it at that.'

In 1990 there would be more nuptials on the horizon. 'You'll never guess what', Raine said to Peter Constandinos her hairdresser, as she bustled into the salon: 'Charlotte's getting married – he's got money and a title'.

The calm that had settled over Althorp after Charles and Victoria's wedding did not last long. As the boom and bust, shoulder-padded eighties went out with a whimper and the housing bubble burst with a bang, recession was setting in and biting at the heels of even the wealthiest. Charles Spencer and his wife were now living in the grounds of Althorp in The Falconry, which made both parties feel uncomfortable.

The Viscount's marriage was soon in trouble, which in itself was deemed newsworthy, but not as newsworthy as the details which cartoonist Sally Ann Lasson, apparently the object of his short-lived affections, was happy to divulge. Lasson told *Daily Express* diarist Ross Benson that Charles Spencer had regaled her with tales of the Spencer children and their family squabble which was, as Benson put it, 'nothing less than distasteful'.[13]

The situation reached breaking point for Raine and Johnnie (who had, up until then, maintained a fairly dignified and restrained approach to the constant press leaks and accusations) when the press suddenly paid rapt attention to the potential sale of forty estate cottages. Matters were not helped by some of the tenants, who raised a petition to protest the sales which they said would make them homeless. There was carping too that the prices were unfair – the press couldn't make up their minds whether they were too cheap (and therefore being sold off at a loss to the estate) or too expensive (for the tenants to buy). The sales, they noted, were being handled by Raine's staff and not by an estate agent. There was gossip too that Johnnie was buying Raine a new home with the proceeds. Actually, he'd already bought her the house in Farm Street which was under renovation.

Matters intensified when the couple gave a spontaneous interview to immaculately suited, well-spoken, monocle wearing star *Daily Mail* journalist Brian Vine, who by wit or sheer good luck just happened to be on the same plane as them heading out to Nice, where they were to join a cruise on 10 September 1991.[14] For once Raine let her guard down. She was exhausted by the internecine family feud: 'Do you think for one minute if I didn't love Lord Spencer that I would put up with all this hassle and bad blood. I don't need it', she told Vine who described her as: 'immaculately coiffured . . . her nail varnish blood-red, her cheeks rouged [she] breathed fire over the coals'. Vine, a former foreign correspondent who was acknowledged as a genius at achieving the sort of scoops both Evelyn Waugh and his character Boot could only have dreamt of, managed to elicit what counted as a confessional from Raine. 'Why do people do this feuding. Isn't it just wonderful that the family are well, that no one's got cancer, no

True blue: Raine and her son Rupert at a Mayfair polling station during the general election of 1970 which returned a victory for new conservative PM, Edward Heath. *(Evening Standard/Getty Images)*

Picture this: celebrating with Roy Strong, director of the National Portrait Gallery, and cartoonist Osbert Lancaster, Somerset House, 7 December 1971.
(John Minihan/Evening Standard/Getty Images)

Family matters: Earl Spencer standing beside his former wife, Frances Shand Kydd, at the wedding of their daughter Lady Jane Spencer to Robert Fellowes, 20 April 1978. Raine, now Countess Spencer, stands far left.
(Popperfoto/Getty Images)

Celebration: Johnnie and Raine with Sir John and Lady Mary Mills at All Saints Church, Northampton, 12 May 1979, at the service of thanksgiving for Johnnie's recovery *(Popperfoto/Getty Images)*

Grand design: with Johnnie outside Althorp House, 1980. *(Tim Graham Photo Library / Getty Images)*

Proud papa: Raine with Johnnie outside Buckingham Palace on the day of Diana's engagement to Prince Charles, 24 February 1981. *(Anwar Husein/Getty Images)*

Garden party: Diana, now Princess of Wales, with Raine in the grounds of Althorp, 1983.
(Jayne Fincher/Princess Diana Archive/Getty Images)

Sunshine and showers: with Johnnie at his son's, Charles Althorp's, wedding to Victoria Lockwood.
(Tim Graham Photo Library / Getty Images)

Stepping up: seated with Johnnie on 'that' staircase for a photoshoot, Althorp, 1986.
(John Downing/Getty Images)

Freedom? When Diana is granted the Freedom of the City of London at the Guildhall on 22 July 1987, the family attend. From left to right Raine, Johnnie, Charles, Diana's mother Frances Shand-Kydd and her grandmother, Frances's mother, Lady Fermoy. *(Hulton Archive/Getty Images)*

Sunnier climes: with Johnnie on holiday in Athens, Greece, July 1989. *(P Anastasselis/Shutterstock)*

Grieving: with Princess Diana and Charles Althorp at Johnnie's funeral, March 1992. *(David Hartley/Shutterstock)*

Third time's a charm: Raine and Comte Jean-François de Chambrun announce their engagement to the press, London, 10 May 1993.
(Jacques Lange/Paris Match/via Getty Images)

Mummy dearest: the happy couple with Dame Barbara, 11 May 1993.
(PA Images/Alamy Stock Photo)

A quiet wedding: Raine and Jean-François surrounded by press and photographers as they leave Westminster Registry Office in Marylebone after their marriage ceremony, 8 July 1993.
(Rex Lentati/ANL/Shutterstock)

The country bride: Raine, resplendent in pink Ungaro for her ecumenical wedding service at the Holy Trinity Church, Cold Ashton, 10 July 1993.
(David Cooper/Alamy Stock Photo)

Chic at the château: with Jean-François at Château Garibondy, 22 October 1993.
(Jean-Claude Deutsch/Paris Match via Getty Images)

(left) The rapprochement: Diana and Raine lunch in Mayfair, 28 March 1997. *(Tim Graham Photo Library /Getty Images)*

(above) Social scene: Diana and Raine, together for the launch of the Christies Auction of the Princess's dresses to raise money for The Aids Crisis Trust and The Royal Marsden Hospital Cancer Fund, 2 June 1997.
(Tim Graham Photo Library /Getty Images)

ieving: Raine arrives at the funeral of Diana,
ncess of Wales, at Westminster Abbey, 6
ptember 1997. *(Julian Parker/UK Press via Getty Images)*

'Till girl with a title': Raine with Daryl Hannah at
the opening of the Harrods sale, 9 July 1997.
(Alex Lentati/Evening Standard/Shutterstock)

bove) Suits: arriving at the High Court for the
quest into the death of Diana, Princess of Wales,
ndon, 12 December 2007. *(Cate Gillon/Getty Images)*

ght) Big spenders: Raine with friend Shirley
ssey at the Chelsea Physic Garden, in aid of the
lapagos Conservation Society, 17 June 2004.
an Davidson/Shutterstock)

Last party: Raine photographed at one of her final social appearances in Apsley House, London, 15 June 2015. *(Richard Young/Shutterstock)*

one's got Aids'?' she asked, seated in First Class, seat 1C, with
Johnnie reading his magazines in his seat 1A across the aisle, after
telling Vine, 'yes I've heard myself called "wicked stepmother".'
She was, she said, only interested in her love for her husband and
what he was trying to do for posterity. 'I have all the money I'll
ever need . . . I have a fascinating job as a director of the British
Tourist Authority, I own my own home still and I have my health.
People are so ungrateful don't you find that?' She continued telling
Vine that she had not been responsible for the decision surrounding
the sale of 'paintings or cottages' – 'I get my orders from him' she
said, gesturing to Johnnie in the opposite seat. Now Vine turned
his attention to Lord Spencer, 'dressed in blue yachting blazer and
eye catching yellow trousers', who willingly chimed in telling Vine
that Diana had been on the telephone complaining about 'Raine's
new décor', and then he added a zinger which one couldn't help
but think he'd been harbouring for some years, 'But why she has to
make such a fuss I don't know because she seldom visits, only at
Easter and Christmas.'

'I love my children', Johnnie confessed, 'but they have gone a bit
haywire . . . You know children aren't grateful. They never even
thank you for pocket money apparently.' The Spencer children were
going to inherit a bit more than pocket money. Johnnie told Vine
that he'd already given Diana 'a helluva lot of money . . . between
half and a million pounds' which she in turn had apparently passed
on to Prince Harry 'as the heir will be pretty well taken care of'.
'Diana has no experience of money', he would later say, 'she's too
young.' He did not spare the other siblings either, calling his son
Charles 'a little immature', saying, 'he'll get over it all'. And then he
addressed the matter of the selling of the estate cottages, which had
caused the family rift: 'I can do what I like with my properties . . .
Someone is trying to make out that I am a heartless landlord
. . . Everything I do is for my home, Althorp.' It was the most

outspoken interview he'd ever given and it garnered plenty of column inches in the next few days. Johnnie felt no remorse: 'He thought they were acting very badly and he was terribly hurt', says a close friend of the couple. But neither of them would have spoken out without Vine's prompting: 'Neither of them believed in airing their dirty linen in public, so Vine got quite a story', says the friend.

Had Raine set the whole thing up? Was it a complete coincidence that Vine was on the same plane as the couple and in the same cabin? What were the chances? There were those who speculated that it had all of her hallmarks – two men, thoroughly in her thrall in a perfectly handled press encounter with an element of faux spontaneity, offering the perfect setting for Johnnie to finally unburden himself without reproach. He was already in holiday mode – as he told Vine – and they would be away for enough time for the reverberations to die down. Vine was no 'second class' journalist though – he travelled in First as a matter of course as befitting a man with vowels to match Bertie Wooster. He had owned racehorses too and a Long Island summer retreat.

Vine was the man 'most likely to' when it came to getting the Spencers to talk – a suave ex-private school journo with the sort of credentials which conveyed a 'one of us' persona and gave the upper classes a false sense, both of security and discretion. If any member of the press was taking the plane to Nice for the weekend it would have to be Vine – a man who could actually afford the lifestyles he was writing about.

It was 1992 – the year the nineties really got down and dirty. Staggering job losses, rising crime figures, the announcement of a general election to be held in April, with John Major's Tories ahead in the polls were partially responsible for the pall of despondency, which hung over the country. AIDS figures were increasing amongst the homosexual and heterosexual population, inducing panic and prejudice over a killer disease no one knew how to treat. As if to underline the mood, someone called Damien Hirst had sliced a shark in half and pickled it in formaldehyde. Many British teenagers were high on avoidance – still getting off their heads on something called Ecstasy and raving to Acid House music. You couldn't really blame them.

At Althorp the mood was also sombre. Whilst the rankling over Johnnie and Raine's interview had died down, Johnnie was feeling unwell. He was uneasy over the continuing problems in Diana's marriage, which were being slavishly reported by the press. On 19 March, the Palace announced on behalf of the Queen, who was celebrating her fortieth year on the throne, that Prince Andrew and Sarah Duchess of York were to separate, adding to the intense speculation as to whether Diana and Charles would be next. A poll published by the *Daily Express* had revealed that two out of three members of the general public thought that the monarchy was out of touch. But the number one slot in popularity still went to Diana at 29 per cent, with the Queen coming in second at 15 per cent and Charles lagging behind piteously in fifth place, with just 11 per cent of the votes.

In mid-March, Johnnie's weakness and malaise was diagnosed as a chest infection by his London doctors. At both Raine's and his doctor's insistence he was confined to bed for a week in Farm Street. On his return to Althorp he seemed listless and disconnected. Staff realised the seriousness of the situation when Raine informed them that she would be taking care of the wine choices from now on: 'We knew he must have been ill because not in a million years would he have let Her Ladyship near his beloved cellars if he could help it' one staff member told Angela Levin. On Saturday 21 March, Johnnie was admitted to the Humana Wellington Hospital in St Johns Wood, London, suffering from pneumonia. On the Sunday he was visited by Diana, William and Harry who were due to go off on a skiing holiday. Raine was shuttling between the hospital and Althorp where she was anxiously making preparations for a large event the following weekend. On Thursday 26 March, a Humana Wellington hospital spokesman told the press that the Earl was making a good recovery, indeed visitors reported him as tetchy and anxious to return home. It was not to be. On 29 March, Johnnie suffered a fatal heart attack, brought about, as Charles Spencer later reported, by 'bruising around his heart caused by the earlier stroke'.

It was a pale, shocked Charles who would give a statement to the press and cameras gathered expectantly outside the hospital, after escorting a shattered looking Raine, still resplendent in red coat and matching lipstick, and two of her children, Henry and Charlotte, to her waiting limousine. 'We all thought he was fine. My stepmother was at home overseeing something, I was at home with my family . . . It is a matter of regret for the rest of us that nobody was with him when he died, but he died instantly', Charles said. Would Raine have rather that she had spoken to the press on the occasion of her beloved Johnnie's death? Of course. But it was characteristic of a woman who had been brought up to be rigorously respectful of proper etiquette and ritual to defer to her stepson who was, after all, now the new Earl Spencer. The cameras captured her pale but still composed and immaculately coiffed, staring straight ahead as the car pulled away from the hospital. The woman who once claimed that 'nobody was going to destroy Johnnie whilst I was by his side', had, in the end, been powerless to save him.

9

Don't Look Back in Anger

———————•◆•———————

Raine had not expected any sympathy or empathy from the
Spencer children and, in this at least, she was not to be
disappointed. 'She didn't want to leave Althorp so quickly but she
was effectively thrown out' says a close friend. It seemed as if Charles
Spencer and his sisters moved at lightning speed to remove all traces
of their stepmother from their lives. It was also as Johnnie – a man
who had seemingly grown increasingly weary of his family's demands
– might have predicted. Which is why he had made such extensive
provision for his beloved wife in his will and had provided her,
before his death, with a home and an income of her own.

Raine had confided in a close friend after the visit they had made
to the family solicitor after Johnnie had returned to Althorp post-
stroke: 'Raine told me that the solicitor actually said to Lord Spencer
in front of her: "Lord Spencer I feel I must ask you, before you sign
[your will], do you really wish to leave *all* of this money to your
wife?" Whilst Raine was horrified at the solicitor's impertinence she
said nothing. Meanwhile Johnnie's response was fulsome: "If I could

leave her even more I would."' The will was said to have left Raine with £6 million, the houses in Farm Street and Bognor (plus contents), a vast collection of jewellery and an annuity.

The retribution – for that is how it appeared to everyone – was swift and decisive. On the night of her husband's death Raine had repaired to her home at 24 Farm Street W1 and Charles, who had driven down the motorway a Viscount, swept back through the wrought iron gates of his new home, Althorp House, as the 9th Earl Spencer. 'From a Champagne Charlie to ninth Earl' was the headline in the *Daily Express*, riffing on Charles's much reported upon and, it should be noted, possibly apocryphal, predilection for champagne, nightclubs and rambunctious behaviour. He was the godson of the Queen the paper reminded us.

One of the first people Raine called was her personal assistant, Sue Howe, asking her to send her some appropriate clothing down to London in a taxi. The fact that Raine, the woman who was known by her friends to possess the rare capacity to be prepared for everything and anything, was in London without her widow's weeds, only serves to illustrate that Johnnie's death had come a complete shock. 'She was heartbroken', Sue told cameras for the documentary, *Princess Diana's 'Wicked' Stepmother*, 2017, 'as we all were.' When Sue arrived at Althorp she was surprised to find herself being escorted to Raine and Johnnie's Wardrobe Room by the housekeeper: 'I had been in and out of that house for nearly twenty years . . . I said to her what do you think I'm going to do, put a Van Dyke in the suitcase?'

Howe tells in the documentary of how, the next day upon returning to collect more of Raine's personal belongings, she found the Princess of Wales and her brother present. According to Howe, they didn't agree to her taking Johnnie and Raine's Louis Vuitton monogrammed suitcases, removing the contents and stuffing Raine's belongings into bin bags, at which point she says they were 'thrown out onto the tarmac'. In other newspaper reports, the garbage bags of possessions were booted down the steps. Hyperbole or truth? It seems very unlikely that Howe would have consented to an on camera interview if these accusations were untrue, but it's also a fact that there's no tarmac outside the front of Althorp, only gravel. As Queen Elizabeth II so succinctly put it during a more recent family spat 'recollections may vary'. One of the first acts of Charles's stewardship was apparently to remove the Sancha portrait of Raine from its place in the gallery and replace it with a portrait of the 3rd Earl Spencer. Of this action at least, we can be almost certain.

Other friends of Raine endorse the tales of chilly treatment: 'Of course Raine had her own rather wonderful collection of paintings and furniture which she had taken with her to Althorp in the first place. Naturally she wanted those back', says Frank Partridge. There are rumours that Raine had to ask her first husband to corroborate which antiques and paintings had belonged to her before her marriage to Johnnie in order to persuade the Spencers. 'I went back to Althorp with Raine before the funeral service', says Peter Constandinos, 'and Raine wanted to go up to her room. They agreed and someone was stationed outside to check that Raine didn't leave with anything. But what they had forgotten (or didn't know) was that Raine and Johnnie's rooms were adjoining so we simply walked through the connecting door into Johnnie's room, took some more of her things which were laying around and packed them into my hairdressing bag. We then left again through Raine's room and no one was any the wiser. It was a great shame that she wasn't allowed the time and dignity to remove her own things without the pressure.'

Charles Spencer made no secret of how he felt about Raine in his book, *Althorp: The Story of an English House*:

Immediately after my father's death Raine appeared at Althorp armed with stickers to be stuck with prominence to all the things in the house that were hers. It was the grimmest tour of the house I had ever undertaken; reaching a crescendo at the end when Raine handed over the catalogues of chattels dating from Grandfather's time with the words 'You'll find a lot of these are missing. Still you have more than most people, so don't complain.'

The only person from the family who seemed to be in control of their emotions at the funeral of the 8th Earl Spencer, held on 1 April 1992, was the widow herself. Raine, looking utterly composed if pale, stood straight backed and smiling in a black Hardy Amies wool skirt-suit, black stockings and shoes, her hair piled high around a black pillbox hat, her white gloved hands clutching a black leather Lachasse handbag. Was she wearing a vast brooch of starburst diamonds above her heart that Johnnie had given her, or one of her favourite pieces of costume jewellery from Butler and Wilson? Whichever it was, the overall effect was one that Johnnie would have approved: dignified, chic and quietly confident. Stoically she glided between groups of guests and stood supportively beside a tearful, Chanel clad Princess of Wales and her sisters in the damp chilly atmosphere of the churchyard at the Spencers' local parish church, the thirteenth-century St Mary the Virgin in Great Brington, a few miles from Althorp, as the coffin processed from the church.

The new Earl looked depressed as his wife Victoria, newly pregnant with twins, stood sobbing silently by his side. A devastated Charles was apparently unable to read the lesson, leaving the task instead to his brother-in-law, the Queen's private secretary, Robert Fellowes. 'Birds twitter and peck in their nests, even when they are gilded ones in the media eye' said family friend Lord St John of Fawsey, who delivered the eulogy, 'but love is not so easily disarmed'.[1] Really? The funeral was notable for two things, the coldness of the

Spencers towards Raine (although one newspaper report had Diana and Raine arm and arm – friends dispute this) and the lack of attentiveness of Prince Charles towards his grieving wife. The couple, who were by now living apart, had arrived separately and, directly after the service, the Prince took a helicopter back to Buckingham Palace to attend to 'pressing business'. The next day the papers would be full of what commentators saw as Charles's dereliction of husbandly duty, alongside pictures of the grieving family and wreaths from the Queen and Prince Philip, the Queen Mother and the Princess of Wales. It was the Princess's handwritten note attached to her flowers which was front and centre: 'I miss you dreadfully Darling Daddy, but will love you forever' it read. A similar envelope, placed on an arrangement of flowers and addressed simply 'Mummy', would capture a grieving public's imagination five years later.

The Princess had more than the death of her beloved father to worry about. The clock was ticking on the time bomb that was to be the publication of the sensational book *Diana: Her True Story* by Andrew Morton, with whom she had co-operated. The book would divulge details on the heir to the throne's ongoing affair with Camilla Parker Bowles and the Princess's suicide attempts, bulimia and self-harming. Whilst she cannot have been aware of the catastrophic damage the book would do to the royal family, Diana must have had an inkling and she would have been counting on the man she loved most in the world – her father – for support.

As the party moved off to follow the coffin, which was topped by a huge bouquet of yellow spring flowers, to a service of private cremation at Towcester crematorium, Raine, supported by her children, flashed a small, brief smile to the waiting press pack. She had told friends that she did not wish for the funeral to be a sad day because 'Johnnie hated people to be gloomy'. It was a testament to her determination and her own personal strength that she managed to make it through to the end of the day without breaking down. 'That', says a friend, 'was simply not Raine's style. She knew that the eyes of the world were upon her and she also didn't want to let herself down for Johnnie's sake. Her grieving she did in private.'

The family presented a much more united front some weeks later at Johnnie's memorial at St Margaret's Church Westminster, on 29 May, so much so that photographs of Diana and her two children hugging and kissing Raine featured in most of the newspaper coverage. Prince Charles, who also attended, was said to have penned an extensive letter of condolence to Raine and their friendship was to continue for the rest of her life. During the service, Robin Leigh-Pemberton, Governor of the Bank of England, gave the address, managing only to draw greater attention to the family rift by saying 'I take this opportunity to say that there was never a split'. One of the hymns, 'I vow to thee my country', was notoriously a favourite of the Princess's since schooldays – she had chosen it to be played at her wedding. All of Raine's family were present, including Barbara Cartland swathed dramatically in black, looking like a grieving widow herself. Charles Spencer, who had overseen the memorial service, sat at the front of the church with his wife Victoria, his sisters and their mother. On the other side sat Raine, resplendent in a black and white Hardy Amies suit, with an enormous wide brimmed black hat and fire engine red lips, sur-rounded by her own children. Royals in attendance included the Duke and Duchess of Kent and Princess Alexandra with Sir Angus Ogilvy. 'He would have loved it', Raine triumphantly announced to the waiting press as the last guest left, before making her way back to Farm Street from where she planned to focus on rebuilding her life.

Meanwhile, Charles Spencer was losing no time in re-making Althorp to his own specifications. 'There was a massive house staff of fourteen many of whom had had little to do in the previous years except form cliques and bicker', Charles writes of that time. 'It would be fair to say then that in 1992 I inherited Althorp in a state that none of my ancestors would have recognised.' He goes on endlessly and implicitly criticising Raine, describing the house as 'candy floss pink or flock wall-papered like a Balti house', he talks of the 'shrieking over gilding' and the 'embarrassing tartiness' of chairs and sofas and claims that 'through a failure to grasp even the most basic lessons of book keeping the house . . . was running at a loss of over £400,000 per year'.[2]

With the blame laid successfully at his stepmother's feet, it is little wonder that she told friends – and anyone else who would listen – that she never wanted to set foot in Althorp again. In July she went so far as to release a statement to the Press Association: 'As far as I am concerned my life at Althorp is finished. I do not want to say any more about my life there, now or ever. I am a widow and I would be grateful if the press would leave me alone to rebuild my life.' The statement was less than convincing. Raine was deeply distressed and in putting on a 'brave front' she allowed the press to use her comments as evidence for everything that she was trying to deny. 'It shows that the public display of togetherness shown by Earl Spencer's children towards Raine at his funeral . . . after his death last March was nothing more than a sham' pronounced the *Daily Mirror*.[3]

There were few who knew the family history who would argue with the *Mirror*'s sentiments and even fewer who expected never to see or hear from Raine again. This was the age of gossip columns and salacious front pages, a time when the newspaper industry was booming and press barons like Rupert Murdoch, Robert Maxwell and Tiny Rowland were still coming into their own. The year before Johnnie's death, in 1991, a computer programmer named Tim Berners-Lee had introduced the World Wide Web and the concept that information could be globally and immediately available to users was still very much in its infancy. If anything, 1992 was the year of the 'red top': 11 April saw the iconic headline: 'It Was The *Sun* Wot Won It', suggesting that the paper and its readers had anointed the Conservative government by providing them with their fourth successive victory.

But politics did not sell newspapers (the *Sun* only ended its forty-four-year 'tradition' of topless Page 3 girls in 2015). Controversy and prurience sold: entitled aristocrats, badly behaved politicians and drunken celebrities were all grist for the mill. And that mill was ardently, avidly, unrepentantly misogynist. Male journalists like Margaret Thatcher's former press secretary Bernard Ingham or the celebrated 'gossips' Nigel Dempster and Ross Benson seemed unable to accept that women could behave as men did and 'get away with it', which is why they very often didn't. Female columnists like Jean Rook, Lynda Lee-Potter and Mary Kenny, often referred to as 'The Wednesday Witches', were in the main little better, taking delight in the downfall of women cleverer, more successful, richer, more popular, more aristocratic (the list goes on) than they. Rook famously provided the template for *Private Eye*'s satirical hack: 'Glenda Slag'. The 'witches' readership, mainly women, lapped it up. Never was this more evident than with the separation and divorce of the Prince and Princess of Wales and – by an association from which she would never rid herself – Raine.

'Di's father leaves £89m . . . but why was it not more?' Asked one newspaper after the reading of Johnnie's will. 'The sum involved is really quite tiny. I was expecting it to be 200 million', exclaimed the lofty Harold Brookes-Baker,[4] publisher of Burke's Peerage. Brookes-Baker failed to point out that the value of the entire estate was certainly in excess of £200 million if the house and its grounds were included. In any case, figures in cases such as this were often fudged by accountants and lawyers in an attempt to mitigate against a vast death duty bill. The will provided yet again the opportunity for the airing of dirty linen, particularly Raine's, in public. Whilst she did not comment on the will, Raine was entitled to feel vindicated by its instructions. As the newspapers so faithfully recounted, Johnnie had left her: cash and investments held by Global Asset Management believed to amount to somewhere in the region of £6 million, an annuity of £10,000, also specified were an ivory inlaid travelling box, three stools and a writing table all originally from Althorp and hers until her death. She was also left the two Bognor homes and their contents together with their Mayfair home and contents. Johnnie also revealed a rather bizarre hobby, leaving his collection of Third Reich postcards to his grandson Alexander Fellowes. His daughters were left a memento each to be chosen by his trustees and his grandchildren were awarded £1,000 each. If it seems strange that a man as wealthy as Johnnie should only leave 'trinkets' to his daughters. Such remains the antiquated feudal ruling of primogeniture, whereby an estate and wealth passed directly to the eldest son and heir, the assumption being that any daughters would and should have made 'good' marriages of their own. Although if Johnnie had already given Diana 'between half and a million pounds' as he had confessed to Brian Vine, one could be pretty sure he'd done the same for his other two daughters. When Charles Althorp dies, he has said that his estate will pass directly to his fourth born, Viscount Louis, rather than his first born, Lady Kitty Spencer.

Neither male nor female journalists could fathom why Raine, an intelligent, wealthy, successful female – a countess twice over, once divorced and now widowed – would not, to borrow the words which would be memorably uttered in 1995 by her stepdaughter, 'go quietly' and live a life of sober seclusion. But then why should she? A devout non-apologist who had said many times that her motto was 'never complain never explain', she was determined to live the rest of her life as she chose, which happened to be, once she had finished grieving, fairly outrageously: 'Raine absolutely did not believe in looking back, life was for now and for living to the utmost', says Michael Cole. She'd already told friends that she confidently expected to marry once more. It had been Johnnie himself who had commented that she'd be 'hopeless as a widow'.

In February 1993, Raine arrived to fanfare in Palm Beach, Florida, the winter playground (alongside Aspen) of America's richest men and women. She was the guest of her great friend Anne Fisher, wife of the shoe magnate Jerome (co-founder of Nine West shoes) and was staying at their 35,000 square foot mansion. Palm Beach welcomed her – as she perhaps had never been welcomed before – as bona fide royalty. 'Practice those curtseys and dust off that tiara' the *Palm Beach Daily News* exhorted its readers, informing them that Raine had arrived. Diplomat and socialite Francis Kellogg, seventy-five, squired her to a garden party, whilst at the glittering Bal des Arts – the event of the Palm Beach season – she danced with her host Jerome Fisher and giggled with her new pal, ex actress and fellow Brit, Celia Lipton Farris, one of the world's wealthiest women and owner of the palm tree fringed Lakeview House, nicknamed the 'glam pad' or 'the other Versailles'.

Her appearance as 'the merry widow', as one sniper put it, ignited the gossip columnists again – how dare a sixty-something grieving woman be seen to be enjoying herself in the company of powerful, wealthy men and women, and in an Eden-like setting surrounded by the crème de la crème of the world's most powerful nation? Nigel Dempster trumpeted a scoop in the *Daily Mail*, malice dripping from his keyboard, sniping that Raine was being courted by Kellogg, 'even though it is only eight months since Earl "Johnnie" Spencer died'. 'She has jetted about here and there', he scolded, as if Raine should have been interred with Johnnie or at least shut herself in her bedroom for the remainder of her life. The announcement provided yet another excuse for a run through of all the old Raine tropes – the titles, the wealth, the mother, the destruction of Althorp. 'She is pretty but not dramatically beautiful, bright but not academic and neither of her husbands made special mention of her cooking' bleated Dempster.

Never mind, because Raine didn't. She just continued having fun, travelling widely, cruising with Greek billionaire widower and friend of Prince Charles, John Latsis; visiting friends like retired hotelier Douglas Barrington, attending openings, parties and social events. Now that she was rid of the Spencer children, she spent more time with her own: Rupert was by now a married novelist with two children, whilst she also visited with Charlotte, married to Duca Don Alexander Paterno Castello di Carcaci and living in Milan.

Shortly after the Dempster column appeared, Ross Benson, Gordonstoun-educated *Daily Express* diarist scooped him by revealing that Raine was now on the arm of Italian lawyer, Count Carlo Colombotti, 'fondly known as Carlo the Dish', and later rumoured to be the consort of Naomi Campbell's mother. Less than a month later the intrepid Fleet Street grandee Benson had another scoop: he had spotted Raine 'widow of the Princess of Wales's father', entering upmarket lingerie store Janet Reger. Having had it confirmed that Raine was a customer by Aliza Reger, Janet's daughter, Benson went on to pass censure 'Raine Spencer is 63. The Mind Boggles'.[5] Did it? One wonders what Benson, who died in 2005, might have made of another columnist passing judgement on the lingerie choices of his then wife, editor of *Majesty* magazine, Ingrid Seward. Better still, what about a female writer condemning Benson's age and his underwear? In the nineties, the male dinosaur, in all of his foul-breathed, small-brained, big-footed, reptilian glory dominated the newsprint canyons of Fleet Street, Wapping and Kensington. Some might say they still do.

Raine met Comte Jean-François Pineton de Chambrun, direct descendant of the Marquis de Lafayette, hero of the American revolution and co-author of *The Declaration of the Rights of Man* and *The Citizens* (which he based on the American constitution), at a dinner thrown by mutual friends in Monte Carlo in early 1993. She was rumoured to be in Monaco secretly visiting Prince Rainier. If this was true, then nothing would come of it after she met Jean-François: 'It was love at first sight', he said. She was, in the first instance, more reticent, although she cannot have been insensible to the charms of a very good-looking man: slim, fit, tanned, six years her junior (with a full head of glossy brunette hair and the prerequisite perfect nose) who hailed from one of France's most established families. With a title and a chateau in Southern France, Jean-François was exactly what the doctor ordered. But he was also the father of two children and Raine, cognisant of the implications, held back. 'I tried so hard with those Spencers and I cannot go through that again', she later told Valerie Grove in *The Times*,[6] adding that she had stipulated that she was not prepared to be a mistress. Not to be deterred, in fact seemingly encouraged, Jean-François, the owner (at that time) of a high-tech water treatment business for fish farms,[7] flattered and pursued Raine, via telephone, faxing her love letters and calling her his 'Reine Raine'. She hinted that their relationship had been consummated in Antibes, 'well at our age no one would think we had just held hands', and when, twenty-five days later at a candlelit dinner in Paris, he proposed, she said yes.

'I feel like I have been struck by lightning' was Jean-François' Gallically gallant response to press interrogation, once the engagement had been announced. The event had been expertly stage managed by the bride-to-be who understood all too well the imperative to get 'ahead' of the news in order to control her own agenda. On 10 May 1993, the engaged couple introduced themselves to the world when they appeared for a photo call outside Farm Street. Raine, looking soigné in an uncharacteristic black bouclé suit trimmed with white, was instantly hailed as a beacon of hope for the 'older woman'. 'What you give out you get back like a boomerang', she said when pushed for a message to women in a similar position, extending her hand, upon which shone a diamond engagement ring, to exemplify matters. The bride had already designated the S. J. Phillips ring as 'the one' long before she met 'the one' – she'd seen it whilst visiting her friends the Nortons and perspicaciously earmarked it, for her third engagement – should the opportunity ever arise.

Few other women, if any, would ever find themselves in a 'similar position' to Raine, as the press frenzy which mounted throughout the week proved. On Tuesday, the *Daily Mail* published a one-page story with the headline 'Raine just can't live without a man'. By Wednesday, Dame Barbara had been prevailed upon to give comment, which was characteristically inappropriate: 'The French are not faithful. You wake up in the morning and you think: "What kind of girl will he go off with?"'

This blatant negativity was given some counterweight by the evidence of royal approval. The Princess of Wales, Raine confided, had bumped into the couple in Claridge's and offered her warm congratulations. Later she'd sent flowers and a hand-written note. An onlooker in the same restaurant noted that the friendliness between Raine and Diana was at odds with their public reputation as sworn enemies. And in fact, whilst she was keeping it to herself, Raine had begun seeing the Princess every few weeks for lunch to offer sanguinity and support on the upcoming royal divorce. Not to be outdone, the Prince of Wales had apparently already met Jean-François when, as Raine told the press, they had motored down to Highgrove for Sunday lunch the weekend before.

Jean-François looked awfully good on paper (and in photographs). Tall and debonair, he was the owner of the eighteenth-century Chateau de Garibondy, a three-storey turreted mansion on a hillside overlooking the Mediterranean Bay of Cannes, with sweeping gardens and an azure-blue tiled swimming pool. He was divorced from American/French heiress Josalee Douglas (presented at Les Bal des Debutantes in Paris 1964 and niece of the US Ambassador to the UK). He had two daughters, who were by all accounts polite, charming and unlikely to present the kind of challenge offered up by the Spencer children.

Was this the sort of good news story the papers loved to run, offsetting the most recent glut of terrible headlines – the tragic murder of the teenager Stephen Lawrence, the IRA bombing of Bishopsgate in the City of London and the fact that the Conservative Party was trailing Labour in the polls by sixteen points? Well, it definitely had legs – as Raine likely knew – and she wisely battened down the hatches for the rest of the week, barely moving from Farm Street and resisting further comment. She was probably already aware that Princess Angela Von Hohenzollern of Germany would surface (which she did on the Thursday of that week). The Princess, who was separated from Prince Carl Alexander Von Hohenzollern, first cousin once removed of Prince Michael and apparently dubbed by the German newspapers as 'the sexy twit' for his intellectual shortcomings. She was happily photographed, head to toe in white, holding a glass of champagne by her swimming pool in Cannes, declaring that Jean-François had proposed to her after just three dates and calling him 'an incurable romantic'. 'If I married everyone who proposed to me', she added without a hint of irony, 'I would never be out of church'.[8] According to the *Daily Express*, the Princess had once been the mistress of Von Hohenzollern's father and her credibility seemed far from assured.

Meanwhile Jean-François' two daughters distinguished themselves by behaving in precisely the manner Raine might have hoped, heaping warm praise on their stepmother-to-be, calling her a 'truly lovely kind woman'. 'They are just like teenagers' one of them declared of their father and his new fiancée. And then his former wife, Josalee Douglas, chimed in with her own good wishes: 'He was a good husband to me and I'm sure he will be a good husband to Raine', she said diplomatically.

By Saturday the papers had two other 'scoops': the brother of Jean-François, Charles de Chambrun, a former minister in the de Gaulle government, was revealed to be a supporter of the extreme right-wing politician and president of the National Front, Jean-Marie Le Pen. '[This] is bound to embarrass her', said one newspaper hopefully. It didn't. Neither did the other hints and claims that the Count was 'impecunious'. 'It was always accepted that when it was over, for it would be over, he would walk away with a nice settlement, which I believe he did', says Lady Colin Campbell. And why not? Raine was nothing if not fair and it was entirely plausible that she and Jean-François would have signed some kind of pre-nuptial agreement, although this was never confirmed.

What was clear was that Raine was a woman very much in love, so much so that she told the magazine *Paris Match* that she had conceded to Jean-François' wish that she go on a diet before her wedding: 'He demands that I weigh myself every day . . . it is extremely difficult because I am very greedy'. She lost 2 stone before the event but confided to writer Valerie Grove in a *Times* interview that her fiancé would still like to see 'another sliver off the derriere'. For some women this type of control would have been a warning sign, but for Raine, who had grown up in an environment wherein to please a man was all, her manic dieting, something which she had resisted her entire life, was simply a sign of fealty.

'Raine was rejuvenated by Jean-François. She brought him in to meet us and she was almost girlish in her happiness', says Michael Cole. Mohamed Al Fayed, who had been asked by Johnnie to 'take care of Raine if anything happens to me', counselled caution, 'be careful Raine', he said, 'take your time'. Raine had no intention of heeding anyone else's advice. 'In the words of the song she was simply "Mad About the Boy"', says Cole, 'and let's be clear: she certainly wasn't marrying him for his money.'

The couple were at every social event of the summer season, culminating in their appearance, hand in hand, on Ladies' Day at Royal Ascot with Raine in a daffodil yellow jacket and jaunty flying saucer hat and Jean-François in morning dress, clearly enjoying himself. The couple were guests of Raine's good friend, Lady Stevens of Ludgate. 'She was having fun and enjoying every moment of that romance', says Valerie Grove, of her meeting with the Countess for *The Times*. 'I adored her. When she held out her gloved hand, with her immaculately powdered face and her huge hair – she was the absolute, complete personification of herself.'[9] Having booked a suite at The Connaught Hotel within which to hold the interview, Raine welcomed Grove with the question guaranteed to engender from journalists, the world over, a warm glow of gratitude: 'Now, would you like a blow by blow?'

'She was definitely intent on getting out ahead of the story', says Grove, 'she knew what she was doing.' As Raine began to unburden herself and explain to the UK how and why she was marrying so swiftly and for the third time, a flunkey wheeled in a silver cart piled high with lavish luncheon delicacies. Grove soon found herself (as all journalists did interviewing Raine) being treated as a confidante and seduced by the force of her full attention. 'Of course she may have been pure poison in private', says Grove, 'and I'm not sure how it would have been to be her stepdaughter, but she was heaven.' Was she aware of what she was getting into? 'Oh yes. But then she lived the kind of life where you were constantly on the move – flitting across the surface – from Le Touquet to St Tropez.' Grove was enthralled too by Raine's particular intelligence: 'she was bright. She could recite lines from this and that but she'd also had the kind of upbringing whereby she'd learned to play the piano, paint watercolours and dress immaculately'.

Grove had a feeling too that Raine understood completely the unspoken (or perhaps even spoken) arrangement that had been struck between herself and her fiancé in return for their marriage certificate. 'I think she absolutely knew that he had not a bean to his name.' But it was Raine's actions at the close of the interview that astonished Grove and remained with her most vividly: 'she went around the room vigorously pummelling the cushions: "My mother" – biff, biff – "always said you must" –biff – "leave a room exactly as you" – biff, biff – "found it"'.

As if to underscore the need for financing, the couple had signed a deal with *Hello!* magazine to allow them to photograph the wedding exclusively. The royal family and the Spencers were said to be appalled by this blatantly commercial gesture, which as history now illustrates, was later to become all too commonplace amongst lesser royals with a 'name' and a desire for some ready cash. Inevitable carping in the press and jokes about the infamous 'curse' of *Hello!* magazine, whereby those featured were almost certain to be seeking their decree nisi before the magazine hit the newsstands, followed.

In *Paris Match*, that spring, not only had Raine astutely praised French design (she was after all soon to become a partial resident): 'I've been buying my clothes in France for 25 years because I'm a maniac for detail'. She had even defied tradition by allowing the magazine to photograph her in her Ungaro wedding dress before the ceremony. When *Paris Match* took pains to make the point that as a third son, the Count had no right to the title, which he had adopted regardless, Raine dismissed the accusation with a show of bravado: 'It doesn't matter. I would have married him even if he wasn't from an aristocratic family.'

Was it the overwhelming rush of love that blinded Raine to her husband-to-be's weaknesses? Was she aware that not only was he in debt, but that like every other stereotypical upper-class Frenchman of those times, Jean-François would also expect to carry on relations with his existing mistress, as well as his new wife? It was unlikely that she did not. She had always said she would marry again after Johnnie, and marry she would, no matter the consequences or circumstance. She was ready for yet another big adventure and the fates had presented it. Here was a handsome Frenchman, with whom she undoubtedly enjoyed some of the best sex of her life (at least she would hint at such to her friends), he had a title (purloined or not), a chateau and the ability to make her feel good – and she him. What was not to like? 'The glorious life-enhancing quality about Countess Spencer is that she doesn't care what other people think . . . You won't find her saying middle-aged women are anonymous or expect to get ignored by men. She demands adulation and total attention – and gets it', wrote Lynda Lee-Potter admiringly in the *Daily Mail*.[10]

The press did not need to wait long for yet another story: The day before the wedding, Parisian businessman Jacques Audier surfaced, revealing that a debt of fifteen years, owed by the Count and his politician brother Charles to Monsieur Audier, of £350,000 for a swimming pool business they had jointly purchased in 1979, had been almost entirely settled by a mysterious payment 'from England'. The brothers had been ordered to pay the money to M. Audier after a 1979 court ruling and he had been pursuing them fruitlessly ever since. Until now. 'I am very happy that I have got my money after fifteen years. I am also very happy that Raine and the Count are happy', said a delighted M. Audier.[11]

The scene outside Westminster Registry Office in Marylebone, on 8 July 1993, resembled more of a red carpet film première than a small, quiet, third wedding ceremony. Granted, the 1920s building formerly known as Marylebone Town Hall had been the location of some of London's most iconic weddings, including those of Sir Paul McCartney and then Sir Ringo Starr, but even the pre-requisite attendant 'Bobbies' stationed around the cordoned off front steps seemed surprised by the insistence of the surging press pack. Raine pleaded for space: 'please, please, let us through we just want a quiet wedding', she said, beaming graciously and waving her bouquet of red, yellow and white roses, which picked out the colours on the butterfly print of her dress. Her hair was traditionally and immaculately swept upwards and topped by a broad-brimmed black raffia hat. In her white pearls, vast gold earrings, white tights, and black patent shoes she looked like the star of a 1950s Hollywood film. He was dressed in an immaculate double breasted Savile Row suit with white shirt and navy patterned tie. Raine's weight loss was evident in her nipped in waist and her defined cheekbones, and they made for a sensationally urbane couple as the wedding pictures, in which Raine looks radiantly happy, illustrate.

The ecumenical wedding service two days later, was an altogether more formal affair: held at Holy Trinity Church, Cold Ashton, near Bath, the church where Rupert, Raine's second son, worshipped. The *Telegraph* dubbed it 'the summer's most flamboyant and public romance'. Certainly, the press and public attention outside the church (with only *Hello!* permitted inside) was acute. With some of France's top families in attendance, the women in bright block-coloured bouclé suits of yellow, red and white with wide brimmed hats, clutching Chanel quilted bags and the men in wing-collared morning dress, all streaming into the church alongside members of the British establishment (and an entirely pink attired Barbara Cartland), it made for an unusual spectacle. This was a village more used to hosting the 'meringue dress' attired brides of Britain's middle classes, who were still aping the Princess of Wales more than a decade on.

That Barbara turned up in her trademark cerise would not have come as a surprise to anyone but Raine, who had telephoned her mother weeks beforehand with a specific plea, which she repeated verbatim to her hairdresser Peter Constandinos. She called BC and asked: 'Mummy darling, as it's my third marriage, I can't possibly wear white, so I have this most beautiful pink dress to wear, so please Mummy darling, please choose a different colour to wear just this once, for me.' The Ungaro dress was by one of Raine's favourite designers and the cost was in the region of £20,000. That Raine still needed to plead with her mother for a favour, said everything about the sixty-three-year-old Countess's relationship with her ninety-three-year-old mother, who had recently been made a Dame of the British Empire for her literary, political and social contributions. The honour had been a long time coming and it was apparently granted after the Queen was prompted by Princess Margaret.

Dame Barbara's outfit was not the only issue: villagers complained of paparazzi invading their gardens, crowding the pavements and jostling locals out of the way in order to get the best shot. The bride, a traditional six minutes late, took her son Rupert's arm to walk up the gravel drive and into the church smiling beatifically in the warm July sunshine. Five minutes beforehand Jean-François had drawn laughter and cheers of encouragement from the onlookers as he paced anxiously, awaiting the arrival of the blue Rolls-Royce which conveyed his bride.

Inevitably Raine stole the show. Dressed in the riotously untraditional long Ungaro dress of pink and white flowers with lace bell undersleeves, accessorised with a matching pink pillbox hat and pearled pink short veil, diamond necklace and earrings and post-box red lips and nails, she was the epitome of the 'third time lucky' bride. She even garnered the front cover of the satirical *Private Eye* magazine – a dubious honour only granted to those 'important' and famous enough to lampoon. The front cover had possibly never before been granted to a third time bride, who was featured exiting the church on Jean-François' arm, with a speech bubble emitting the words: 'You only married me for my mummy'. Whilst she would have claimed not to have seen the cover, one can imagine Raine taking a sneak peek and giving a delighted chuckle at this acknowledgement of her level of relevance in late-twentieth-century Britain.

She had certainly been smiling throughout the service and as she walked back down the aisle with Jean-François on her arm, looking like the proverbial feline *qui a eu la crème*. Not everyone was convinced: 'to my mind it was rather an odd service, there we all were thinking it was unlikely to work, but keeping up the façade. And he (Jean-François) was winking at all the pretty girls as he came back down the aisle', says Lady Glenconner, who was in attendance.

Even the reception, which was held at the seventeenth-century Lucknam Park Hotel near Bath, would turn out to be controversial. The event itself, organised entirely by Raine and held in a vast cream marquee on the lawn where guests, seated at cream taffeta clad tables, sipped champagne and nibbled on canapes, passed off without a hitch. Later though, when the couple were living in France, a story that Jean-François was to be sued by the hotel for not settling his bill hit the British newspapers. There was speculation that Raine finally settled the account because she was finding Jean-François' inability to pay embarrassing. This might have been so, but the couple were doing a very good job at appearing to be the model of a modern continental partnership, flitting between the South of France, Paris and London.

Raine was immediately at work restoring the Chateau de Garibondy, which the couple planned to continue to rent out. And what of the Count? Well, he was . . . indulging himself in his twin passions. The two-week walking and climbing tour he embarked upon with Swiss friends just a month after the marriage sparked headlines in the British press, during what can only be described as a 'slow news month'. In response to the rumours Raine gave a statement: 'a husband and wife cannot be together every minute' she said pragmatically, adding 'people can say what they like, I just don't care'. On this point she was at least correct. But what she would never admit to was that she was already struggling with a life so far from family and friends. She worried that renovating the chateau would not be enough to keep her occupied and that French society was not as welcoming as she might have hoped or expected. Privately she was telling friends that Jean-François had already gone back to his mistress, who the papers had tapped as forty-five-year-old Nicole Bruggemann (this was never confirmed), something he had given her his word he would not do. He was also seemingly very keen to spend her money and was making noises about buying a new yacht.

Whilst these circumstances might have sunk or at least depressed a lesser woman, Raine was telling everyone that she considered herself enormously lucky: 'the weather is beautiful, I can have friends to stay, I have my health, everything else is a bonus' she would repeat like a mantra, when anyone enquired. She was making headway in the manner that only Raine knew how: getting things done. Determined to make herself useful she had offered her services to the Nice Council of Tourism, 'They said if I'd stand as a councillor they'd do their best to make me head of the tourism committee' she later said, 'Me! Une Anglaise!'[12] In fact she did rather better than that, ending up on two councils – the council of tourism and the council for the improvement of the Promenade des Anglais. 'I was told by that she was one of the most effective members they'd ever had' says Cole.

In pictures Raine looks the best she'd ever looked – two stones lighter she was dressing twenty years younger in the BCBG (bon chic bon genre) style adapted by French aristocrats and no doubt influenced by Jean-François, who was no slouch himself in the style department. Gone were the big taffeta skirts and flounces, instead Raine was photographed in neat shouldered, belt waisted dresses, fitted round necked three-quarter sleeved cashmere sweaters, pearls, narrow pencil skirts, dainty heels and Hermès scarves. In a shoot by Jean Claude Deutsch for *Paris Match* in October 1993, entitled 'Rendevous with Raine and Jean-François de Chambrun dans leur château' the pair appear for all the world like a modern-day Edward and Wallis Simpson, or Jack and Jackie Kennedy, beaming at each other playfully in the early autumn Côte d'Azur sunshine, strolling through the chateau grounds. The journalist, diarist and power broker Woodrow Wyatt records his impressions of Raine when he came across her at a dinner at the Berkeley Hotel: 'As we were going (we left rather late because we had drunk so much) I went over to the amazing woman, Raine Spencer, step-mother of Princess Diana, now married to a Frenchman and having a blissfully happy time. She says she is madly in love with him and has the best sex ever. She has been, though she looks very cool, a very hot piece indeed, and still is.' His view of Jean-François is rather less flattering: 'I thought her husband a fairly miserable looking fellow.'[13]

Within months reality took hold for Raine too: 'It became obvious that it wouldn't work within about a year' says an old friend of Raine and Johnnie's, 'and I think this was quite a setback for her. She really thought that once she set her mind to anything she could achieve it.' But being married to Jean-François was different. He was not devoted like Gerald, neither was he besotted like Johnnie: 'he achieved the impossible and got rid of Raine's "Cartland hips"', but once she couldn't bed him (because he'd returned to his mistress) 'she divorced him' says Peter Constandinos.

For a woman who lived in the present, Raine's divorce from Jean-François would be one of her few real regrets as she later admitted to Michael Cole: 'There we were at Nice Town Hall, about to be divorced in floods because we were both so unhappy, asking ourselves why we were parting when we loved each other'.

Friends had known there was something amiss the minute Raine was spotted back in London on what she termed 'a little break'. She told them she simply couldn't adjust to living in the South of France in what she saw as 'the country', without her London friends and nor, privately she confided, was she prepared to do what Jean-François wanted which was to hike in the mountains or spend time on his yacht. 'I think it was terribly hard for her that it didn't work out', says Anne Glenconner. And indeed Raine carried on for quite a while pretending that all was well. When they were in the UK together and staying at Farm Street, the pair put on a united front, visiting the opera, having lunches and dinners with old friends of Raine's and doing the same in Paris. Raine struck up a particularly close relationship with one of Jean-François' daughters, Elizabeth – one suspects she must have been delighted to have come upon a 'step' relationship that was far easier than the out and out hostility of the Spencer children. With the Spencers there was a history, with Elizabeth there was an opportunity for a fresh start: 'there was no one as wonderful to me as Raine' she told Cole after Raine's funeral.

By the time she had married Jean-François, Raine was already back in full on 'speaks' with the Princess of Wales, whose separation from Charles had been announced in December 1992. The olive branch had been extended from the Princess's side initially. Raine later admitted it was not something she would ever have done, not because of obstinacy, but because quite simply she thought that side of her life was over for good. In fact, it was during one of Raine's stays in Paris at the Ritz, where Mohamed Al Fayed's previous close friendship with Raine and Johnnie always guaranteed a warm welcome, that a hand-written letter with Kensington Palace letter-head was delivered. In it the Princess of Wales had invited her stepmother to lunch. Both women were still grieving the loss of

Johnnie. Despite misgivings, Raine accepted the invitation, curious but also guarded, reasoning that Diana must want or need something from her. It was unlike the Princess to meet even her closest of acquaintances (outside her immediate circle of friends) for a simple chat, let alone the woman whom she had christened 'Acid Raine'. But Diana seemed to want to feel closer to Johnnie via Raine: 'I was absolutely astonished by Diana's gesture and very touched by it', Raine later told Piers Morgan for the *Mirror*, speaking publicly about her friendship with the Princess for the first time in 1998. 'It was a complete surprise and because of it we became enormous friends.' By her own admission the women were 'initially a little bit wary of each other. But we became closer and closer'.[14]

Before she and Jean-François married, Raine had received another invitation from the Princess to lunch at Kensington Palace. The Princess had expressed that she was keen to meet the Count and Raine was delighted to be able to introduce him. It was early days in the reconciliation and the couple approached with caution. As they were seated, a jittery, light-hearted conversation about how Jean-François and Raine had met ensued. Uncharacteristically, Raine let Diana take the lead, which she did by announcing that she wanted to take the occasion of the couple's engagement to say something from the heart, which Raine recounted later to the journalist Piers Morgan as: 'Thank you for looking after my father. I know you loved him'. In a letter published by *The Times* on 13 July 1993, and written by Jean-François in defence of the two women's friendship, the Count confirms that statement and relates what happened next: 'Raine and HRH fell into each other's arms and they kissed goodbye in the most affectionate way'. It was a line that could have been penned by his mother-in-law (and with hindsight it possibly was). But no matter: 'It was Diana's way of saying sorry' Raine told Morgan. 'Jean-François was so moved by it he started crying.'

Weeping aristocratic Frenchmen aside, all three guests at the Kensington Palace luncheon were to benefit greatly from that afternoon's events: Raine and Diana from a cemented friendship which would develop into a quasi-mother–daughter relationship and Jean-François (whom the Princess of Wales nicknamed 'the healer' for his benevolent energy) who was destined to be forever remembered in the history books as the witness to this remarkable turnaround.

It is all too easy to speculate on the Princess's motives and con-venient to assume that she 'saw the light' where Raine was concerned. Whilst this could be true, many who knew both women suggest that there was an element of self-interest on both sides of the spec-tacular 'make-up'. The Princess was a woman who was about to be jettisoned from the Buckingham Palace bubble and for whom the future looked exceptionally uncertain. She'd burned bridges with friends, been thwarted in love and turned on many of her advisors and confidantes. She sorely missed the steadying influence of her father and continued to feud sporadically and spectacularly with her mother. After her notorious BBC interview with the now dis-credited journalist Martin Bashir, in which she exposed the fissures at the heart of the British Monarchy and insinuated that her hus-band, Prince Charles, the future King, was not up to the job, there was no going back. 'I don't think anyone understands the extent of the coldness towards Diana after the Morton book, the TV inter-view and her divorce – she was horribly shunned in court circles', says Lady Colin Campbell. 'She would walk into a room and it would fall silent. Backs would turn. I mean she was reduced to talk-ing to the likes of me and we were never, how shall I put it – "great friends"!' Raine provided the Princess with a link to the past and a discreet support mechanism for the future. 'Diana was often at Farm Street when I visited' says, Peter Constandinos, 'she would sit for hours in her father's study – she said she could sense that he was there somehow.' Raine welcomed the Princess's presence in the house: 'We both felt that each other was the only person with whom we could share John', she told Morgan.

Meanwhile Raine viewed the Diana reconciliation as only positive, telling friends that it made her enormously happy. After all, she reasoned, she needed some good news: after twenty-four months she and Jean-François had mutually and amicably agreed to part, but the situation had been complicated by the amount of her own money that Raine had sunk into the chateau renovations. She wasn't about to leave the marriage without her investment being returned. Constandinos remembers the scenario: 'she said to me "Peter darling everyone is telling me to get lawyers on the case to get my money back but once it's made public that we will divorce and it's known we have to sell the chateau the price will plummet"'. In the end she took Constandinos's advice to forget the solicitors and trust that Jean-François, who was promising to return her funds once the sale of the chateau went through, would be true to his word. He was.

By the time that the newspapers reported, in May 1994, that the chateau was up for sale and began to speculate about the marriage, the couple were already divorced. Although it was something of an open secret, the couple did not go public with the truth about their divorce until 1996. Their love and respect for one another continued, with Jean-François and his new wife often present at Raine's social gatherings. When he was in London visiting alone, the Count would stay with Raine, who was by then living in a large one-bedroomed flat in Grosvenor Square, where she had gilded the plaster cornices just as she had done at Althorp. She would often joke with Constandinos about their ongoing relationship – 'and you know Peter', she would giggle, 'that the flat only has one bed'.

10

Mother's Nature

———————•◆•———————

Raine's return to the British social scene in 1996 was notable in the main for two things: rampant press interest of an undoubtedly schadenfreude-esque nature and the frequency with which she and Diana were spotted together (also covered avidly by the newspapers).

Raine shrewdly gave one statement about her divorce to the press on 11 November 1996, standing on the doorstep at Farm Street looking immaculate and poised. She maintained the pretence – as did the newspapers – that she'd been living in France since 1993, whereas she'd actually spent more time in the UK than she had on the Côte d'Azur in the past forty-eight months. The papers kept their side of the bargain (it made for a better story this way) and faithfully reported that the marriage was over and Raine was returning to live in London. The *Express*, never a particular fan of Raine's, gave her the best PR she could ever have hoped for, splashing her across its front page with the headline: 'Divorced Raine is radiant but the Count is crushed'.[1]

It was true though, Raine looked terrifically poised. With her hair sculptured glossily, and a silk Hermès scarf at her throat, she looked every inch the continental countess. She was soon to drop 'de Chambrun' and revert to Spencer – as in Raine, Countess Spencer, a title to which she was not technically entitled because she had married again. Characteristically, she decided to adopt it anyway and, after early grumblings in the right-wing press, she would be known as Raine, Countess Spencer until her death. 'I have great affection for my former husband. I wish him every happiness', she told the reporters gathered at her door for comment, with a broad smile.

So as not to appear be too sympathetic after its glowing front page, the *Express* then ran, on page 48 of the same edition, a full-page article by Virginia Blackburn on Raine's failed marriage with the headline: 'If only Raine had listened to mummy'. The writer had turned once again to only one of two people who were ever willingly fulsome in their responses about Raine on the record – her mother (the other was Charles Spencer). BC, who had worked full-time herself since her teenage years, was nonetheless, fond of making deprecating remarks about women in employment. In this she sometimes included her daughter: 'the divorce rate is always the woman's fault. They go out and have careers and then the poor man comes home and there's no one to make him happy and look after him'.

The 'poor man' in this case, was, in tabloid parlance 'gutted'. And he was homeless. Pictured looking moribund aboard his yacht, which he informed friends and reporters was, after the sale of the Chateau de Garibondy, his 'life ' and his 'home', Jean-François was open about what had driven the couple apart. 'An example of our differences came one weekend when I told Raine that I was going hiking in the mountains. But she said she was having Mr So and so around for dinner. On that occasion I accepted that dinner was

more important but it made me think how different we were.'² It
was a heroic attempt to shift the spotlight from himself, but it was
more likely that he had been unable to keep his side of the marriage
bargain. And for Raine, loyalty was all.

Was Raine happy with the situation? She was certainly relieved
to be no longer living a lie. She was also delighted to be able to
socialise openly again in London, appearing on the arm of old
friend Robert de Stacpoole amongst others. Privately she despaired
of ever finding another mate: 'the men I'm drawn to are all taken
or gay' she complained to a friend. It was the beginning of a reconciliation that she would never marry again. 'Raine is a star of society
in England' Jean-François had said. But was she still? She was feeling the pressure of re-finding her feet and friends reported that she
was also putting them under pressure to 'host' weekend house parties for her, often ringing them not simply to invite herself, but also
offering a guest list of others she'd like to 'see'.

It was perhaps inevitable that Raine and Diana would ultimately
become great friends. Their paths, although different, had led them
ultimately to a very similar place. They were both living in a city
they loved without the man they loved most, both recovering from
broken hearts and unsure of what the future would hold. Both
women had reinvented themselves on numerous occasions, both
had been effectively outsiders in male-dominated infrastructures –
Raine in politics and Diana a victim of Palace mandarins not to
mention her husband's entourage. Both had suffered at the hands of
a misogynistic, male-dominated press (although it should be noted
that most female journalists hadn't been reticent in their venal
attacks on both women either).

The press liked them now though. As they lunched and dined
their way through the winter, spring and early summer of 1997
they were snapped at The Connaught and Claridge's, shopping
together at Harrods and attending parties such as the auction of the

Princess's dresses for charity at Sotheby's and a drinks party at the Russian embassy. Gossip columns disclosed to their readers such intimacies as: 'they called each other darling', 'Raine was the perfect person for the Princess to have in her corner to advise on the divorce', 'they spoke every day on the telephone'. Whilst all of these so-called 'facts' might have been true (and by all accounts they were) what really mattered to the Princess was discretion and Raine was and always had been the ultimate keeper of secrets – her own and those of her friends and family, whether she was on good terms with them or not. According to Paul Burrell, Diana and Raine would speak every morning towards the end of Diana's life and cards and gifts would fly back and forth between the two with extraordinary regularity. 'She would sit on my sofa and tell me her troubles'[3] Raine later admitted, although she went to her grave without disclosing a word. 'The Princess told me: I'd rather speak to Raine than to my mother. She is the mother I never had', writes Ingrid Seward.[4]

For all of her off-the-record briefings to journalists like Richard Kay of the *Mail*, the Morton book and *that* BBC Panorama interview, the Princess had plenty of matters that she still wanted kept under wraps. She'd never gone public about her relationship with Hasnat Khan, the so called 'dishy doctor' – a thirty-six-year-old heart surgeon at the Royal Brompton Hospital, although the papers had speculated on this since 1995, when Khan had first invited her to witness one of his open heart surgeries. The Princess was deeply in love with Khan, an emotion which was intensified by his apparent ambivalence regarding her fame and status. In fact, he ardently disliked any form of publicity and when Diana visited Lahore to stay with Jemima and Imran Khan and ended up taking tea with his extended family, it was a step too far. The papers had already prevailed upon Khan's father – also a doctor – to give them a quote: 'He is not going to marry her . . . we are looking for a bride for him . . . She must belong to a respectable family . . . preferably to our own relations or tribe, which is Pathan . . . She should be at least a Pakistani Muslim girl.'[5]

When Raine once more re-entered Diana's life full-time, the Princess was desperately in need of a shoulder to cry on. She had been devastated not by the divorce from Prince Charles itself, which was made 'absolute' on 28 August 1996, but more from the loss of her HRH title, which, although she put a brave face on it, had underlined the fact that she had all but been forcibly ejected from that 'bloody family', as she had once referred to the Windsors. Now she had to fend for herself. On attending the preview for the Christie's New York auction of her dresses in aid of The Royal Marsden hospital in June 1997, the lack of her HRH title suddenly hit home when she realised to what degree it exposed her to less than exalted treatment. 'It was awful', she told a friend, 'so familiar'. She was grieving three times over for the loss of the bedrocks in her life: for her father, for her rapidly diminishing relationship with Khan and for any semblance of the mother–daughter relationship which might still have existed between herself and Frances Shand Kydd.

Shand Kydd appeared to be going out of her way to antagonise her daughter. Not only had she been publicly critical of her daughter's relationship with Khan (in return Mohamed Al Fayed would later accuse her of being racist and a snob), Diana regarded her as untrustworthy. She told friends that her mother was drinking too much: Shand Kydd had been banned from driving in 1996 after being stopped near her home, in Oban, Scotland, on 6 April with 2.5 times the legal amount of alcohol in her blood. During her trial it emerged that the morning of the offence she had received a letter 'from someone' containing distressing news which had caused her to cry all day. Was the letter from Diana as some speculated? Maybe, but it was more in the Princess's style to ignore letters and return them unopened, than to write poison missives herself. Even during her worst times with Raine, Diana had persuaded school friends to send Raine anonymous hate mail rather than putting her own pen to paper.

Diana had consciously widened the mother–daughter gulf between herself and Frances by excluding her from Prince William's confirmation on 9 March 1997. Instead Shand Kydd had paid for a notice in the newsletter of the St Columba's Catholic Cathedral, Oban, 'For my grandson William on his confirmation day, love from Granny Frances'. She then agreed to two interviews on subsequent weeks with *Hello!* magazine, the proceeds of which would also go to St Columba's Cathedral. She told *Hello!* that her daughter's loss of her HRH title was 'absolutely wonderful' because it would allow her to establish her own identity. If she was trying to be supportive, she failed. Her daughter was incensed by her remarks, and failed to return any further letters or phone calls from her mother.

Raine had proved herself to be the consummate keeper of secrets. She had rarely (other than the notorious Rook and Vine interview and her later interview with *Times* journalist Valerie Grove) given her opinions on the Spencer children publicly, nor had she spoken out about their treatment of her after Johnnie's death. Her ability to remain aloof, detached, but always smiling and gracious impressed the Princess; even more so now that she was confiding in her step-mother on a daily basis. There were few other close friends or family with whom she could speak in confidence: 'She would not speak with Jane – her marriage to Robert Fellowes – by then the Queen's private secretary, made her untrustworthy, she had made up with her brother Charles, but that rapprochement after he'd withdrawn his offer to her of a house on the Althorp estate, was fairly recent. There was only Sarah to trust' says a friend. And Sarah lived in Lincolnshire, the wife of a landowner, with three children – she was not always available for cosy tête-à-têtes or as a party 'partner'.

Raine was fun, she was upbeat and optimistic, she knew how to navigate forwards skilfully – away from her past and into her future – and the Princess was more than happy to be borne along on the same tide. 'Raine absolutely hated negativity, and living in the present as she did, she never bothered with past quarrels or difficulties. In fact, I do not remember her saying something nasty about anyone', says Julian Fellowes.[6]

The two women also had another man in common: Prince Charles, with whom Raine continued to be friendly and with whom Diana was anxious to maintain their recently achieved, hard won, uneasy truce. Raine's wisdom on that relationship and much more would prove invaluable. She was and always had been of the opinion that maintaining a cordial relationship with one's ex was critical to a harmonious life. As such she never failed to be positive about Gerald and she and Jean-François would remain friends up until the time of her death. She was instrumental in persuading Diana that she should be positive about Charles whenever possible, and it was rumoured that the Prince had begun to drop in on Diana occasionally for tea at Kensington Palace. 'Raine's influence was certainly steadying and influential in that direction and I think the Palace knew it' says a friend.

Conversely, Raine would have as much to thank Diana for. It had been the Princess who had helped her through her divorce from Jean-François and later it would be Diana who would suggest to their mutual friend Mohamed Al Fayed that he hire Raine as a director at Harrods because: 'Mohamed, this woman can organise *anything*'.

The Spencers' friendship with Mohamed Al Fayed had long been the subject of nasty, barely veiled racism on behalf of the British establishment and the press. Johnnie's lifelong love affair with Harrods had extended to him filing all of his personal papers in the white paper Food Halls shopping bags with their gold signature logo, where they were found after his death. The couple had first met Al Fayed whilst staying at the Ritz in 1985 when they were invited to meet the new owner of Harrods. The Spencers' friendship with the Al Fayeds had never wavered since, despite public hostility towards the man who owned not just the famous department store, but also the House of Fraser chain and the London football club, Fulham FC. Raine and Johnnie were stalwart supporters and would happily turn up for events, give speeches and open new ventures. Later Raine and Rupert would appear in the directors' box for Fulham at home games, chauffeured there and back in the Rolls.

That Al Fayed had never received a passport in spite of having four children in the UK, employing thousands of people and paying millions of pounds in tax spoke to a number of issues that the so-called 'Establishment' had with the Egyptian businessman, and he with them. Having been embroiled in a Department of Trade and Industry inquiry (1987–89) over his takeover of Harrods in 1985 and then the rest of the House of Fraser Group (at the insistence of Lonrho boss Tiny Rowland, who held 29.9 per cent of the Group's shares), Al Fayed had revealed in 1994 to a Parliamentary Inquiry, that ministers had been paid by him to ask questions on behalf of Harrods during the Lonrho controversy. Two cabinet ministers, Neil Hamilton and Tim Smith, were fired as a result of the 'cash for questions' scandal. Critics said Al Fayed's disclosures were a tit-for-tat response to the rejection of his citizenship application. They were wrong, says Cole, who notes the application was rejected 5 months after the scandal and not before. Al Fayed blamed Tiny Rowland and the DTI inquiry for his thwarted attempts to gain a British passport.

And then there were the additional allegations of arms dealing, when Jonathan Aitken, the then Tory Minister of State for Defence Procurement, and Chief Secretary to The Treasury at that time, was outed by Al Fayed and the *Guardian* as having had his room at the

Ritz paid for by Prince Mohammed of Saudi Arabia. Was it a coincidence that Prince Mohammed's intermediary just 'happened' to be staying at the hotel at the same time as Aitken? Probably not. Aitken was jailed for eighteen months for perjury and perverting the course of justice.

In 1999, the then Home Secretary Jack Straw would again decline Mohamed's passport application. So, was it personal? If it wasn't then we have to assume that the British Government didn't mind seeing three of its own – all be they Conservatives – taken down by the Egyptian owner of what had once been a thoroughly British institution. And that seems unlikely.

When Al Fayed sent round a year's contract for Raine to become a director of Harrods International she could hardly believe it. 'I thought he was joking', she said, 'Happily he wasn't.'[7] That Al Fayed felt a level of responsibility towards Raine was unquestionable – he was fond of saying that Johnnie had asked him to take care of her and to keep an eye on his children if anything happened to him. But he was also no idiot. Whilst he realised that Raine desperately needed a challenge to engage her at this new stage in her life, he recognised that with her connections and societal position, she could be an asset to the store. At the time, she was slowly getting back into the swing of London life, lunching, going to openings and working as a volunteer one day a week for stroke victims. She had her collection of 'walkers' (mainly gay says a gay friend who played that role) – male friends, mostly from the rarefied worlds of high-powered banking, politics, design, art and antique dealing happy to accompany her to parties, openings, the theatre or the opera without attachment. Her girlfriends were few, but loyal.

She didn't spend much time thinking over Mohamed's offer. She didn't need to. Ever the optimist, she saw an opportunity and grabbed it. Not everyone agreed that it would work. When she arrived at the store at the staff entrance on Basil Street in her

Rolls-Royce, chauffeured by the redoubtable Brian, the managing director was unmoved. 'He said, "Well it is all very well Mohamed giving you a job, but I don't know what to do with you".'[8] She figured it out for herself, quickly becoming an asset, working with high-net-worth customers and forging new sponsorship and partnership deals at Harrods International, the arm of the business which dealt with the store's interests at British and foreign airports and overseas. 'The person who knew the facts and figures in every business deal was Raine', says her friend, interior designer Philip Vergeylen, who met Raine via a deal Harrods were doing with American Express where he was marketing director, 'she was incredibly impressive.'[9]

On the afternoon of Friday 29 August 1997, Raine called in to see her friend Michael Cole in his Harrods office. She regularly swung by for what she would have no doubt termed a 'cosy chat'. Cole's office was on the fifth floor, two doors down from Al Fayed's, and his door was always open. 'Raine never gossiped', he says, 'she imparted information she had gleaned.' This particular Friday, Cole was a very busy man. Diana was in the throes of what seemed to be a full-blown love affair with Mohamed Al Fayed's son, Dodi, which was playing out on a global stage thanks to the paparazzi. The press coverage was reaching fever pitch as the couple were pictured cruising around the Mediterranean together in Mohamed's yacht, *Jonikal*, on their third vacation together.

When Raine popped in to Cole's wall papered comfortable 'clubby' office with its flame stitched sofa and winged easy chair, they did not discuss the press storm, despite the fact that they were both intimately acquainted with both players; rather they chatted about Raine's weekend, which was to be spent with a female friend who owned a Palazzo on the Grand Canal in Venice. Before leaving, in a move which was completely out of character, Raine took a piece of paper from Cole's desk and wrote down the details of where she'd be staying in Venice 'just in case' she told Cole. 'It was not something she ever did and it struck me at the time as being unusual, but I put the paper in my briefcase and thought nothing more of it', he says before he bid Raine a good weekend and returned to dealing with the barrage of press calls which were besieging his office.

The relationship between Dodi, Al Fayed's son from his first marriage in 1956 to Samira Khashoggi, and Diana, had been kindled thanks to an initial invitation from Al Fayed for Diana, William and Harry to holiday with him and his family at their villa in the south of France. The invitation had been extended during a post-performance dinner at the Churchill Hotel on Portman Square, for the English National Ballet's new production of *Swan Lake* (sponsored by long term supporter Harrods). Raine had been positive about the invitation. Diana, she had reasoned, needed somewhere fun to take the boys, which had all of the necessary security they would require.

Diana, who was feeling the pressure to compete with the traditional royal family holiday at the Queen's 50,000-acre Balmoral Estate, had been weighing up the options of a vacation on her friend Teddy Forstman's yacht, a stretch in The Hamptons, Long Island, or returning to an island off the Thai coast she had visited and loved in the past. Ultimately she had dismissed all options on security grounds. Might Al Fayed's villa, situated on a private estate outside St Tropez, with its hot and cold running staff, Al Fayed's security team and her own private guest villa be the answer? She called Cole to understand what exactly would be on offer and he had passed on what he knew of the property, which ostensibly had all of 'the toys' that her two young sons might enjoy – a pool, two yachts, a speedboat and jet skis. Finally, she checked with the palace (otherwise known as Prince Charles) and to her surprise, the go-ahead was given. In addition to Al Fayed's own security service, two Scotland Yard security officers would accompany the Princes.

The background to the Al Fayed vacation, the acceptance of which surprised even her closest of friends (of which there were increasingly few with whom she remained on speaking terms) was the Princess's deep depression over the recognition that Hasnat Khan would never marry her. Ironically it was ultimately her fame rather than her religion that made it impossible. Khan hated the limelight, the rumours and the inevitable lies and fabrication peddled by the press that came with any close association with Diana. Her fantasy that they would escape Britain together and live somewhere warm, both working on humanitarian causes, had manifested in her attempt to persuade the world-famous heart transplant specialist Professor Christiaan Barnard to employ Khan in South Africa, so that they could move there together. It was an idea which both medics could immediately see would never come to fruition. Diana's attempt to meddle in Khan's career, and a sudden spat of speculation in the press that the couple were already secretly engaged, destroyed any hopes that the relationship might continue long term. Khan began to withdraw. The knock-on effects of what looked to be almost certainly the beginning of the end of their relationship, contributed to a distressed Diana accepting an invitation which she might, it can be reasonably supposed, in other circumstances, have politely declined.

The sight of the future King of England alongside his younger brother, and the world's most famous woman holidaying alongside one of Britain's most notorious multi-millionaire 'shop keepers', had been almost too much for the British establishment and the general public to bear. 'Di gets it wrong again' blared one headline. Thanks to the tabloids the world watched their every move: Mohamed Al Fayed with his arm around the Princess, her arm on his shoulder, Diana racing across the bay on a Jet-ski with Harry, executing a perfect swan dive with William. And then came a bizarre impromptu ten-minute 'press conference' given aboard a motor dingy moored next to a launch carrying photographers and reporters from media outlets which included the *Daily Mail* and the *Mirror*, with a swimsuit clad Diana telling the press, 'You are going to get a big surprise with the next thing I do.' Hinting that she was planning to leave the country, she motored back to the Al Fayed villa leaving the journalists astounded and speculating wildly. And then came the first appearance of Dodi, who had arrived from Paris and was staying on board a yacht with Calvin Klein underwear model, Kelly Fisher, who it turned out later had pre-supposed herself engaged to Dodi.

That Diana believed herself to have fallen in love with the forty-two-year-old playboy is hard to dispute. The evidence was writ large in the letters that were later made public by the Paget enquiry, written to him on Kensington Palace letterhead, addressed to 'Darling Dodi', and the fact that she had, by their third holiday together, made a gift to him of her father's gold cufflinks, something which after her two boys, were possibly most precious to her:

> Dear Dodi, these cufflinks were the very last gift that I
> received from the man I loved most in the world – My Father
> – They are given to you as I know how much joy it would
> give him to know they are in such safe and special hands.
>
> Fondest Love
> From Diana x

Did Dodi have any idea of what he was getting himself into? It seems unlikely. By all accounts he was a gentle soul, indulged, unworldly and very much in the thrall of his powerful father. His most notable role had been as an executive producer of the Oscar-winning 1981 film *Chariots of Fire*. Producer Lord Puttnam told the *Daily Mail* in 2012 that he'd thrown Dodi off the set for trying to supply a cast member with cocaine and he was not exactly complimentary about his EP skills either: 'He had the attention span of the average flea', MailOnline quoted him as saying.[10] Dodi knew a beautiful woman when he saw her though and Diana was undeniably gorgeous. In the face of Khan's rejection and in the aftermath of her divorce she was skittish and needy – even more so after her friend Gianni Versace was murdered in Miami on 15 July 1997. It was at this point that she turned to Dodi for solace, something which, with time and funds at his disposal and possessed of an empathy and compassion devoid in most British men she knew (but which Khan had also possessed in spades) he was more than equipped to provide. On 25 August 1997, *People* magazine in the USA ran a front-page story: 'A Guy For Di?' it asked, ' . . . Is he a dreamboat or a deadbeat?'

By the time Raine headed off to Venice on a British Airways early evening flight, Diana and Dodi were cruising into Porto Cervo in Sardinia, where they would disembark, stroll around the town and eat dinner in a local restaurant. 'They went unrecognised', reflects Cole, 'which was in itself at that point something of a miracle'. Cole packed up and headed out to his country home in Suffolk for the weekend, reasoning that since he was not in direct contact with Dodi, he was unable to confirm or deny any of the press enquiries. He remembers the Saturday for two things: the sultry late August heatwave and the spat he had with his wife, an event which was so out of character after a twenty-year marriage that it is still riven in his memory: 'it was an exhausting week with all of the Diana and Dodi furore', he acknowledges, 'and I may have been a bit bad tempered and ratty'. He took a number of further calls about the vacationing couple throughout the day, promising the press a response on Monday, and looked forward to a quiet Sunday.

Consigned to 'solitary' as he puts it, Cole sat up watching *Match of the Day* and then turned in, disgruntled and tired. His bedside telephone rang at about 12.45am. and he answered to hear a young Scottish reporter from the *Sunday Times* asking him about rumours of a car crash involving Princess Diana and Dodi Al Fayed. Cole understood but chose not to reply. He hung up, disturbed. As he swung his legs out of the bed, the phone rang again. This time it was Clive Goodman, Royal reporter for the *News of the World* – one of Cole's least favourite individuals. 'Is it true about the crash?' he demanded. Cole's recollection is that fury overtook him, jolting him fully awake: 'There's been a car crash in Paris' said Goodman. 'Diana's been hurt but I am sorry to tell you that reports say that Dodi is dead'. It was the false tone of concern, that incensed Cole. 'You make me sick', he told Goodman, the man later to be jailed in 2007 for hacking the phones of Princes William and Harry, 'you've spent the summer pursuing them and this is the end result.' He hung up the phone and called Mohamed Al Fayed at home at his country estate in Surrey. Mohamed had already heard the news and had called his helicopter pilot to take him to Paris. 'Let us pray it is not true', he told Cole, 'I am going to Paris to find out what has happened'.

Cole hung up and glanced at the clock. It was 1.15am. He began 'bashing the phones' as he calls it, ringing everyone and anyone who might be able to provide more information. He rang the Ritz in Paris, trying to establish some rudimentary details. They confirmed that the couple had been at the hotel for dinner and that the crash had occurred, whilst the Mercedes carrying the couple had been trying to evade paparazzi on the way back to Dodi's flat in the Rue Arsène Houssaye. They too had heard Dodi was dead but they could not confirm. The Paris police HQ confirmed the basic facts that a crash had occurred. Next, Cole rang the hospital where he'd been told Diana had been taken. Yes, the Princess was there, but as Cole was not family they would not release any more information. Cole hung up and wondered what to do next. Then he remembered the paper Raine had given him two days before. Had he brought it home with him? He scrabbled urgently through his briefcase and found the details written in Raine's clear, sloping hand. He picked up the phone again and dialled the number in Venice.

Cole's Italian was what he calls 'Trattoria Tested', but unequal to the circumstances. Nonetheless, he managed to convey to the confused Italian who answered the phone that he needed urgently to speak with Raine's American Hostess, who could then wake Raine. There had been a party the night before and Cole anticipated a long wait.. 'After a few minutes Raine came to the phone and I told her briefly everything I thought I knew. That Dodi was dead and Diana was injured and that they would provide a family member with more details.' Raine immediately snapped into action. Cole gave her the number of the Pitié-Salpêtrière Hospital where Diana had been taken.

Her French was fluent and as a family member she would be able to ascertain the situation. Within five minutes she was back on the line: 'Michael, Diana has not survived, I am afraid that they are both dead'. Cole remembers falling to his knees and weeping whilst still holding the receiver with Raine at the other end, his wife Jane now standing beside him. As ever, Raine had already mastered herself and the situation. She was in practical mode: 'It's a terrible thing but there's nothing we can do. We must think of how we can help now and what we can do to make things easier', she said to Cole calmly, trying to ease his own distress. 'Raine knew before anyone else that the Princess had died' recalls Cole, who switched on the TV to see ITV reporting that Diana had sustained a broken arm. They both recognised that it was not their place to break the devastating news.

Raine would take the first flight back to London whilst Cole headed to Harrods to deal with the press. Arriving at 6.30am he found the streets around the world's most famous store deserted. Within hours they would be thronging with mourners and the media, all hungry for answers. Cole spent the next twenty-four hours without sleep, in the same clothes he had left his home in, fielding questions, giving press interviews and trying to keep a lid on the rising hysteria.

By the end of the day Raine was back at Farm Street, dealing with both the barrage of publicity, her own grief and her concern for Al Fayed, who it was reported was inconsolable. 'We were in the house together, the morning after Raine arrived home. There were no staff on duty so we spoke freely together and for a long time. There were a lot of tears shed between us but Raine was philosophical and practical as ever. She could see the difficulties a long-term relationship might have brought the couple.' says Peter Constandinos. A few days later Raine would be photographed, in a black short-sleeved bouclé shift dress and sunglasses, with a silk scarf tied at her neck, crouching down to read some of the cards attached to the mountainous bouquets of flowers which had been left outside Buckingham Palace in memory of the Princess by the grieving public. At Raine's side was a police officer; a measure of the establishment's concern over the rising hysteria and outright hostility for the aristocracy and monarchy, which Diana's death had wrought.

For Al Fayed, there were pressing practical matters to be attended to. In accordance with his religion Dodi would need to be buried as soon as possible. Al Fayed brought Dodi's body back with him from Paris in his helicopter and a brief service was hurriedly convened at Regent's Park Mosque soon after nightfall on Sunday 31 August, where Dodi's coffin, draped in black and gold cloth, arrived in a hearse with police escort. After the short twenty-five-minute ceremony, attended by Egypt's ambassador to Britain, Dodi was buried at Brookwood Cemetery in Surrey, just outside London, some time before midnight that same day, as his religious tradition dictated.

The simplicity and dignity of Dodi's funeral was in direct contrast to the collective grief and hysteria that gripped the nation over the death of a woman Tony Blair would dub 'The People's Princess'. Britain was under new management thanks to a recent landslide victory for the Labour Party, ushering in not only a new era of government, but also a very different way of looking at the world. Gone was the 'stiff upper lip' Toryism of the past and 'in' was the touchy-feely, 'emotions based' zeitgeist, popularised by Diana and then seized upon by Blair as a means of underlining Labour's new direction: the so-called Third Way – a modernised social democracy emphasising social justice, social cohesion and meritocracy.

Suddenly nothing looked more out of step with the social and political mood than the monarchy, who the public, somewhat irrationally, seemed to be blaming for the Princess's death. Ironically, it was largely thanks to a Labour administration that the monarchy survived at all. Blair, whose wife Cherie, a successful QC, refused on principle to curtsey to the Queen, continued to press courtiers for Her Majesty's return to London. The new PM, already adept at reading the country's mood, rightly judged that the tide of public opinion was turning against the monarchy, a fact underlined by the traditionally monarchist *Sun* front-page headline exhorting the Queen to: 'Show us You Care'.

Whilst his press team, led by the irascible and infamously grouchy communications supremo Alistair Campbell, moved into Buckingham Palace to oversee operations for the funeral, Blair worked the phones with a hotline to Balmoral, the Scottish estate where the royals were sequestered with the young Princes. Only when the Queen and Prince Philip emerged from their black limousine in London on 5 September, in a carefully stage-managed event to view the thousands of bouquets left by the public in front of Buckingham Palace, with hundreds of cameras present, did Number 10 breathe a collective sigh of relief. That the establishment were unprepared for the death of Diana, Princess of Wales is to grossly underplay the situation. The fact that the plans for the Queen Mother's funeral (codenamed operation Tay Bridge) were used as the basis for the ceremony (viewed by an estimated 2.5 billion people across the globe) illustrates the scale of the dilemma. The co-opting of the guest list which had also been prepared for the QM's death, resulted in any number of surprised but flattered individuals receiving invitations. It also meant that, to put it bluntly, the Queen Mother was able to watch her own funeral, whilst still very much alive and seated in one of the pews.

When the Al Fayeds and Cole entered Westminster Abbey for the royal ceremonial funeral of Diana, Princess of Wales on 6 September, they were pleased to find an immaculately coiffed Raine, dressed in the same black and white Hardy Amies wool suit with broad brimmed black hat and white gloves, she had worn for Johnnie's memorial service, waiting for them. As she embraced the couple warmly, first kissing Al Fayed's Finnish wife Heini Wathén and then Mohamed himself, hundreds of heads in the Abbey turned to watch the 'outsider' being embraced by the 'insider'. 'I was so relieved and grateful to see her' says Cole, 'she had every right to be sitting in a prominent seat with the rest of the Spencers, but she seemed to have chosen to sit with us. She was the only good thing about that terrible day.'

Throughout the ninety-minute service, during which Diana's coffin, draped in the Royal Standard with an ermine border (denoting that she did not have a personalised standard of her own), lay before them, Raine sat between the Al-Fayeds silently holding their hands. It was a gesture of solidarity from his Countess, of which Johnnie Spencer would have been justifiably proud. 'Raine was not a fair-weather friend, she had an immense sense of loyalty. She would never let you down',[11] says Andy Kerman, Raine's lawyer, executor and also a long-time friend. After the ceremony, Raine would lead the Al Fayeds through the throng to her own family, who had been seated in the choir, introducing them left and right as she wove her way. It was a dignified, warm gesture of acknowledgement for the grieving couple, who without Raine, would in that uneasy climate have been treated as outsiders at best. Later Heini Wathén would tell Cole of the enormous fun and laughter they had all shared with Diana and the boys during their family vacation that summer, before adding that in Sweden they had a saying: 'After too much laughter, tears.'

There were more tears that year for the Dartmouth family, although less publicly shared. In December 1997, Gerald died after a short illness. He was buried after a simple service in the country at the church in Chipping Norton. For Raine, Gerald, who had re-married four years after their own divorce, and who had always been 'darling Gerald', a 'wonderful husband' and a 'great friend', would be another huge loss. Throughout all of Raine's ups and downs Gerald had been there, silently observing and supporting in the background. She would feel his loss for the rest of her life. 'I don't know how she did it', says a friend, 'but she managed to maintain great friendships with both of her ex-husbands and they with her, there was always a great warmth and affection between them.'

One positive, if there was such a thing to be had at the end of such a tragic year, was that Gerald's death also seemed to mark a turning point in Raine's relationship with her children. She'd always been close to Henry and Rupert and she had grown closer to William and Charlotte since her marriage and subsequent move to Milan. There were more grandchildren too: Victoria Otley, Rupert's wife had given birth to Edward in 1986 and Claudia in 1989, whilst Charlotte had three children: Miranda born in 1993, Chiara in 1995 and Tancredi born in 1997.

'It was the one thing about Raine which did not add up', says Andy Kerman, 'she was an incredible woman – so successful, intelligent and a wonderful friend – but she seemed to have very little interest in her children or her grandchildren. Was it that Raine had no interest in her grandchildren or that children in general did not interest her? It was more likely the latter. When called upon to provide she never failed: friends note that on 'big' occasions, such as the Spencer Christmas children's party, she was at pains to ensure that every child had a good time. And her godchildren, of which there were many, spoke of her with fondness and enthusiasm, especially of her kindness and generosity during their teen years and later: 'Raine was quite literally the fairy godmother who could easily have stepped out of one of her mother's romantic novels',[12] says her godson Ivor (Lord) Plymouth. 'She was an amazing godmother to my daughter May, there was always a lovely lunch and a gift', says Anne Glenconner.

And what of her own children? Two of the Legge offspring were notable for one thing: they did not appear in the press. In strong contrast to her, their mother, Charlotte and Henry had actively striven to keep themselves and their children out of the public eye. It was almost as if, between them, they had agreed to adhere to the tenet of a quote Charlotte had once given to the *Daily Mail*: 'I don't want to talk to anybody about anything.'

But William was different – he had political inclinations and as the titular head of the Dartmouth clan, the new Earl would inevitably attract a greater wattage of the spotlight. Raine instantly felt that she could offer advice and support to a son who had finally found his calling, which was ultimately similar to her own: politics. As the eldest, William had suffered from the pressure of having a strong mother (much as Raine had done with Barbara). He was effectively a 'grown up' when his mother left his father for Johnnie and he'd very much gone his own way, choosing, after Eton and Christ Church, Oxford, to head first to Harvard where he'd been awarded an MBA and then to Australia to make his own way in the world without the pressure of his influential 'celebrity' mother.

After becoming a chartered accountant like Gerald, his first foray into politics had proved unsuccessful when he contested Leigh Lanarkshire for the Conservatives in 1974. By the time Gerald died in 1997, and William had assumed the title Earl of Dartmouth, there was a lot to unite son and mother. The uncomfortable bone of contention was that William remained stubbornly unmarried, and marriage was something which Raine told friends she considered necessary for a successful political career.

But times were changing fast: William sat in the House of Lords until 1999, when the Blair government's House of Lords Act removed most hereditary peers, leaving only ninety-two (Charles Spencer, William's stepbrother would be culled at the same time). If William wanted a political future then he'd have to carve one out for himself and not rely upon what would have traditionally been his birthright.

11

The Joy of Raine

---•◆•---

At a time when most women of her age and class were hanging up their stilettos, browsing the small ads in the *Telegraph* for elasticated waistbands and passing on their tiaras to younger family members, Raine was doubling down on the business of being Raine. Which is to say that she did not let up for a minute where her image, her workload or her socialising were concerned. 'Raine was from another age – the era of glamour and she never let that go. She was great company and she was alluring. She was almost Elizabethan with that tiny waist, that enormous skirt, the beautiful skin, always made up with lipstick expertly applied, a scarf tied at her neck and jewellery. Always lovely jewellery', says Robert Mountford,[1] a friend from Harrods days. 'She liked men', says Julian Fellowes, 'and she had the ability to make you feel like you were the most attractive man in the room. As a clever, funny woman, she liked to be appreciated by clever men.'

On Christmas Day 1997, when the Queen's Christmas message was broadcast to the nation, complete with sorrowful images of

Diana's funeral, upbeat shots of the Queen and Prince Philip on their fiftieth wedding anniversary and mention of the peaceful handover of Hong Kong to China, Raine was at Heathrow Airport. She wasn't waiting for a flight to Barbados or some other far off, warmer clime, like so many others of her ilk. Instead, she was working the tills at the Harrods concession at Heathrow's Terminal 4. 'I thought the other staff have to be here so why shouldn't I?' she told a reporter. After all, the previous year she'd manned the cash desk at Terminal 3.

Was she lonely and at a loose end for Christmas? Possibly. Farm Street, which by now, with all of her art and antiques in place, was looking like a mini-Althorp according to her brother Ian, only served to remind her of Christmas seasons spent with Johnnie and the McCorquodales. The family tradition of meeting at Camfield Place with BC and the rest of the extended family on Christmas Day, which had gone on for decades, had all but petered out. Raine's children were all living their own lives with their own interests and families. Dame Barbara was frail, but still able to recount to friends the days, when surrounded by the entire family on 25 December, each, including the children, was required post-lunch to stand and give a speech and a toast. 'Here's to Raine', she would fondly recall Johnnie saying, 'and I love her so much.'

Friends were less than inclined to invite Raine – the attendant drama she created meant having her to stay was a full-time, full-on immersive experience, as friends would recall: 'You'd have to be really up for it', says one, 'she was exhausting and her timekeeping was appalling – dinner would be at eight and she would emerge an hour late having kept everyone waiting. The food of course was ruined'. Sir Roy Strong agrees: 'She bounced off the walls. You couldn't say, let's just have some supper and put the TV on. She made Princess Margaret look easy.'

But self-pity was not Raine's style, nor was it her intention to live in the past. Where others would have wallowed, Raine worked and when she did she positively enjoyed herself. 'She really liked people', says Cole, 'she could connect with anyone.' Working and socialising had always been her way of dealing with her own personal crises and this time was no different – so Christmas at Heathrow it was. She made the papers too, pictured smiling benevolently as she handed over merchandise in Harrods bags to satisfied customers – evidence if any were needed of the type of thoroughly modern aristocrat to which the upper classes in Blair's Britain were supposed to be aspiring.

As far as her appearance was concerned, Raine concentrated her efforts as she grew older, but her routines always remained simple. During her weekly or sometimes twice weekly wash and 'set' with Constandinos, she would sit under the dryer carefully analysing notes from and for business meetings. 'She was always the only one in the salon with business notes on her lap', says Constandinos, who was effectively the architect of the much commented upon trademark bouffant, which at times verged upon the vertiginously preposterous. 'Raine was a bit like Salvador Dali with her hair', he says, 'it was how she expressed herself', adding that sometimes Raine added hairpieces to pump up the volume to an even greater extent. He admits to once giving her a thoroughly modern short cut.

> Oh my god did she give me hell. She looked fabulous and it took years off her, but then she went to a reception at Buckingham Palace and the Spencer tiara was required. The thing was an antique: it was designed for when women wore wigs. Raine said she spent the entire evening feeling like it was sliding off her head. From that moment on the 'tiara hair' would remain.

Raine was famously opposed to having any facial 'work' at a time when her peers were experimenting. 'She would never have anything "done", she refused to even dye her hair. Her porcelain skin was thanks to her sun umbrella', says Constandinos. But it wasn't just the parasol that had preserved the famous skin, or Constandinos's attentions that had maintained her envious head of hair: Raine believed in the power of jojoba oil, which she applied to her face religiously three times per day and a 'mask' of oil and egg which she combed into her dry hair once monthly. She applied her make-up twice daily and was not afraid – at a time when it was considered bad manners – to whip out her compact and carry out the entire procedure in public view, on a train or at a restaurant. It was a thoroughly modern, unashamed approach to beauty, well before its time.

There was no accounting though for her marvellously youthful embonpoint, which through to her eighties was remarkable and which she showed off to best effect garlanded with jewels, in her low neck-lined ball gowns from Balmain, which were otherwise, with their long hemlines, entirely modest. 'Raine had unbelievable breasts', agrees Constandinos, 'they were like a girl's – she always said it was because she had never worn a bra and the muscles had developed.'

'She was a true Grande Dame – was tall and imposing and she wore jewellery as it should be worn as "decoration", she thought it should be large and be seen, otherwise her attitude was "why bother?"' says Nicolas Norton, remembering her Van Cleef ruby parure in particular. 'She very much liked the company of men but she also liked women too. She got on famously with my wife for example. Women she did not like were those that she regarded as a threat', adds Norton.

Proof if any were needed that in her late sixties Raine still had 'it', was underlined in Bernard Donoughue's Diairies. Donoughue, former advisor to Harold Wilson and James Callaghan, and Minister of Farming and Food under Tony Blair, invited Raine to a dinner given at the Barry Room (named after the architect of the Palace of

Westminster Sir Charles Barry and priding itself on its à la carte menu), in February 1997 in the House of Lords. Later he recorded the event:

> Sat Raine Spencer (now Countess de Chambrun or something) next to my friend the singer Adam Faith. They got on like a house on fire. He is terrific fun and gently stroked her back throughout. She in return virtually sat in his lap. Beneath her glitter is a seriously effective operator.[2]

'Raine got on famously with Robbie Williams at a Harrods catwalk fashion show – almost flirting with him. And then at a Fulham FC celebratory dinner she chatted animatedly in French with handsome French footballer Louis Saha' laughs Cole, marvelling at her ability to engage men well into her later years.

Gerald's memorial service at the Guard's Chapel in March 1998 also made the news and not just because Raine was present, alongside his widow, Gwendoline Seguin, whom Gerald had married in 1980, four years after he and Raine had divorced. It had been a happy and settled life for Gerald – living between Grosvenor Square and a country home: the Manor House, Chippenham. He had been a warm, steadying influence on his children, all of whom adored him, a good husband and a successful businessman and supporter of the arts serving as Chairman of Ocean Wilson Holdings Ltd (an investment and maritime services company based in Brazil) and also Chairman of the Royal Choral Society and the Anglo-Brazilian Society. Raine had relied on him for his friendship and advice throughout her life. It was a huge loss. Nigel Dempster was predictably less bothered by respecting the sombreness of the occasion than he was by the date: '[the service] is certain to be packed out', he sniped, 'despite being held on Cheltenham Gold Cup day: the family are clearly not racegoers'.

The nineties had been a decade of loss for Raine, and it was not over yet: On 2 September 1998, the death of the last great press baron, Lord Vere Rothermere, owner of the *Daily Mail, Mail on Sunday* and the *London Evening Standard* was announced. The cause was a heart attack. The families had long been close and Raine and Vere had grown up alongside each other, going to the same parties, mixing in the same circles. Newspapers were after all in the McCorquodale's blood. Barbara's initial success had been based almost entirely on the MO of Lord Northcliffe (Rothermere's great uncle – considered to be the founder of popular journalism in the UK) and repeated to her ad infinitum by Max Beaverbrook, the proprietor of the rival *Daily Express*, during her first stint as a columnist: 'get names into everything you write, the more aristocratic the better'. The trials and tribulations of love between aristocrats was the mainstay of Cartland's fiction and, as her biographer John Pearson writes: 'snobbery was an important selling point'. And so it was for the *Daily Mail*, at that point one of Britain's biggest selling newspapers (it is at the time of writing the biggest). For although the *Mail* loved to 'take down the "nobs"' as one hack put it, the aristocracy and the monarchy were the bread and butter of middle-class newspapers.

Old Etonian Rothermere had been at heart a snob too – when once asked which class he belonged to he replied 'nobleman'. It was then lost on few at his funeral that at the time of his death he had switched his allegiance to the Labour Party after a lifetime as a Conservative supporter. He had married his second wife, Maiko, a former hand model, after the death of his first wife 'Bubbles' (so named for her love of champagne) in 1992, attributed to an accidental overdose of sleeping pills. Raine was one of the few people outside the family invited by Maiko to visit in the days leading up to and following her husband's death.

It would be the year 1999, rather than the turn of the century the following year, which would prove to be a turning point for

Raine. As for so many others, the year preceding the new millennium would be a time for reflection, taking stock and in Raine's case at least, making some life-changing decisions. This was her seventieth year and she was determined to make it count. At Lord Rothermere's memorial service in January, a black-suited and broad-brim-hatted, white-gloved Raine was pictured amongst the hordes of the great and the good – including Margaret Thatcher, Tony Blair and Rupert Murdoch – looking thoughtful and reserved, but still managing the glimmer of a smile for the cameras.

In Blair's Britain it looked as though 'aristos' were about to go through a tough time. Not only were all but ninety-two hereditary peers removed from parliament, but the first meetings of the Scottish Parliament and the National Assembly for Wales were fuelling rumours of the breakup of the United Kingdom and a destruction of the old order. To add to this, a spate of bombings in London in April, which left two people dead and eighty-nine injured, underscored the mood of deep unease in a country which was, depending upon how you looked at it, either going through severe growing pains or a complete implosion.

On 12 May Raine celebrated her seventieth birthday, four months earlier than her actual birthday on 9 September, with a glamorous party thrown at the Ritz. With typical efficiency she had already determined what she'd like as a gift and asked guests for a donation towards a gift from S. J. Phillips. With all of her children present it was to be a family celebration par excellence – they had between them invited 350 guests and she would be footing the bill. 'Normally if you get to seventy you shoot yourself but I am giving a party for old friends', she said.

As the year drew to a close the climate in Britain became even more uneasy. In October, the government circulated a leaflet to all households entitled 'What Everyone Should Know About the Millennium Bug' referring to the potential 'Y2K disaster', which according to some experts, would leave computers unable to cope with the new millennium dateline and cause amongst other things, planes to fall from the sky, stock markets to crash and a shortage of food and water. The zeitgeist was, then, fuelled by uncertainty, doubt and fear, none of which seemed to bother Raine particularly, but all of which undoubtedly influenced her decision-making process for the year ahead.

She was planning to move from her beloved Farm Street, telling friends that it was just too big and that the stairs were becoming unmanageable. It seems that she was also considering William's position – she had decided, despite her lack of affection for the muddy British countryside, to buy a stately home with him to use as his base. They would share it she said, but no one really believed that she would ever spend much time there, rather that she thought that for a man with political aspirations, the 9th Earl of Dartmouth should own a country estate. In moments of solitude, Raine was homesick for Althorp and besides she needed another all-consuming project to take up her weekends when she was not working at Harrods. The purchase of a new home for William would also be financially shrewd – some might call it sensible tax planning.

The only disasters which seemed to have occurred in the twenty-four hours between 31 January 1999 and 1 January 2000 were PR related. The pictures of the Queen looking uncomfortable and undignified, gingerly linking hands with Tony Blair and the Duke of Edinburgh for a chorus of 'Auld Lang Syne', whilst standing in Peter Mandelson's shockingly inept excuse for a monument to the millennium, 'The Dome', might have presaged the difficult year that was to follow. What was heralded as the *International Year for Culture and Peace* began with the murder of twenty Coptic Christians at the hands of Muslims in the village of El-Kosheh, Egypt, on 2 January and would end with Christmas Eve bombings on behalf of Al Qaeda and Jemaah Islamiyah in Indonesia killing eighteen people. Closer to home, 2000 was a year when the PM would finally meet his match at the Women's Institute's National Conference, where he would find himself booed and slow handclapped by a hostile, entirely female audience; when the much-celebrated Millennium Bridge, spanning the Thames from St Paul's to the newly opened Tate Modern, would close within a few days of opening thanks to safety concerns and a new TV show called *Big Brother* would revolutionise the way we watched 'the box'.

For Raine, the first few months of the new Millennium were not entirely positive. BC would die in her sleep on 21 May, aged ninety-eight, just a few months shy of her ninety-ninth birthday. Raine's relationship with her mother had never been easy, most likely because they were two equally strong characters intent on being heard and getting their own way. The phrase 'no love lost' could have been written for this particular mother–daughter pairing. And yet and yet . . . For Raine her mother had been a constant presence – her link to where she'd come from and a permanent reminder of a father she'd effectively lost very early in life. She had been proud of her mother too – a woman who had struck out on her own and achieved global success. There weren't many people who could say that of their 'mummy'. It was hard to ignore the fact that Raine's life was slowly emptying of those closest to her. At her mother's funeral – a surprisingly modest affair, held at the Dame's home, Camfield Place, Hertfordshire – Raine read a passage from the First Letter of John ('In the beginning was the Word and the Word was with God, and the word was God', 'The Word Became Flesh' – appropriate somehow) whilst William read one of BC's own poems about love and the afterlife.

BC was buried in her own garden in a cardboard coffin, wearing one of her favourite pink chiffon dresses. Her resting place had been carefully chosen too: beneath the ancient oak, which she always claimed had been planted by Queen Elizabeth I. It was an appropriate location for a woman who was, at the time of burial, the global record holder for the amount of bodice ripping romances published. It would have surprised no one who knew her that BC had, in 1986, penned her own obituary and delivered it to the obituary desks of each of the national newspapers tied in pink ribbon. To cap off the funeral, the 150 mourners sang Perry Como's ballad 'I Believe'. Amongst the mourners was Lord Brocket, the pulchritudinous peer and notorious insurance fraudster with whom Dame Barbara had struck up a pen-pal friendship whilst he was serving time in Springhill Prison.

Farm Street sold on 29 March 2000, for £2,900,000, and Raine moved into a redbrick mansion flat in her beloved Grosvenor Square on the corner of South Audley Street. She couldn't stay away – she'd lived there first with Gerald and then again with Johnnie. The historic garden square (the second largest in London) was, after Buckingham Palace, nominally at least, still the centre of the London universe for the aristocracy. Owned by the Duke of Westminster (Grosvenor is his surname) the square was brimming with history, although many of its historic buildings had been demolished and replaced by faceless blocks of flats, anodyne hotels and officious looking embassies. The square was dominated by the Eero Saarinen's 1960s American Embassy, an overbearing reminder, if one were needed, of a long-held US presence in the square, initially Georgian in origin. The first US 'mission' to the Court of St James had been established in the square by John Adams, who had lived in a house which still stands on the corner of Duke and Brook Streets between 1785 and 1788.

BC's presence was felt here too: the south-east corner of the square had been the home of her great pals: the Bentley Boys, who had leased adjacent flats, parking their racing green sports cars askew outside and throwing legendary parties during the twenties. Such was their reputation that for decades afterwards, London cabbies referred to that part of the square as 'Bentley Corner'. Oscar Wilde, a Grosvenor Square resident between 1883 and 1884, had referenced the location in *An Ideal Husband, Lady Windermere's Fan, The Importance of Being Earnest* and *The Picture of Dorian Gray.* Latterly, Grosvenor Square featured as the home of the Bridgertons and the Featheringtons in the *Netflix* bodice-buster, *Bridgerton.* A little over a year after Raine moved back into the square, the events of 9.11 would cause the American Embassy to close traffic access to the Western side as an anti-terrorist precaution. A memorial to the sixty-seven British victims, under which is buried a piece of wreckage from the towers, stands in the eastern corner of the gardens.

If Raine was feeling nostalgic (and the signs were that she was) she was not one to mope. She took the lead at her brother Ian McCorquodale's wedding to ex-Royal Ballet lead Bryony Brind, whom he married quietly a few months after his mother's death, by choosing to read one of her mother's love poems for the couple. Raine's seventies were to be for her a time of consolidation and in many ways a new beginning. She found herself in demand socially, so much so that when *Tatler* published its top one hundred party guests of 2000, Raine came in at number 46, behind the Earl and Countess of Derby and ahead of 'new entry' Frederick 'Freddy' Windsor, only son of Prince and Princess Michael of Kent (and now married to Sophie Winkleman, half-sister of Claudia). *Tatler* had collated the guest lists for almost every prestigious party of the year so it wasn't entirely surprising that Raine, whose mailbox was bombarded daily with invites, would feature.

The same year, after much consideration (and likely some pretty tough bargaining) she and William purchased the Whiteway Estate in Chudleigh, Devon for £5 million.[3] The estate came with sporting rights – mixed duck and pheasant shooting and deer stalking – over its 659 tenanted acres of land (they bought 281). The eleven-bedroomed Grade II listed home had been recently renovated, although that would not stop Raine from getting to work as soon as the deal was inked. William would be in charge of a money-making concern too: according to details from the time, the estate also had another nine properties which would be included with the sale: 'These with the farm business tenancy on the land and farm buildings, generate about £61,500 per year', recorded the particulars.

Those friends who had sniffed that Raine would never make a go of it in the country were in for a surprise and, if they were fortunate, an invitation. After she'd finished the renovations, which took well over a year, Raine began inviting friends for country weekends. She'd redone the place from top to bottom with the familiar gilding, swagging and peaches and pinks. The newly renovated indoor swimming pool had been hung with pictures by artist Teddy Millington-Drake and the walls in the house were festooned with her favourite artists including Boucher, Fragonard and Vernet. Philip Vergeylen visited for a weekend with his partner Paolo Moschino:

We went for the weekend thinking this could be tough but it was the easiest because of course Raine knew exactly how to entertain: there was no formal breakfast, it was always ordered the night before and brought to you in bed. Then we'd meet in the library for drinks before lunch and you could do whatever you'd like for the afternoon – there'd be a car at your disposal or you could walk in the grounds. You would meet again in the library for drinks before dinner. It was a perfectly calibrated mix of private and personal and it was pure Raine. The only issue I ever had was that I needed to hang out of the bedroom window to smoke my cigarettes as she hated the smell of tobacco smoke.

For Raine, the country was no reason to sacrifice one's personal style and she continued wearing her well-cut day dresses and court shoes during daylight hours and gowns and jewellery for evening dinners. Her one concession was her hair, which she swept up behind her head into a chignon using a floral clip, acknowledging perhaps that only her beloved Peter could really manage to pull off 'the do'. One thing Vergeylen remembers vividly is accompanying the Countess to the village to buy flowers for a dinner that evening: 'she negotiated very hard about the price of two lillies, then winked at me saying "C'est pour épater la bourgeoisie" (loose translation: 'it's for shocking the respectable middle classes') which made me laugh'.

True to form though, Raine's interest in gardening and the outdoors was zero. To welcome her to Devon, one particular set of landowners had prepared a luncheon beside their swimming pool. Hearing of this upon arrival, our Countess looked askance: 'I don't do outside', she said with a firm but charming smile. The food and drink was swiftly moved into the dining room without further comment.

It was likely her ambivalence about her home's surroundings that led to the gardens at Whiteway being deeply underwhelming – 'you could almost imagine you were at Versailles and never leave the building' she once said of Althorp. Although she appreciated swathes of parkland (whilst she was motoring through it) there was nothing of the Vita Sackville-West about Raine. She would have positively disliked the grubby bohemia of the Bloomsbury and Charleston set. The mistress of Whiteway had a far greater interest in her guests than in the external fauna and flora. This became all too obvious when, during the Sunday morning of his stay, Vergeylen was taking a bath only to hear a sharp rap on the door, swiftly followed by Raine making an entrance: '[she] sat on the end of the bath talking to me to organise the day. I'm really no prude but the bubbles helped!'

Not everything about Whiteway would prove to be smooth sailing. In 2002, Raine and William would come under scrutiny in an employment tribunal brought by the former gamekeeper Paul

Davis and his wife Liz, the Whiteway housekeeper. Both claimed unfair dismissal after Mr Davis was made redundant by William just five days after his wife had agreed her own severance package with Raine. According to Davis, his wife had become 'seriously ill due to being run down as a result of working extremely long hours to prepare the mansion on her own'. Davis also claimed that the butler had collapsed from the stress and exhaustion of working over Christmas for Raine and her house guests. Although the tribunal claimed the dismissal was fair (William was ordered to pay £2,186.20 in redundancy, commission and expenses)[4] the incident did little to improve either Raine or William's reputation as hard taskmasters where staff were concerned.

In 2004, the tabloids had a new subject: the friendship of one Victoria Beckham and Raine, Countess Spencer. It was convenient if nothing else, because it gave the papers a new angle for their grinding pursuit of the Beckhams in the face of claims by David Beckham's former PA, Rebecca Loos, that she and the former England mid-fielder had had an affair. Raine and Victoria had been spotted lunching together at Harrods, deep in conversation. The papers speculated that Raine was dispensing marital advice to her new designer-clad pal. In truth the pair had much in common, not least being the subject of relentless tabloid conjecture and negativity, a savvy, dry sense of humour and a delight in luxury labels. What was certainly true was that any advice from Raine would have amounted to counsel for the Beckhams to stay together and keep their heads down until the paparazzi moved on. 'Raine was firm on family values, she was extremely moral and she believed in the sanctity of marriage', says Nicolas Norton, adding that 'she [Raine] was devastated when her marriage to de Chambrun broke down.'

In any event, when Victoria announced that she and her two children were moving to Madrid to be with Beckham, full-time, whilst he fulfilled his contract with the club (for which read keep any eye on him), there were those who felt sure of the guiding hand of a certain Countess in the decision. Raine made another big celebrity appearance that summer which got the paps snapping, when she was spotted hand in hand with her friend the music sensation and diva, Dame Shirley Bassey. The unlikely couple were pictured together wearing co-ordinating polka dot ball gowns for the *Some Enchanted Evening Party and Fashion Show* in aid of the Galapagos Conservation Society at the Chelsea Physic Garden in London.

Even the replacement of both hips between 2005 and 2006 was newsworthy. Both operations were carried out by the orthopaedic surgeon to the Queen Mother, Sarah Muirhead-Allwood. This fact alone should not have been enough to make the 'gossips'. But an added 'spice' in the mix as far as the tabloids were concerned was the fact that Muirhead-Allwood had, until 1996, been known as William – to which these days one might rightly enquire 'so what?' It was, instead, a measure of the times that Raine's hip replacements were utilised as an excuse to discuss the good surgeon's gender/sex change in full detail. Raine ignored the prurience and instead chose to focus on the surgeon's excellent work, telling the Princess of Wales's former favourite, Richard Kay of the *Daily Mail*, that Muirhead had given her a mantra to repeat as she climbed the stairs, 'Good leg leads to heaven, bad leg leads to hell'.

The replacement hips provided her with a new lease of life – she'd struggled for years with the stairs at Farm Street and was enjoying the simplicity of living in her flat in Grosvenor Square. Plus, she was looking better than ever. She would have been thrilled to find herself mistaken for her idol Margaret Thatcher (no matter the latter's advanced age) as she was at a reception at the Russian embassy that summer. Her 'shop girl' career was going from strength to strength too. 'She'd never earned her own money', says Cole. 'She loved the independence. She used to send her chauffer Brian to Coutts in Mount Street to bank her cheque and he'd come back with her cash.' It was Brian, who was employed not only as a driver but as a butler too, whom she was starting to rely upon more than anyone else. Raine's daughter Charlotte acknowledged how much her mother depended upon him: 'She was the least domestically inclined person one could ever hope to meet – when her beloved butler, Brian, was away, she would eat off paper plates rather than have to wash up – but she always changed for dinner, donning a cocktail dress and jewels, even when alone.'[5]

'They were absolutely thick as thieves', says Julian Fellowes of the Countess and her butler: 'At one point Raine lost a tooth and to my absolute amazement I later noticed that Brian was missing the very same tooth. I began to wonder if he'd had it extracted in sympathy.'

'She was paid a lot by Harrods', says a friend (not Cole), 'but for every contact leveraged by Al Fayed, Raine paid back in spades.' In fact, to the surprise of almost everyone except possibly herself, Raine was a natural. A loyal, dedicated hard worker and a consummate diplomat, her background and her self-assurance meant that she was exactly the type of representative Harrods needed when dealing with high-net-worth individuals. Inevitably though it was her title that gave her the edge. She displayed it prominently on the gold Harrods badge she wore above her left breast (almost always balanced by a diamond or paste brooch on the right) which read: *Harrods* and then below it: *Raine Countess Spencer,* with the French tricolour flag indicating her fluency in that language. Her ability to make every customer feel special, whether they were purchasing a home in The Little Boltons or a pair of cashmere socks, made her a talking point, in a world where commerce was universally derided as both cut throat and somewhat 'common'. 'She passed the grand person's ultimate test', wrote one journalist who lunched with her at the Basil Street Hotel during her Harrods lunch hour: 'she was extremely polite to the waiters.'

There was also no escaping from the simple fact that as a Harrods Management Board Director, she also knew her stuff. Her eye for detail was also legend and she was spotted at one particularly important Harrods launch, checking the loos, which she pronounced as 'perfect'. 'She regarded Harrods as simply an outpost of her own home and she wanted everything to be just so', says a friend.

'She possessed the zeitgeist until the day she died' says her beloved godson Ivor (Lord) Plymouth.[6] And indeed, it was one of her greatest pleasures to be able to destabilise a conversation with an aside which proved that she was more avant-garde than her interlocuters. When she told the *Daily Express* that she owned a 'digibox' (the latest TV cable device at the time) at the launch of Harrods *Truly British* in June 2005, the column reported it the next day. Albeit – as she happily admitted – she actually used it to watch old classics like *Fawlty Towers*, *Yes Minister* and *Dad's Army*, 'which is heaven'. She was a grandmother once again too – William's former girlfriend, TV producer and magistrate's daughter Clare Kavanagh, had given birth to an 8lb 10oz boy in 2005 . There was no talk of marriage though. In fact William, who was by now fifty-five, was already dating former model Fiona Campbell who he would go on to marry in 2009 and divorce in 2015.

Raine's love-life also appeared to have taken a turn for the better. Whereas previously she had been seen on the arm of various friends and walkers, she was reported to be openly entertaining 'handsome forty-something banker' William Bachetti at Whiteway. They were also spotted hand in hand at a Covent Garden restaurant party thrown by PR supremo Liz Brewer for Shirley Bassey, with the papers making much of the thirty-five year age difference, which would of course have gone unmentioned were their positions reversed. Bachetti was later the subject of tabloid conjecture when he appeared on the arm of Cilla Black, although Black dismissed him as the man 'who sorted out her money'.

On 31 January, Raine purchased 2a Sprimont Place, an end of terrace house, just off the King's Road in Chelsea SW3, moving closer to daughter Charlotte. Before she could move in, she carried out her customary renovations – changing carpets, walls and kitchen amongst other things and staying with friends, including Philip Vergeylen and his partner Paolo Moschino, until the work was completed. 'She was a thoroughly easy and very charming guest, although my housekeeper did complain about her prolific use of talcum powder', laughs Vergeylen. He also recalls a night spent in at home, something which one imagines would be to Raine anathema: 'when I told Raine that after a week of going out we'd be staying in for supper and watching a movie she was delighted. In fact what she said was "I've got the perfect outfit for this"'. The perfect outfit was red lace and maribou. The movie was *Geisha*.

In July 2006, Raine was promoted to a new role as director of Harrods Estates which meant she travelled extensively to Shanghai, Moscow and the Middle East. 'Selling property is just like selling Fairy Liquid' she told a reporter 'and I learned all about the techniques of selling from my days canvassing as a local politician in London. I love it when a deal comes together.' She was also engrossed in another project, this time in her own home: she was Marie Kondo'ing, long before Kondo came along – paring back and selling off her clothes on eBay. Her successes were faithfully recorded in the papers: three fur hats by Frederick Fox and Simone Mirman, a white fur shawl and bolero jacket by Maxwell Croft and a pair of black silk vivaldi court shoes (size 6).

In September 2007, she would accept an invitation sent out by Clarence House on behalf of William and Harry, who had taken the lead in organising a memorial service marking ten years since the death of their mother. The tenth anniversary memorial service for Diana, Princess of Wales was to be held at the Guards' Chapel, Wellington Barracks, where so many family events – both happy and sad – had taken place. Effectively the royals' local place of worship, situated just down Birdcage Walk, minutes from Buckingham Palace, the Guards' Chapel remains the location of choice not only for royal family events, but for the majority of smart London weddings and memorials for anyone with even a distant military or royal connection. The neoclassical chapel was rebuilt after a V1 Buzz Bomb destroyed it in 1944, tragically killing 121 soldiers and civilians and seriously injuring 141 more who had been attending a Sunday service at the time. Despite the carnage, the six silver candles standing on the main altar reportedly did not extinguish and have remained lit ever since. The chapel is a place of worship for Her Majesty's Household Division, which is comprised of the five regiments of Foot Guards and two regiments of the Household Cavalry. Privacy at the chapel, which is hung with battle flags and holds up to a thousand people, is guaranteed since it is situated within the barracks itself and access is gated. In other words, services at the Guards are paparazzi proof.

Attendees that the papers managed to snap on their way in and out included the Queen in lilac, the sombre Duke and members of the extended royal family in all of their dubious, crumpled, dog-haired finery. Diana's family were notably more glamorous and afforded the paparazzi one of their first collective views of the ambitiously blonde and grown up 'Spencer girls' – Diana's nieces Kitty, Eliza and Amelia. Celebrities included Elton John, David Furnish and Cliff Richard, alongside representatives from Diana's favourite charities. Harry would eulogise his mother as 'simply the best mother in the world' and William would read from the bible: Ephesians 3.14–21: to know the love of Christ that surpasses knowledge, that you may be filled with all the fullness of God. Pointedly not invited was Mohamed Al Fayed, although his daughter Camilla, who had maintained contact with William and Harry, was deemed to be worthy of an invitation. The Al Fayed family were after all in mourning too. A fact which seemed to have been all too often forgotten.

Had the Princes been nudged by Prince Charles to invite Raine? As the invitations were sent out from Clarence House it was hard to tell. There was little doubt that after their mother's death the boys would pay 'Aunt Raine' scant regard and she would not be present at any future royal celebrations. Was this because they viewed Raine as tainted by the Al Fayed connection? It was later reported that William, if not Harry, had felt uneasy about the French holiday from the start. Or was it simply that as teenage boys, closeted by the Windsors and influenced by their Uncle Charles and their 'real' Granny Frances, they preferred to look to the future and not back into the painful past? Raine never spoke of their 'disconnect' but as a proud royalist, close friend and confidante of their mother, and their former step-grandmother, that disregard would not have gone unfelt or unnoticed.

Looming on Raine's horizon and undoubtedly on that of most members of Diana's immediate family – royal and otherwise – was the inquest into her death, which began the month following the memorial on 2 October 2007. Seated in Room 73 at the High Court in The Strand on that first day were Mohamed Al Fayed, the Princess's sister, Lady Sarah McCorquodale, and Jamie Lowther-Pinkerton, representing Diana's sons, Princes William and Harry. Together with the eleven-person jury (six men and five women), they listened as Lord Justice Scott Baker, the fourth coroner nominated to lead the inquiry, explained: 'Mr Al Fayed had maintained throughout that the crash had been in furtherance of a conspiracy by the establishment, in particular his Royal Highness Prince Philip, the Duke of Edinburgh who used the security services to carry it out'. It was a shocking and some said scurrilous accusation and the trial promised to excavate the claim in full. Before the hearing officially began a letter from the Princes was read out by the second royal coroner Baroness Butler-Sloss, who was handing over to Lord Justice Baker, appealing that the inquest 'should not only be open, fair and transparent, but that it should move swiftly to a conclusion'.

This particular request was going to be made more difficult by the ten-year delay between the death of their mother and the beginning of the inquest. There had been justifiable hold ups. First the French police investigation, which had lasted until 2003, and then an independent British Police investigation – led by Lord Stevens – which began in 2004 and culminated in the public release of the 832-page Paget Report, together with the findings of the criminal investigation on December 2006. The findings stated simply and baldly that Diana and Dodi had died in a 'tragic accident' because their car, driven by Henri Paul (over the legal limit of alcohol), was driving too fast.

Michael Mansfield QC, for Al Fayed, had criticised the timing of Lord Stevens's report into the crash, arguing that it had given the impression that the Diana case was now closed. 'The public, as well as national and international media, have regarded what is printed in the report as the final and the official verdict.' On the other hand, just three years previously, in 2004, the *Sunday Express* had run a telephone poll, the results of which indicated that one in four of their readers believed that the Princess had been murdered. These sentiments, in spite of the evidence to the contrary, seemed to be shared by a good proportion of the British public.

The royal family's attempt to hold Diana's inquest in private, with a jury made up solely of senior courtiers, seemed suspicious and had been thwarted. Al Fayed had argued successfully that, contrary to the Palace's contention that Diana was 'royal' when she died and therefore due a royal inquest, the princess had died a commoner and thus was entitled to a public inquiry with jurors made up of the general public. The Palace claim was a curious one, given that the Queen had stripped Diana of her HRH as part of her divorce settlement, the corollary to which was that she was not protected by Royal Protection officers on the day she died. When Baroness Butler-Sloss handed over to Lord Justice Scott Baker, the stage was set for what in the public's minds at least was to be a showdown, with the spectres of Diana and Dodi in one corner and the royal household, very much on the ropes, in the other.

The Windsors had much to fear. The most fundamental allegation was the question of criminal intent. To quote from Paget:

> It is alleged that the Princess of Wales was pregnant with Dodi Al Fayed's child. The Princess and Dodi Al Fayed told Mohamed Al Fayed this information. The 'Security Services' became aware of this information through telephone monitoring thus providing the motive for the alleged murders. The Princess of Wales was illegally embalmed on the instructions of the Palace to conceal the fact that she was pregnant with Dodi Al Fayed's child.

And then there were the accusations of racism against the Al Fayeds which were implied, as were the suggestions that the late Princess of Wales was effectively being 'slut shamed' in today's parlance. Could it really have been considered acceptable within the royal family, for the heir to the throne to behave in a way he so chose, but not acceptable for his former wife, from whom he was now divorced, to do the same – to the extent that they would have wanted her to be 'extinguished'? Furthermore, whilst the trial threatened to throw a forensic light onto the private life of the Princess, it would not, it seemed, subject the future king and his family to the same level of scrutiny. Instead the 'firm' had offered up the Duke of Edinburgh's private secretary to give evidence instead of the man himself, who had refused even to entertain the idea of taking an investigator's phone call on the matter of his ex-daughter-in-law's death.

There were plenty of loose ends and unanswered questions. Even so, that they pointed to the murder of Dodi and the Princess seemed implausible, simply because some of the biggest conspiracy 'notions' had already been disproved. The notorious white Fiat Uno for example, which had been implicated in the crash by several signed witness statements, had been first traced to a French photo journalist, James Andanson, who had been present amongst the paparazzi. When French police analysed paint samples from his Uno with those from the wreck of the fatal Mercedes, they found no match.

This should have been the end of the matter, but the story gathered pace because of a tragic twist, when Andanson's body was subsequently discovered inside the burned-out wreck of his BMW on 4 May 2000, in Nant, southern France (verdict: suicide). A suspicious hole in the left side of his temple had been rationalised by the French coroner as the result of the intense heat of the burning car. But it was there nonetheless. And then, on the night of 15/16 June 2000, Andanson's press agency, Sipa in Paris, where he kept his archived photography, was burgled. Was this all a very unhappy set of coincidences? Probably. But you could see how and why some might think otherwise.

The fact that the Paget report had identified, but not named, another Fiat Uno owner, suspected to have been at the scene of the crime, was also unfinished business. The suspect, who was later named as Le Van Thanh, a French born bodybuilder, had given a witness statement to the French police which would later be read out at the inquest. He had declined to give evidence in person and was protected by French law. (In 2019, he claimed that the French Police had told him 'It's not the same law as in France, don't go there'.)[7]

There were also unanswered questions about the driver of the Mercedes – Henri Paul – whose reckless driving it was claimed had caused the crash. There was evidence not only of alcohol levels of well beyond the legal limit in Paul's blood (in a man whose friends testified that he was barely a drinker) but also inexplicable levels of carbon monoxide (between 12 and 21 per cent). This, according to experts, would have suggested that a few hours earlier Paul's blood would have had a carbon monoxide saturation of approximately 40 per cent which would have induced such a state of instability that he would have been unable to stand, let alone tie his shoelaces, as he was caught on CCTV doing at the Ritz. Certainly he would have been unable to subsequently drive the fateful car. The suggestion was that the bloods tested in the autopsy had not been Paul's at all, but had been substituted before testing.

And then there was the file note written by the Princess's lawyer, Lord Mischon, who was disturbed enough after a visit to see the Princess at Kensington Palace on 30 October 1995, to go on record, stating amongst other things that: 'the Princess had been informed by reliable sources that efforts would be made if not to get rid of her (be it by some accident in her car such as pre-prepared brake failure or whatever) between now and then, then at least to see that she was so injured or damaged as to be declared "unbalanced"'.

At face value the claim that the Princess of Wales had been carrying Dodi Al Fayed's child and that she had been illegally and prematurely embalmed on the instructions of the Palace to conceal the fact that she was pregnant seemed plausible, if unlikely. It was against the law both in France and in the UK to embalm anyone who had died in suspicious circumstances before an autopsy had been carried out. That a diplomat from the British Embassy in Paris and another officer from the French police had supposedly been able to give the order for the Princess's body to be 'partially embalmed' (from the waist up) within a few hours of her death 'with the full consent of St James's Palace' beggared belief. The heat in the Paris hospital had been blamed for the speedy decision, but had no one considered moving the Princess's body to a mortuary?

Even the simplest of individuals (which one must assume the British Consul General – Keith Moss[8] – was not) might have wondered whether or not there would be more than a few questions to be asked about the untimely, tragic death of the world's most famous female? The only certainty was they would be unable to be answered once the embalming fluid did its job.

To answer at least part of the charges would require the raking over once more of the minute details of the Princess of Wales' personal life, leaving no intimate details spared. Was this right or even decent? Did all of the evidence need to be played out again in the full view and knowledge of her sons who were now young men? Al Fayed's appetite for justice was unassuaged and so, to some extent, was the public's. For many, the accusations of Mohamed Al Fayed, that the royal family would regard a Dodi/Diana marriage as an embarrassment, did not seem ridiculous – it seemed entirely possible. Especially given the further accusations that the Duke, not known for mincing his words or shying from comments that would these days be regarded as 'unwoke' at best and racist at worst, had sent Diana a series of aggressive threatening letters during the breakdown of her marriage to Prince Charles. The letters, which several people testified to having seen, had now also mysteriously vanished. They had been either shredded, it was speculated, by the Princess's own mother, or seized by police who had raided the home of Paul Burrell in 2006 and carried away many personal items belonging to the Princess. Either way the public's suspicions, and those of Mohamed Al Fayed, all added up to pretty much the same thing – that, in Al Fayed's words, quoted in the Paget Inquiry Report: 'the Royal Family *"could not accept that an Egyptian Muslim could eventually be the stepfather of the future King of England"'*.[9]

In analysis, the ongoing claims by Al Fayed that the Princess was carrying Dodi Al Fayed's child seemed baseless. For starters, there was the simple fact that the infamous Gottex Animal Print bathing suit pictures to which the press and Al Fayed referred as proof of the Princess's so called 'baby bump' had been taken on 14 July 1997, the same day that the Princess was actually reintroduced to Dodi Al Fayed in France and before they began their relationship. They had met previously some years before when Prince Charles and Dodi had played polo at Guards Polo Club, Windsor Great Park.

Another key piece of evidence had been offered up by the Princess's former lover Hasnat Khan. Khan had given a written statement to Paget in 2004 in which he stated that the Princess was rigorous about her use of the contraceptive pill.[10] Putting this fact aside for a moment, consider the additional evidence: the Princess had been in a serious relationship with Khan for almost two years previously . By his own admission, Khan had spent the night with her at Kensington Palace before she and the Princes had jetted off to the South of France the next day. In which case, surely the baby (had there even been one) would have been much more likely to have been Khan's than Dodi Al Fayed's?

Amongst the revelations made by Khan in his 2004 statement to Lord Stevens's Operation Paget was the fact that Diana had asked her butler, Paul Burrell, to find out whether the two could marry in secret (a fact which was said to have appalled Khan). He also said that the Princess had considered living abroad – in Pakistan, South Africa or Australia – that she had on one occasion changed her car because she said that the brakes had been tampered with and that he received death mail during his relationship with the Princess. He said that Diana had stopped speaking to her mother after Frances had expressed her disapproval that her daughter was seeing a Pakistani and a Muslim. And that, contrary to press reports, it had been Diana rather than he who had ended their relationship after she began seeing Dodi Al Fayed in August 1997.

Perhaps regretting the fullness of his previous statements and wary of the media spotlight, Khan had refused to give evidence either in person or via videolink at the inquest. Instead, he was in Pakistan, where he was beyond the jurisdiction of the court and where he would remain until after the inquest had closed and the findings been made public. In February 2008, his responses to written questions which had been put to him by the solicitor to the inquest, Martin Smith, would be read out in court. Their content would reveal very little that was new.

The *Guardian* would later describe the events in Court 73 that day as: 'PG Wodehouse meets Bourne Conspiracy'[11] – one could see why. When she was called to the stand on 12 December at 2pm, Raine was uniquely torn between a lifelong loyalty to the monarchy, in particular Prince Charles, and her close friendship with her boss Mohamed Al Fayed, upon whose accusations the entire trial pivoted. Witnesses for both the Stevens Report and now the inquest were all actively vying for BFF status with the late Diana. All, in their various ways, were claiming that they were the 'closest' confidante to the Princess; all were 'sure' that Diana would have confided in them had she planned to get engaged or, for that matter, were she pregnant. Amongst those claiming to be her most intimate 'confidante' were Diana's sister Sarah; her friends, the Honourable Rosa Monckton and Lucia Flecha de Lima; and Rita Rogers, her medium.

'If you want to get something done then send for Raine', the Duke of Edinburgh once famously intoned. And so it would prove at the inquest. Where information was lacking, Raine provided just enough of it to indicate her 'inside track'; where discretion was called for, she sweetly smiled and demurred. She knew the Princess's heart but she wasn't going to offer it up on a platter: 'Certain things she told me which I could never say because, after all, if people are dead and then, you know, they still would not want all very intimate things to be told', she said to Ian Burnett QC, counsel to the inquest, who was asking questions on behalf of the coroner, whilst twinkling at the coroner himself, Lord Justice Scott Baker.

The royals would see and hear nothing to concern them from Raine at least. She was a pro. She'd been through this sort of rigour before, and she knew all about the royal twin codes of privacy and secrecy.

She begged the court's indulgence whilst she explained: 'If I could just divert to prove my point? John and I used to be asked the most incredibly impertinent questions about not only Diana, but the rest of the royal family, do you know, and people used to listen agog at dinner parties waiting for our reply'. She went on: 'We developed a reply which always amused Diana very much, when we used to say, "It is very kind of you to ask. I am afraid we cannot possibly answer that because we know too much". It always annoyed people very much indeed, which was quite deliberate, because the questions were extraordinarily impertinent.'

That was all very well, but what the world and Lord Justice Scott Baker most wanted to know about was Raine's relationship with the late Earl Spencer's children, and one child in particular.

'It is right, is it not, that your relationship with his children was not an altogether happy one during the course of your marriage?' asked Mr Burnett.

'Correct', the Countess responded dryly, offering the enquiring Mr Burnett no further elaboration.

He pressed on.

'But in the years following his death, you re-established a cordial relationship with the Princess of Wales; that is right, is it?'

'Yes', said the Countess, adding that the pair had gone on to 'become very close'.

'I feel so happy, your Lordship, that at that particular point in her life, when she really was very, very down, that I was able perhaps to help her a little. She would ring up and at a very short notice would come round and sit in my house on the sofa or talk or ring up and say – or plan ahead, even, for lunches. And she wanted us to be seen in public, which was so nice', said Raine, knowing full well that this information alone would put her firmly in the driver's seat. 'She always said that I had no hidden agenda', the Countess added pointedly. 'I think that so many people, because she was so popular and so world famous, wanted something out of her.'

Friends would not have been surprised to see and hear the Countess's legendary wit emerging as the two-hour testimony continued.

When Burnett asked for a summation of the Princess's relationship with the Duke of Edinburgh, which reports suggested had been less than amiable, the Countess had a bright idea.

'Why don't you read the next two sentences?' she asked, smiling benevolently, referring to her written statement, 'because I think that covers it'.

'My problem, Lady Spencer', replied the esteemed QC dryly, 'Is that you are giving evidence and not me'.

'I see', responded Raine, looking appropriately chastened and a little exasperated, waiting for the giggles from the public gallery to die down.

'Well I apologise. Would you like me to read it instead?'

And then there was the infamous ill-fated relationship with Dodi – did the Countess know much about this, the court wanted to know? We already knew the answer. The Countess was the mother lode, but again, access was restricted. Here again she skilfully skated the thin line between truth and loyalty: after all the man who had employed her as a director of Harrods for the past decade and paid her wages was Dodi's father, Mohamed Al Fayed, with whom she famously had a close friendship, whilst the royal family, with whom she also had close connections – particularly to Prince Charles – famously did not.

Diana and Dodi had been very much in love, she assured the court. 'As I think I have intimated earlier, her life was a great strain with always somebody wanting something. Do you know? I, in my small way, was in public life for so many years, and there is always somebody wanting you to do this, do that, do the next thing, solve a problem, open the bazaar, visit the hospital, et cetera, et cetera, which of course is only a pleasure and a duty if you are a councillor and it is your job to look after your people. But with her it was so extreme that to meet a man who then wanted to please her and only do what she wanted to do and think up wonderful outings and lovely dinners and wonderful holidays was suddenly the most marvellous thing to happen to her.'

'Diana was madly in love with him', she pronounced, initially referring to Dodi, 'whether she was on the rebound from Hasnat Khan, I do not know.' So there it was: not only had Diana's relationship with the dishy doctor been serious, it had also been accepted as a matter of course by those who knew her well. This would be confirmed in later testimonies.

By now, the Countess had fully hit her stride and she proceeded at a pace, flatly denying some speculation and bolstering other conjecture. Yes, she said decidedly, she thought that the Princess and Dodi were likely to get engaged and then married, or at the least live together. At this statement, Ian Burnett, QC, put up a valiant fight: 'Was that something the Princess herself said or is this a close friend divining what is likely to happen from the tone and nature of what has been said?'

Raine remained calm, but one might sense from her words a level of exasperation: 'Diana would never have said', she smiled patiently. 'Don't you see, even though she trusted me completely, it was too newsworthy a thing to admit to anybody that she had made any kind of decision of that nature?'

Mr Burnett was revving up for the showstopper. 'Now, I take it then that, in the light of what you have just explained to us, there was no question of the Princess mentioning to you that she was pregnant?' he asked provocatively. The Countess remained impassive and unblinking: 'No', she said flatly, before explaining Diana's old-fashioned values and finishing with a zinger which undermined her initial answer and had the unintended result of feeding the rumours rather than killing them: 'But I do not know if she was or not.'

As Raine's measured, polished, unfailingly polite testimony came to an end after almost an hour of questioning from both sides, it was glaringly obvious who actually knew most about the Princess's state of mind, leading up to the moments before her death. The one person who had never and would never sell out the Princess was her once despised stepmother. Raine was the consummate keeper of secrets and the ultimate diplomat. Despite having had many reasons and countless opportunities to do so, she had rarely uttered a word against her famous stepdaughter in the entire twenty-five years or so that the two had known each other. 'She was famously completely silent on Diana. Once though she let slip when we were hurrying through Kensington Palace to a recital, one sentence: "Silly girl. All this could have been hers"', says Philip Vergeylen.

The press coverage the following day was radiantly positive. Raine was 'captivating' according to one paper and 'the Fairy Godmother' according to another. If they'd been hoping for a scoop, the papers had something that might play even better: a reverse fairy tale for the modern age, the one in which the wicked stepmother makes good and rehabilitates her public image. And the Countess had touched upon much that the papers could revisit. The Princess's predilection for soothsayers and horoscope readings, 'Well we all want the dark handsome gentleman to walk through our door'; her feelings of foreboding, 'she did very often discuss the possibility of accidents'; and the Princess's role in the Countess's own current employment, 'it was Diana who suggested to Mohamed that he give me a job'.

There had been no doubt, the papers concluded, that Raine knew much of the affairs of the Princess's heart and that before she died she had become perhaps Diana's greatest intimate, supplanting even her butler Paul Burrell. Burrell, who Diana had nicknamed her 'rock', had, in the decade since the Princess died, swiftly chipped away at that particular nomenclature by selling his story to various media organisations. Later, in his summing up, Lord Justice Scott Baker would remind the jury that Burrell had become 'quite a porous rock'.

'The irony', one royal writer was quoted as saying, 'is that at the time of her death, Diana was on far better terms with Raine than with her real mother.' 'Diana was very fond of her', confirms Anne Glenconner, a friend of Raine's and former lady-in-waiting to Princess Margaret, 'she had a terrible relationship with her own mother Frances'. Ingrid Seward, author of *The Queen and Di: The Untold Story*, published in 2000, claims that the Princess told her, 'I'd rather speak to Raine than my mother. She is the mother I never had'.

When it was all over, the Countess had asked for a moment to make a short statement.

'I beg you to do your utmost to solve this mystery, to tear aside anything that could be a cover up and sift everything possible and indeed impossible to allow poor Diana and poor Dodi to at last, truly, rest in peace.' And with that she left the stand and made her way outside, pursued by flashing cameras, to her Rolls-Royce, where her faithful chauffeur Brian ushered her into its leather-clad interior, took the wheel and together they purred off into the drizzling gloom.

Any way you looked at it, Raine had given a Command Performance, masterful in its delicacy and understatement. Those who might have assumed she would break the royal code of silence were inevitably disappointed. 'Those who don't know speak and those who do, don't', says Cole of the unwritten rules of the royal circle.

Raine's beloved husband, the late John Spencer, the 8th Earl Spencer, and father of Princess Diana, would have been proud.

Unlike almost every other witness in this unfolding drama, Raine had been schooled in the ancient diplomatic art of saying everything and nothing whilst maintaining a warm smile throughout. It was a skill she had learned at her mother's knee and it was something she had been doing her whole life, to great success.

'What did we learn?' asked many publications on the day after the verdict was read. The answer, after 278 witnesses were interviewed in a six-month trial estimated to have cost the public more than £6.6m, was very little. The nine–two majority verdict was that the deaths of both Dodi Al Fayed and Diana, Princess of Wales, had been caused by 'grossly negligent driving'. The prepared statement which was read by the forewoman of the jury stated:

> The crash was caused or contributed to by the speed and manner of the driving of the Mercedes, the speed and manner of driving of the following vehicles, the impairment of the judgment of the driver of the Mercedes through alcohol, and there are nine of us who agree on those conclusions. In addition, the death of the deceased was caused or contributed to by the fact that the deceased [were] not wearing seatbelt(s), the fact that the Mercedes struck the pillar in the Alma Tunnel rather than colliding with something else, and we are unanimous on that, sir.

Whilst Dodi had died on impact, Diana had died from a chest injury detailed as laceration within the left pulmonary vein and the immediate adjacent portion of the left atrium of the heart, at La Pitie Salpetriere Hospital, at around 4am on 31 August 1997.

The Princess had quite literally died of a broken heart.

Had Raine decided that the inquest was to be her last big public appearance or was it simply coincidence that after this point she seemed happier to live a quieter life, more frequently out of the spotlight than in it? She certainly didn't let her age deter her, she had turned seventy-eight a few months before the inquest and she was still working at Harrods, lunching with her friends and upon occasion could still be seen on the dance floor of smart private clubs like Lou Lou's or Annabel's. Friends who still jealously guard the privacy of her final years, tell of a secret 'close companion' who would accompany her to select events and parties.

Work was different though and she would happily turn out for a Harrods event, chatting effervescently and greeting friends with her customary kiss on both cheeks. Her finger was still firmly on the pulse: at a party to celebrate the opening of a new Bamford and Sons concession in March 2008, she discussed with journalists (who might have been hoping for something more juicy) the fact that she was still travelling – 'next month I'm flying to Mumbai on behalf of Harrods Estates to take part in a trade show with them' – and the prevailing ecological dilemma of the availability of cheap flights for all.

'How does she manage to look so young?' asked the *Sunday Express*'s Adam Helliker column, in 2010, after spotting Raine enjoying a giggly lunch at the Ritz with her friend barrister Karen Phillipps, former girlfriend of the late rock star QC George Carman, before revealing Raine's age: eighty-one. If the snippet was designed to irritate, it failed. Age for the Countess was certainly just a number – 'I will never retire', she told a friend, 'if I gave up work after two weeks I would be twiddling my thumbs.' That same year she gave an astonishing performance in the BBC series *One Foot in the Past* presented by Kirsty Wark, expounding on the virtues of 'the most exotic pavilion of love in Europe' – the Brighton Pavilion. Outfitted first in an Ungaro mohair coat, boots and fur hat, then a day-dress and pearls and for the finale a full teal-coloured Pierre Balmain ball gown complete with feather headdress, long white gloves and diamonds, Raine glided through the vast building, examining the Nash architecture, nodding mandarin statues and palatial stables of George, Prince of Wales. The exquisite charm of Raine, Countess Spencer was never more evident. With her poise, confidence and extraordinary diction (rooms are rums, often is orften, jewels are jools) she represented a slice of 'the old England' – one associated with manners, deference and naturally, Her Majesty, HRH Queen Elizabeth II.

It had been her genuine love for the south coast which led to her agreeing to the TV appearance in the first place. And perhaps it was her return which prompted her to once again purchase a home in Bognor where she and Johnnie had been happiest. The house, which she purchased in 2013, was a small double-fronted Victorian villa with an entire room devoted to her beloved ballgowns. It was here that Philip Vergeylen and Paolo Moschino visited her one weekend. 'We found her very happy and at peace. She loved it.'

There were very few incidents that could rattle the cage of the Countess these days and almost none (aside from Harrods events) that could persuade her to speak with the press. But the emergence of letters between Diana and Raine in 2012, alongside photographs and other correspondence, which were being offered for sale by the Northampton-based arm of the auctioneers Humberts, valued at approximately £25,000, were an exception. Naturally the letters themselves and details of their contents featured heavily in the tabloids. Ironically, they vindicated Raine's longstanding assertions that she and the Princess had been close from the start.

In one letter, addressed from her flat in Earl's Court on 28 December 1980, just weeks before her engagement was announced, Diana wrote to her stepmother thanking her for the Christmas she had spent at Althorp with Raine and Johnnie: 'An enormous thank you for making the day so memorable'. Another letter, dated 16 January 1981, indicates that the princess-to-be had discussed her upcoming engagement with her stepmother: 'Dearest Raine, what a touching letter you wrote to me. It contained far too much praise which I'm sure I'm not due for . . . As you saw I went to Sandringham without being noticed . . . Raine you have been extremely kind and patient with all this and consequently I just wanted you to know how grateful I am. A million thanks for all of your support and advice . . . Lucky daddy having you.' There were indications too that they had discussed a difficult relationship for Diana – whether it was with Camilla Parker Bowles or her own mother is not clear. Diana talks about the trip to Australia that she was to take immediately after the announcement of her engagement, to visit her mother who was living on a farm in the outback with Peter Shand Kydd: 'it's not long 2 ½ weeks & will do us both good', she writes. Both letters were signed 'much love', hardly an indication of animosity between the two.[12]

For Raine, though, the violation of the privacy of both herself and the Princess was completely unacceptable, particularly as she worried about the implication that she might have put the letters up for sale herself. In response, she took a page out of her late stepdaughter's playbook and either she or 'a friend' contacted Diana's favourite gossip columnist, Richard Kay of the *Daily Mail*, letting him know that she was furious and demanding to know the provenance of the letters. Kay quoted her via 'an old friend' the next day: 'All the letters I have from Prince Charles and Princess Diana are very much under lock and key . . . I find it distasteful that these letters could be sold'. For further avoidance of doubt, Kay quoted 'the friend': 'Clearly the issue is that the copyright of the letters is Diana's estate and the actual property, the letters, are Raine's.'

The following day Kay trumpeted the good news for his readers: 'Just a day after I revealed the heartache of Countess Raine Spencer over the auction of her private letters from Princess Diana, the sale has been called off.' According to Kay, after a call from 'Raine directly' to Jonathan Humbert the auction house's director, the sale had been cancelled. The letters had apparently, he explained, been brought to the showroom by a former employee at Althorp who was believed to have taken them 'by mistake' during the sale of the Spencer's Bognor Regis holiday homes in the eighties. 'My conversation with Countess Spencer was very good humoured and she has been extremely gracious', Humbert assured Kay. 'There was no finger pointing.' And the fate of the correspondence? Whilst Kay did not seem to have asked that vital question, the answer was almost certainly that the Countess could now triumphantly add these letters to the large stash of royal correspondence she had stored safely in her bank vault.

To say that Raine organised her own demise with the same ruthless efficiency, style and poise which had characterised her entire life would be to imbue her with powers beyond even her steely resolve and perspicacity. If stage managed is the wrong term (and it is because it carries with it a certain cynicism) there was something to be admired about her long, slow, stylish goodbye, the likes of which would have chilled a lesser mortal (or impressed a Buddhist with her calm embracing of the inevitable 'end').

The signs were all there: in 2014 a representative – likely her beloved chauffeur Brian – told journalists who had been accustomed to calling Raine's Sprimont Street number for quotes about matters as varied as manners, sex or schooling that the Countess was no longer talking to the press. (She had said as much to *The Times* in 2004, but this time she said she 'meant it'.)

In 2015, though, she surprised her friends and family by granting a rare face-to-face interview with the sophisticated, niche *Gentlewoman* magazine, complete with pictures shot by acclaimed fashion photographer Alasdair McLellan. It was an inspired choice, representing the mastery of a medium, much utilised by her late stepdaughter. Diana's fashion shoots for *Vanity Fair* and *Harper's Bazaar* were often seen as her way of communicating a change of direction without saying as much.

In Raine's case she took the opportunity to set the record straight both in words and pictures and to record for posterity just how damn good you can look at the age of eighty-five. Did she know then that she was unwell? If she did she wasn't saying and it certainly didn't show. McLellan's portraits of her, in both black and white and colour, taken in her office at Harrods, picture a woman at the height of her powers, immaculately coiffed, made up and manicured with her trademark bouffant very much intact. She was proudly wearing her Harrods badge, pearl earrings and a stonking great pearl ring on her marriage finger.

Were any secrets divulged to writer David Vincent? Well, yes and no. Vincent set the scene by informing his readers of the Countess's dazzling array of titles, her work behind the tills at Harrods and her upbringing at the hands of her novelist mother. His subject demonstrated her notorious sense of humour when discussing that she came out in 1947 aged eighteen – 'It means something different now she hoots', before going on to remind the readers of the reasons for her marriage to one of the most famous aristocrats of our time: John Edward Spencer, 8th Earl Spencer, 'Johnnie was like a whirlwind, a force of nature'. She was effusive about Gerald, 'I loved him and we were always "darling Raine" and "darling Gerald" for the rest of our lives'. She went on record again regarding the restoration and so-called commercialisation of Althorp, 'oh I got flack but it was what John wanted to do', and successfully glossed over her marriage to Jean-François. Seemingly without drawing breath she moved on to Diana, 'we ended up huge friends . . . what was lovely was that she thanked me at the end for looking after him [Johnnie]'. And then there was her totemic hair: 'It just goes into rollers . . . my signature is more swept back and up. When you get older, I think up is good. Droop is bad.' Finally she recalled her recent eighty-fifth birthday party at Spencer House for 126 guests, which Jean-François had attended, 'he came with his new wife and daughter and gave the most beautiful tribute'.

That the writer and the reader would be charmed, impressed and perhaps a little terrified was never in doubt; Raine had lost none of her ability to awe. Her versions of some of the more striking events of her life were never going to be less than definitive: 'Raine is a character of some complexity' Vincent wrote with restrained understatement, before ending with a quote from a Chinese businessman who had witnessed a speech Raine had just given in Mandarin to a group of visitors to Harrods, 'You must come to Shanghai. You will be more famous than Beckham'. She had certainly seen and experienced a great deal more in her life than England's former mid-fielder could ever hope to.

She could still throw a hell of a party too. In 2016, when thirty-five of her closest friends including author Julian Fellowes and his wife Emma Kitchener, Count and Countess Flamburiari, her lawyer Andy Kerman and his wife Joanna Kanska, and Philip Vergeylen and partner Paolo Moschino amongst others gathered at Spencer House for an elaborate dinner. Few of them, if any, had a notion of what was to come. What they anticipated was the delicious food, good wine and sparkling conversation synonymous with all of Raine's immaculately organised dinners.

Close friends and confidantes like Norton and Kerman, joint executors of Raine's will, had an inkling. They knew that the Countess was unwell, and they had both been visiting her at home for the last twelve months to take instructions and keep her spirits up: 'she kept it to herself. She didn't like fuss and really didn't want anyone to know', says Norton. To close friend Dr Ian Weir she had confided: 'I've got a little cancer dear and it has spread to the bones'.[13] Weir knew exactly what the prognosis would be for something like that, but the two never discussed it further. Vergeylen says that on arrival at Spencer House he was struck by Raine's weight loss: 'She was there in one of her dresses that I had seen before, it had not been altered and it hung off her. She said she was having trouble standing for long periods of time and problems with her breathing. She was still magnificent.' Wearing one of her favourite dresses, the black and cream polka dot last seen in that photo op with Shirley Bassey, chandelier diamond earrings and necklace and carrying a black fan, Raine looked ever the sophisticate. The only sign that there might have been something wrong aside from her dramatic weight loss, was that her legendary 'bouffant' was missing. Instead, her hair, now totally white grey, was scraped back into floral clips and gently flowing onto her shoulders. 'She was a little bit late coming through because she had felt faint and had to sit down. But being Raine that was soon put behind her. She might have been physically diminished (by the illness) but she certainly was not mentally', says Fellowes, 'she was absolutely still living in "the now".'

As the last pudding plates were scraped and dessert wine drained, Raine stood with some effort and composed herself. Looking around the table she smiled graciously and thanked everyone for coming. She then began to talk about her memories of each guest in turn, reflecting upon the times they had spent together and the fun they'd had. 'There were no notes', says Kerman, 'she knew exactly what she wanted to say about each friend'. When she got to about the third or fourth person, guests began to realise what was happening. 'The penny dropped with my wife before me', says Kerman, 'she leaned over and said to me in a whisper, "She's saying goodbye. Raine is saying goodbye".' 'She stood for over an hour', says Vergeylen, 'it must have been terribly difficult for her, but she was determined.'

But Raine had still not tied up every loose end. In the aftermath of the party, she rang Michael Cole and invited him for lunch. They met in late July at one of her favourite restaurants, Wheelers in Jermyn Street. There she proceeded to persuade Cole to give the eulogy at her memorial service. 'I said, Raine, like your mother you are going to live forever. I was completely resistant to the idea, but she would not take no for an answer and eventually, it being Raine, I gave in. One always did.' They parted outside the restaurant in the usual way, with Cole accompanying her to her waiting Rolls-Royce on his arm, and the trusty Brian primed and ready to open the car door. They parted with a kiss on each cheek and a promise to see each other again soon. Two days later, Cole received a letter from Raine, dated 1 October, thanking him for 'the great favour in saying you will speak at my service'. Also folded inside the envelope were two closely typed pages of A4 paper, containing details of the accomplishments of which Raine was most proud – from her early years of money raising for 'Polly' buses for the elderly with her mother Barbara, to her time as Patron of the 59th Westminster Scouts, 'who officially changed their name to the "Countess of Dartmouth's Own"', to her final position as Director of Harrods Estates. Her children were listed too and – almost as an afterthought – she had scrawled in biro Henry's position as a QC and William's as, 'The Earl of Dartmouth FCA a member of the European Parliament'.

But it was not the accomplishments that Cole reflected upon when he learned that fifteen days after he received her missive, on 21 October 2016, Raine had died peacefully at home. Rather it was one of the phrases she had used in signing off: 'Life has been' she wrote in her steady script on her beloved Harrods notepaper, 'a fabulous adventure and I feel so lucky and grateful'. Returning from Raine's funeral, which was held quietly and privately, two weeks after her death at North Sheen Cemetery in London, on 1 November 2016, it was a sombre Cole who sat down in his study to re-read Raine's note. It was then that he spotted that she had heavily underlined just one word: *adventure*.

Acknowledgements

Firstly and foremost my thanks go to my stupendously long suffering and enormously supportive agent Eugenie Furniss, who has borne with humour and patience my many exploits over the years. I'm grateful also to my editor Andreas Campomar, who immediately understood my desire to set the record straight on Raine and to Holly Blood, Una McGovern and everyone else at Little, Brown who knocked the book into shape, spotted some howlers and made the whole thing happen.

The McCorquodale/Legge/de Chambrun families have behaved at all times with unfailing courtesy, for which I thank them (Raine would have expected nothing less). Michael Cole, first and always a journalist at heart, guided me with intelligence and pragmatism throughout. His friendship with Raine, which spanned over forty years, provided vital insights into the Countess's personality and drive.

This book was, in the main, written during the periods of our two lockdowns and I am enormously grateful to the many friends and acquaintances of Raine's who came forward, willingly giving of their time and focus via phone, email or the dreaded Zoom, during a moment in history when they could have been forgiven for pulling up the drawbridge and retreating into their gardens, if not always literally then at least metaphorically. Great thanks then are due to: Jeffrey Archer, Sacha Bonsor, Lady Nadine Bonsor, Rory Clark, Lady Colin Campbell, Peter Constandinos, Anne de Courcy, Lord Julian Fellowes, Count and Countess Flamburiari, Valerie Grove, Anne Glenconner, Geordie Grieg, Sir Simon Jenkins, Andy Kerman, Henry Legge, Ian McCorquodale, Nicolas Norton, Frank Partridge, Lord Plymouth, Robert Mountford, Sir Roy Strong, Lucia Van der Post and Philip Vergeylen. My thanks also to those who spoke on background but declined to be named. There had been only one book previously written about Raine: *Raine and Johnnie* by Angela Levin. I am very grateful that Angela paved the way and I have quoted both her and her work at specific points. My appreciation also to Patricia and Merlyn for additional research.

I owe a huge debt of gratitude to my friends in London, Walberswick and beyond, who have borne with humour and grace my grumpy writing demeanour and have variously and unwaveringly offered, encouragement, cups of tea, or walks with the dogs. I could not have completed this book without the love and support of Nick and my two boys (now men): Ethan and Truman, who are undoubtedly, save for an early discovery of the merits of Toblerone, the best things I have ever done.

Endnotes

All references to interviews with individuals are related to the initial footnote unless otherwise stated.

Prologue

1   Coroners Inquests into the Deaths of Diana, Princess of Wales and Mr Dodi Al Fayed

Chapter 1

1   *Guardian*, 29 July 1972

2   Angela Levin, *Telegraph*, 19 August 2013

3   Dr Anthony Clare, *In the Psychiatrist's Chair*, July 1991, BBC Radio 4

4   Tim Heald, *A Life of Love: The Life of Barbara Cartland*, 1994

5   Barbara Cartland, *We Danced All Night*, 1970

6   ibid.

7   *New York Times* Archive, 10 June 1973

8   Cartland, *We Danced All Night*

9   ibid.

10 Henry Cloud, *Barbara Cartland: Crusader in Pink*, 1979

11 ibid.

12 Michael Thornton, MailOnline, 24 October 2008

13 ibid.

14 ibid.

15 Cartland, *We Danced All Night*, p.208

16 David Vincent, *Gentlewoman*, Spring/Summer 2015

Chapter 2

1 Henry Cloud, *Barbara Cartland, Crusader in Pink*, 1979

2 Fiona MacCarthy, *Last Curtsey: The End of the English Debutante*, 2011

3 *Tatler and Bystander*, 23 April 1947

4 Fiona MacCarthy, *Last Curtsey*

5 Interview with Anne Glenconner, 26 March 2021

6 Henry Cloud, *Barbara Cartland, Crusader in Pink*, 1979

7 Anne de Courcy, *Debs at War*, 2005

8 Interview with Frank Partridge, 16 February 2021

Chapter 3

1 Interview with Ian McCorquodale, 29 January 2021

2 BBC.com

3 John Alldridge, *Manchester Evening News*, 4 October 1955

4 *Sketch*, 8 October 1952

5 *Tatler*, 3 June 1953

6 Interview with Anne de Courcy, 2 March 2021

7 Michael Cole, 8 May 2022

8 Interview with Baron Fellowes of West Stafford, Julian Fellowes, 8 February 2022

9 Dick Hobbes, *Independent*, 10 June 1997

10 Various interviews, emails and phonecalls with Michael Cole during 2021

11 Gillian Thornton, *Hertfordshire Life*, November 2020

12 Interview with Sir Roy Strong, 3 February 2021

13 *Manchester Evening News*, 4 October 1955

14 *Northants Evening Telegraph*, 29 June 1957

15 Alamy Stock photo and caption, Keystone Press, 28 June 1957

16 Katharine Whitehorn, *Selective Memory*, 2007

17 Angela Levin, *Raine and Johnnie*, 1993

18 www.ice.cam.ac.uk

19 Whitehorn, *Selective Memory*

20 *Hartlepool Northern Daily Mail*, 5 March 1958

21 Interview with Sir Simon Jenkins, 2 February 2021

22 Angela Levin, *Raine and Johnnie*, 1993

Chapter 4

1 https://www.britannica.com/place/United-Kingdom/Britain-since-1945#ref483684

2 *Daily Mirror*, 19 May 1962

3 *Newcastle Evening Chronicle*, 17 October 1962

4 *Birmingham Daily Post*

5 *Daily Mirror*, 15 April 1966

6 Tina Brown, *The Diana Chronicles*, 2007

7 https://www.gale.com/intl/essays/martin-conboy-language-mirror-idiom-masses

8 Angela Levin, *Raine and Johnnie*, 1993

9 Roy Strong, *Splendours and Miseries: The Roy Strong Diaries 1967–1987*, 2017

10 ibid.

11 *The Times*, January 1972

12 Brian Anson, *I'll Fight You For It! Behind the Struggle for Covent Garden*, 1966–74, 1981

13 ibid.

14 ibid.

15 *The Times*, 11 May 1971

16 ibid.

17 ibid.

Chapter 5

1   Max Riddington & Gavan Naden, *Frances: The Remarkable Story of Princess Diana's Mother*, 2003

2   Interview by Caroline Scott, *Sunday Times*, 13 September 2020

3   *The Times*, 4 June 2004

4   Sarah Bradford, *Diana*, 2006

5   Peter Settelen tapes first aired December 2004 by NBC as *Diana Revealed: The Princess No One Knew*, presented by Ann Curry, written by Dorothy Newell

6   Gordon Honeycombe, *The Year of the Princess*, 1982

7   Andrew Morton, *Diana: Her True Story*, 2017

8   Angela Levin, *Raine and Johnnie*, 1993

9   John Pearson, *Blood Royal, The Story of the Spencers and The Royals,* 1999

10 Charles Spencer, *The Spencers*, 1999

11 Simon Jenkins, *England's Thousand Best Houses*, 2003

12 James Lees Milne, *Diaries, 1942–54*, 2011

13 Charles Spencer, *The Spencers*, 1999

14 Will of the Right Honourable Albert Edward John Earl Spencer, 7 February 1974

15 Mary Clarke, *Diana: Once Upon A Time*, 1994

16 Angela Levin, *Raine and Johnnie*, 1993

17 Charles Spencer, *Althorp: The Story of an English House*, 1998

18 *Daily Express*, 24 April 1976

19 Angela Levin, *Raine and Johnnie*, 1993

Chapter 6

1   Angela Levin, *Raine and Johnnie*, 1993

2   Jean Rook, *Daily Express*, 29 April 1981

3   Brian Vine, *Daily Express*, 11 September 1991

4   Series of email/telephone interviews with Peter Constandinos, 12 February 2021 to 16 October 2021

5   Interview with Rory Clark, 7 October 2021

6 John Pearson, *Blood Royal: The Story of the Spencers and the Royals*, 1999

7 Angela Levin, *Raine and Johnnie*, 1993

8 Interview with Jeffrey Archer, 12 August 2021

9 Interview with Wendy Nicholls, Colefax & Fowler, 9 February 2021

10 Sarah Bradford, *Diana*, 2006

11 Tina Brown, *The Diana Chronicles*, 2008

12 Interview with Lady Colin Campbell, 27 July 2021

13 Charles Spencer, *Althorp: The Story of an English House*, 1998

14 Interview with Nicolas Norton, 1 December 2021

15 Jean Rook, *Daily Express*, 29 April 1981

16 Telephone interview with Jeffrey Archer, 12 August 2021

17 Ingrid Seward, *The Queen and Di: The Untold Story*, 2000

18 *Independent on Sunday*, 15 August 1993

19 *The Times*, 12 December 1982

20 Charles Spencer, *Althorp: The Story of An English House,* 1998

21 Sheila Butterworth, Records Centre Manager, British Library email: 13 April 2022/Press Release, 6 December 1984

22 https://www.christies.com/about-us/press-archive/ details/?pressreleaseid=4199

23 'Why Earl Spencer is selling Althorp's treasures', *Country Life*, 15 April 2010

Chapter 7

1 Charles Spencer, *Althorp: The Story of a Country House*, 1999

2 Kenneth Rose, *Who Loses, Who Wins: The Journals of Kenneth Rose*, Volume 2, 2019

3 Gyles Brandreth, *Charles & Camilla*, 2005

4 Sarah Bradford, *Diana*, 2006

5 Tina Brown, *The Diana Chronicles*, 2007

6 Sally Bedell Smith, *Diana in Search of Herself*, 1999

7 Andrew Morton, *Diana: Her True Story – In Her Own Words*, 1992

8   Peter Settelen 1992 tapes: NBC, Ann Curry, broadcast 2004

9   Ingrid Seward, *The Queen and Di: The Untold Story*, 2000

10 Penny Junor, *The Firm*, 2005

11 *The Journals of Kenneth Rose*, Volume 2, 2019

12 Andrew Morton, *Diana Her True Story – In Her Own Words*, 1992

Chapter 8

1   Lives Remembered, *The Times*, 6 August 2014

2   *Irish Independent*, 19 July 1993

3   *Princess Diana's 'Wicked' Stepmother*, Firecrest Films, 2018

4   Lady Colin Campbell, *The Real Diana*, 2016

5   Interview with Adele Biss, 21 January 2021

6   Alan Clark, *A Life in his Own Words*, 2010

7   Andrew Morton, *Diana: Her True Story – In Her Own Words*, 1992

8   Sally Bedell Smith, *Diana in Search of Herself*, 1999

9   Patrick Jephson, *Shadows of a Princess*, 2017

10 Peter Settelen 1992 tapes: NBC, Ann Curry, broadcast 2004

11 ibid., 53:58

12 *Princess Diana's 'Wicked' Stepmother*, Firecrest Films, 2018

13 Ross Benson, The Diary, *Daily Express*, 10 September 1991

14 Brian Vine, *Daily Mail*, 11 September 1991

Chapter 9

1   Kitty Kelly, *The Royals*, 2010

2   Charles Spencer, *Althorp: The Story of an English House*, 1998

3   James Whittaker, *Daily Mirror*, 14 July 1992

4   *Daily Express*, 20 October 1992

5   *Daily Express*, 21 December 1992

6   *The Times*, 13 May 1993

7   ibid., (the count's CV 'in his own hand')

8   *Daily Express*, 13 May 1993

9   Interview with Valerie Grove, 21 October 2021

10   Lynda Lee-Potter, *Daily Mail*, 12 May 1993

11   *Daily Mail*, 7 July 1993

12   David Vincent, *Gentlewoman*, Spring/Summer 2015

13   Woodrow Wyatt, *The Journals of Woodrow Wyatt, Volume 3*, 2000

14   *Mirror*, 13 July 1998

Chapter 10

1   *Express*, 11 November 1996

2   *Express*, 13 November 1996

3   David Vincent, *Gentlewoman*, Spring/Summer 2015

4   Ingrid Seward, *The Queen and Di: The Untold Story*, 2000

5   *Express*, 9 February 1997 (Tina Brown, *The Diana Chronicles*, 2007)

6   Interview with Julian Fellowes, 9 February 2022

7   David Vincent, *Gentlewoman*, Spring/Summer 2015

8   ibid.

9   Interview with Philip Vergeylen, 15 February 2021

10   Richard Barber, MailOnline, 14 July 2012

11   Interview with Anthony (Andy) Kerman, 18 November 2021

12   Lord Plymouth via email: 1 December 2021

Chapter 11

1   Interview with Robert Mountford, 5 February 2021

2   Bernard Donoughue, *Westminster Diary: A Reluctant Minister Under Tony Blair*, 2016

3   *The Times*, 18 October 2002

4   ibid.

5   *Mail on Sunday*, 9 July 2017

6   Lord Plymouth via email, 1 December 2021

7   MailOnline, 22 September 2019

8   *Daily Mail*, 20 November 2007

9   Operation Paget Inquiry Report Metropolitan Police Download: https://downloads.bbc.co.uk/news/nol/shared/bsp/hi/pdfs/14_12_06_diana_report.pdf

10 *Daily Express*, 3 March 2008
11 *Guardian*, 13 December 2007
12 *Mirror*, 25 September 2012
13 *Princess Diana's 'Wicked' Stepmother*, Firecrest Films, 2017

Bibliography

Brian Anson, *I'll Fight You For It! Behind the Struggle for Covent Garden 1996–74*, Jonathan Cape, 1981

Sally Bedell Smith, *Diana in Search of Herself*, Signet/Penguin, 1999

Gyles Brandreth, *Charles & Camilla*, Arrow, 1998

Sarah Bradford, *Diana*, Penguin, 2006

Tina Brown, *The Diana Chronicles*, Century, 2007

Colin Burgess, *Behind Palace Doors*, John Blake, 2007

Barbara Cartland, *We Danced All Night*, Hutchinson & Co, 1970

Alan Clark, *A Life in his Own Words*, Phoenix, 2010

Rory Clark, *You've Done What, My Lord?*, Constable & Robinson Ltd, 2013

Mary Clarke, *Diana: Once Upon a Time*, Sidgwick and Jackson, 1994

Henry Cloud, *Barbara Cartland: Crusader in Pink*, Weidenfeld & Nicolson, 1979

David Cohen, *Diana: Death of a Goddess*, Arrow, 2005

Lady Colin Campbell, *The Real Diana*, Dynasty, 2016

Anne de Courcy, *Debs at War*, Phoenix, 2005

Anne de Courcy, *1939: The Last Season*, Phoenix, 2012

Arthur Edwards, *I'll tell the Jokes Arthur*, Blake, 1993

Lucinda Gosling, *Debutantes and the London Season*, Shire Publications, 2013

Tim Heald, *A Life of Love*, Sinclair Stevenson, 1994

Howard Hodgson, *Charles: The Man Who Will Be King*, John Blake, 2007

Gordon Honeycombe, *The Year of the Princess*, Little, Brown, 1982

Simon Jenkins, *England's Thousand Best Houses*, Penguin, 2003

Patrick Jephson, *Shadows of a Princess*, William Collins, 2017

Penny Junor, *The Firm*, Harper Collins, 2005

Kitty Kelley, *The Royals*, Warner Books, 1997

Fiona MacCarthy, *Last Curtsey: The End of the English Debutante*, Faber & Faber, 2011

Angela Levin, *Raine and Johnnie*, Weidenfeld & Nicolson, 1993

James Lees-Milne, *Diaries, 1942–54*, John Murray, 2011

James Lees-Milne, *Diaries, 1984–97*, John Murray, 2011

Andrew Morton, *Diana: Her True Story – In Her Own Words*, Michael O'Mara Books Ltd, 1992

Piers Morgan, *The Insider*, Ebury Press, 2005

John Pearson, *Blood Royal: The Story of the Spencers and the Royals*, Harper Collins, 1999

Kenneth Rose, *Who Loses, Who Wins: The Journals of Kenneth Rose, Volume Two*, Edited by D. R. Thorpe, Weidenfeld & Nicolson, 2019

Max Riddington & Gavan Naden, *Frances: The Remarkable Story of Princess Diana's Mother*, Michael O'Mara Books Ltd, 2003

Ingrid Seward, *The Queen and Di: The Untold Story*, Harper Collins, 2000

Charles Spencer, *Althorp: The Story of an English House*, Viking, 1998

Charles Spencer, *The Spencers*, Penguin, 1999

Roy Strong, *Splendours and Miseries: The Roy Strong Diaries, 1967–1987*, Weidenfeld & Nicolson, 2017

Katharine Whitehorn, *Selective Memory*, Virago, 2007

Woodrow Wyatt, *The Journals of Woodrow Wyatt*, Volume 3, Edited by Sarah Curtis, Pan Books, 2000

Documents

What is our Heritage? HMSO 1975

Operation Paget Inquiry Report into the allegation of conspiracy to murder Diana, Princess of Wales and Emad El-Din Mohamed Abdel Moneim Fayed, 2004

Coroner's Inquests into the Deaths of Diana, Princess of Wales and Mr Dodi Al Fayed HM Coroner, nationalarchives.gov.uk

Index